CPL WITHDRAWN

D0819963

GA
20.00

THE GREAT ILLUSIONISTS

(overleaf)
Carmo (Harry Cameron, 1881–1944), a twentieth-century Australian conjurer and illusionist who ran a circus during the nineteen-thirties in Britain. Dame Laura Knight travelled with Carmo's Circus, as recorded in her autobiography OIL PAINT AND GREASE PAINT *(1936), and Mr Raymond Toole Stott, the bibliographer of circus, conjuring and Somerset Maugham, also spent a couple of years on the road with him. This striking lithograph combines a Pepper's Ghost effect of transparency with the shadow of a devil.*

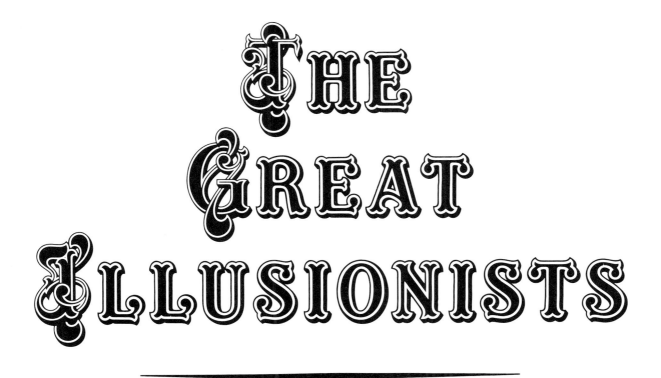

THE GREAT ILLUSIONISTS

EDWIN A. DAWES

The most beautiful experience we can have is the mysterious. It is the fundamental emotion which stands at the cradle of true art and true science. Whoever does not know it and can no longer wonder, no longer marvel, is as good as dead, and his eyes are dimmed.

Albert Einstein, *The World as I See It* (1934)

CHARTWELL
BOOKS INC.

Published by Chartwell Books Inc.
A Division of Book Sales Inc.
110 Enterprise Avenue,
Secaucus, New Jersey 07094

© Edwin A. Dawes 1979

ISBN 0-89009-240-0
Library of Congress Catalog Number 79-50434

All rights reserved. No part of this
publication may be reproduced, stored
in a retrieval system, or transmitted,
in any form or by any means, electronic,
mechanical, photocopying, recording or
otherwise, without the prior permission
of David & Charles (Publishers) Limited

Typeset and printed in Great Britain

CONTENTS

ILLUSTRATIONS

INTRODUCTION AND ACKNOWLEDGEMENTS

Whatsoever I have now done, I hope no
exception can be taken, it is for your
mirth and recreation (and I pray you so take
it,) let such as will needs barke at the Moone,
yell till their hearts ake: Gentle and Gentle-
mens spirits, wil tak all kindely that is
kindely presented.

Sa Rid, *The Art of Jugling or Legerdemaine* (1612)

The fascination of conjuring and illusion is deep-rooted. The marvellous has always excited interest. From the earliest times, practitioners of the art of legerdemain have used their manual dexterity to amuse and bewilder, while purveyors of illusions have always deployed a knowledge of scientific principles, however rudimentary, to create their remarkable wonders. In this excursion into the world of magic and mystery we meet some of the outstanding performers and discover some of the tricks that have baffled countless generations.

The influence of science on the art and practice of magic has always interested me, perhaps understandably since both have been very much a part of my life. Dr Joseph Needham, writing on Chinese civilization, observed that the passage of jugglers and acrobats to and fro merits more attention in the history of science than it has yet received, and this is a challenge that perhaps some future historian will accept. Students of science education are well aware that in the nineteenth century it was desirable to sugarcoat the educative pill. Popular expositors of science and natural philosophy, and some eminent scientists did not disdain this rôle, found it expedient to clothe their instruction with various pastimes, of which conjuring was a favourite. Dr James A. Paris, FRS, produced his *Philosophy in Sport Made Science in Earnest*, 'being an attempt to implant in the young mind the first principles of natural philosophy by the aid of the popular toys and

sports of youth', in 1827. It went through many editions, later ones being dedicated to Michael Faraday, and no doubt many a youth (and his father) learned some magic from the explanation of the show presented by 'Crank Smirky, the celebrated conjurer' at the Osterley Jubilee.

Professor John Beckmann, of the University of Göttingen, in 1797 argued, somewhat unconvincingly, that sleight-of-hand and other entertainers came into being when the occupations most necessary to life were sufficiently filled; those excluded from them 'conceived the idea of amusing the former when tired with their labour'. But Beckmann, unlike some of his academic contemporaries, generally approved of conjurers. As indeed did the late Professor A. V. Hill, distinguished physiologist and Nobel prize-winner, who once advocated that every student of science should be shown in his university classes how the skill of the conjurer deceives the human brain, including the ways that this is achieved; further, that nothing supernatural is involved, only the fallibility of the human senses. Were this done, Professor Hill believed that fewer scientists would publish mistaken conclusions and incorrect observations. And, one might add, the fairly recent scenarios enacted between some scientists and alleged psychics would surely have been somewhat different! It is a well known fact, at least among conjurers, that the more intelligent the audience the more readily will they be deceived by conjuring principles of which they have no knowledge: cause and effect are so rapidly associated that the unexpected *dénouement* catches them off-guard.

This book had its genesis in a series of articles I have contributed over a goodly number of years to *The Magic Circular*, the monthly journal of The Magic Circle of London. Under the general heading of 'A Rich Cabinet of Magical Curiosities' a variety of topics has been treated, most of them embodying some original research or presenting new information. The existence of this series, and therefore, in consequence, of the book you now hold, in one sense may be laid at the door of Mr John Salisse, Honorary Secretary of The Magic Circle, for it was his persuasive manner that first seduced me into writing a regular feature rather than indulging in my previous spasmodic essays. Thus, when Mr Paul Barnett of David & Charles invited me to write a book on conjuring covering principally the eighteenth century to the early years of the present century it was a pleasure to accept. The basis already existed but, as the original articles were written for the specialist reader, those incorporated here have been recast and, together with much additional material, presented in a style that makes no assumption of any conjuring expertise. But in the title of this book I find myself at amiable variance with my publishers, whose insistence on *The Great Illusionists*, instead of my own title of *The Pursuit of Illusion*, will surely offend those magical purists for whom the term illusionist has a special connotation.

While there is a general chronological progression of chapters, it must be emphasized that in no way is this work intended to be a comprehensive history of magic: not even a magician could achieve that within the present compass! Rather is it an idiosyncratic survey of 'Magic and Mystery through the Ages'—to borrow the title of a lecture that for many years now I have given to lay audiences on this topic.

For the benefit of the interested student I have cited primary sources where possible and added some explanatory notes. In the past I have often been frustrated by the lack of references to source material in many of the historical works on conjuring; even when a general bibliography has been appended, the researcher is still left to find his way through the jungle on the trail of his quarry. While acknowledging that the average reader is largely unconcerned with such minutiae, it is hoped that some of the more detailed citations that I have been able to provide will be of assistance to kindred souls who enjoy pursuing the original literature.

The illustrations are of material in my own collection unless otherwise indicated. In this connexion it is a pleasure to thank several friends for their kindness in allowing me to reproduce prints and engravings in their collections. Mr Leslie R. Cole and Mr Robert G. Read have been particularly generous in acceding to my request to reproduce certain of their items, and I am grateful, too, to Mr Alfred Rubens, FSA, FRHistS; Dr David W. Findlay; the Council of The Magic Circle; the Trustees of the British Museum; and the Brynmor Jones Library of the University of Hull, for permission to use illustrations of material in their possession.

My thanks are also due to Mr R. G. Bird, Borough Librarian of Tunbridge Wells; Mr W. S. Haugh, City Librarian, Bristol; Mr P. Pagan, Director of Bath Municipal Libraries and Victoria Art Gallery; and Mr Edward Croft-Murray, former Keeper of Prints and Drawings at the British Museum, for generous assistance in my researches relating to Thomas Loggon, the dwarf fan painter.

It will be obvious that, in a work of this nature, I have benefited from general discussions and exchange of information with many friends over the years and it is a pleasure to thank them all here. While it may seem invidious to single out some for particular mention, especially at the risk of offending others whom I have unwittingly omitted, I am especially grateful to Messrs A. Adrion, W. Alma, L. R. Cole, E. M. Davison, the late J. B. Findlay, J. Fisher, J. F. Gresham, B. Grimshaw, Dr J. H. Grossman, A. Jamieson, G. A. Jenness, D. Johnstone, F. W. Kuethe, R. Lund, the late T. O'Beirne, H. E. Pratt, A. Setterington, S. H. Sharpe, H. A. Smith, Dr W. D. A. Smith, A. Snowden (Editor of *The Magic Circular*), R. G. Read, the late A. M. Stewart (De Vega), R. Toole Stott, P. Warlock and F. White (President of The Magic Circle).

It is a pleasure, too, to acknowledge my gratitude for the resources of the Brynmor Jones Library of the University of Hull and especially to my friend and colleague Dr Philip Larkin, Librarian and poet, and to Mr Alan Marshall who was responsible for most of the photography. Mr Mac Wilson photographed items in the Leslie Cole and Magic Circle Collections.

I should also like to thank Mr Paul Barnett and Mrs Pam Darlaston of David & Charles for their unfailing guidance and courtesy in the preparation of the manuscript for the printer. I am grateful, too, to my younger son Adrian, who fortunately shares an interest in magic, for his forbearance when the little leisure time available to his father was monopolized by the writing of this book to the exclusion of other mutual activities. His willing assistance with the index is also much appreciated.

Finally, but by no means least, my greatest debt is to my wife Amy who has, in every way, shared this voyage of discovery in quest of wonder-workers of yesteryear, and whose own interest and efforts have sustained and supported my writings. And, as if it were not sufficient that she assist my practical performances in the rôle of conjurer's assistant, she also voluntarily undertook the typing of the manuscript. Our modest aim will be accomplished if the reader derives but a tithe of the pleasure that the production of this volume has afforded us and arrives at an appreciation of the fact that there is more to conjuring than mere tricks.

E.A.D.

1
In The Beginning

Thus do they pass, the shadowy host of
magic marshalled from the mists of time . . .
They come from an hundred lands, from
myriads of forgotten graves.

J. N. Hilliard, *Greater Magic* (1938)

Worshippers filed in from bright sunlight to the comparative gloom of the huge temple. They gazed in awe at the closed doors of the shrine that shielded the image of the deity from their sight. To the side of the shrine stood an altar upon which, under the eyes of the faithful, acolytes kindled a fire. A profound silence ensued, broken only by the crackling of the blazing wood. The shooting flames cast flickering, darting shadows across the temple and then . . . slowly but inexorably, the doors of the shrine began to open, revealing at first a glimpse and then, eventually in all its majesty, the mighty idol. Truly the great miracle had occurred again.

As the fire on the altar dwindled and died away, the worshippers saw the huge doors of the shrine starting to move again, almost imperceptibly but then unmistakably, closing with a gentle finality that betokened the proceedings were now at an end. In another temple, not a thousand miles away, other worshippers also watched a fire being kindled, in this case on an altar flanked by two statues holding urns. Miraculously, as the fire took hold, libations poured forth from the urns.

In awesome mysteries of this kind, enacted thousands of years ago in the splendour and solemnity of Greek and Egyptian temples, we may discern the origins of illusions that later brought pleasure to

The machinery for mysteriously opening the doors of a temple shrine in response to lighting a fire on an altar, as described in the PNEUMATICS OF HERO OF ALEXANDRIA, *about 62AD.*

millions of regular theatre-goers, relaxing in their red plush seats and surrounded by gilt rococo splendour of a different kind. The sorcerer-priests of the past, who employed their knowledge of hydraulics, acoustics and optics to produce apparent miracles for the edification of worshippers, may be regarded as the progenitors of those monarchs of mystery who, resplendent in evening dress or flamboyant costume, beguiled and bewildered the patrons of music halls in Victorian and Edwardian times.

It is our purpose in these pages to trace something of the evolution of the magic art from the sacred to the secular. In the hands of many capable exponents it has developed through the exhibitions of the itinerant performers of the Middle Ages, hobnobbing with rogues and vagabonds in the Elizabethan era, to emerge during the eighteenth century with a new dignity. Its practitioners then moved from the tavern and fairground to the Minor Theatres and subsequently to the new music halls, where, during the first decade of the nineteen hundreds, they flourished impressively as magic attained a pinnacle of popularity.

The ancient temple mysteries staged by the sorcerer-priests were, however, susceptible to rational explanations, and much of our knowledge of their mechanism is due to the writings of Hero of Alexandria, who was active about 62 AD.[1] Although Hero has suffered criticism by some authors as being, variously, an ignorant compiler, a mere artisan, and a practical technician and surveyor, and even for being obsessed with toys and such frivolous things, this

The mysterious altar, libations pouring from the vessels after a fire was lit upon it. Explained by Hero of Alexandria about 62AD.

seems manifestly an unfair assessment of an inventor and writer whose works on many aspects of physics have survived some two thousand years.[2] Thus the miracle of the opening shrine doors was precisely explained by Hero. The altar was, in fact, an airtight metal box communicating by a tube with a spherical vessel of water sited in a basement beneath the floor of the temple and away from the sight of the worshippers. As may be seen from the cut-away illustration, when the air in the altar expanded due to the heat of the newly kindled fire it would force water out of the vessel into the large bucket suspended by ropes from a pulley. These ropes wound round two spindles which passed up through the floor and to which the hinges of the doors of the shrine above were attached. Consequently, as the bucket started to descend under the increasing weight of water, the spindles turned and the doors started to open. Later, when the fire was extinguished, the air in the altar contracted and water was withdrawn from the bucket which rose, aided by the counterweight; the spindles thus revolved in the opposite direction and the door of the shrine closed.

The other mystery is explained in a similar fashion; the libations poured from the urns in response to air pressure (generated by the heated altar) on the liquids in the two reservoirs which fed the urns. Pliny recorded an example of a fountain of this type on the island of Andros from which wine flowed for seven days and, alas, water for the rest of the year.[3]

In the Temple of Bel, offerings of food and wine were brought each evening and spread at the feet of the idol. The worshippers retired and the temple was sealed overnight; yet, the following morning, when it was re-opened, all the food and drink had been consumed—a mighty miracle, and ample evidence that Bel was a living God, as King Cyrus of Persia maintained.[4] The solution of this particular mystery is attributed to Daniel and it probably represents the first recorded example of forensic science. One evening, after the offerings had been made, Daniel scattered an arc of ashes around them. The next morning the offerings had gone in the customary fashion but footprints were clearly visible in the ashes. They led to a secret door which opened into the priests' quarters, from whence those worthies emerged after dusk to carry off the prizes and (if we may be permitted to mix our religions!) to indulge in nightly Bacchanalian revels!

Acoustic mysteries abounded, too. There were vocal statues, the speaking head at Lesbos and trumpets that sounded when doors were opened.[3] With the decay of ancient civilizations, the later activities of archaeologists revealed the existence of speaking tubes connecting the mouths of such statues with the priests' quarters, so that the judicious applications of an ear to the tube would enable the priest to receive a question and adroitly serve up the appropriate answer. Trumpet sounds accompanying opening doors were produced mechanically, the door being attached to a funnel-shaped plunger suspended in a tank of water. It was so arranged that, when the door was opened, the plunger was forced down in the water, displacing air upwards through a tube to be emitted *via* the trumpet in an ear-shattering blast.[1]

There are also chronicles of gods being exhibited to the faithful in the temples. Thus Pliny mentions that in the temple of Hercules at Tyre there was a seat made of consecrated stone 'from which the gods easily rose', and there are various other examples which strongly suggest that concave mirrors were employed in conjuring up these apparitions, the existence of such mirrors in ancient times being well attested.[3] Optical illusions of this type were forerunners of the ghost entertainments which, by adapting the magic lantern, became so popular in the late eighteenth and early nineteenth centuries under the title of 'Phantasmagoria' (page 83).

In all these early mysteries we can observe the application of science to the production of apparent miracles, the priests assiduously employing their superior knowledge to create these remarkable effects. Equally, in the present technological age it is certain that we can have no proper appreciation of the tremendous impact that such wonders must have had on the minds of a largely credulous and superstitious people. Their belief in the supernatural was surely fortified by these strange and alarming experiences.

In stark contrast to the ponderous machinery of illusion encountered in the ancient temples is the dexterity of nimble fingers which creates illusion by sleight-of-hand, an individual performer pitting his skills and wits against the multitude, overtly to deceive and entertain.

While the origins of the art of mystifying are themselves shrouded in mystery, it is evident that sleight-of-hand was practised thousands of years before the birth of Christ. The first recorded per-

The discouerie
of witchcraft,

Wherein the lewde dealing of witches
and witchmongers is notablie detected, the
knauerie of coniurors, the impietie of inchan-
tors, the follie of soothsaiers, the impudent falf-
hood of coufenors, the infidelitie of atheifts,
the peftilent practifes of Pythonifts, the
curiofitie of figurecafters, the va-
nitie of dreamers, the begger-
lie art of Alcu-
myftrie,

The abhomination of idolatrie, the hor-
rible art of poifoning, the vertue and power of
naturall magike, and all the conueiances
of Legierdemaine and iugling are deciphered:
and many other things opened, which
haue long lien hidden, howbeit
verie neceffarie to
be knowne.

Heerevnto is added a treatife vpon the
nature and fubftance of fpirits and diuels,
&c : all latelie written
by Reginald Scot
Efquire.

1. Iohn.4,1.

Beleeue not euerie fpirit, but trie the fpirits, whether they are
of God; for manie falfe prophets are gone
out into the world, &c.

1584

[14]

formance of a genuine conjuring feat is to be found in the papyrus acquired by Henry Westcar when he visited Egypt in 1823–4, a document which subsequently passed into the hands of the German Egyptologist Richard Lepsius and ultimately into the possession of Berlin State Museum. This 'Westcar Papyrus' tells of how King Cheops, builder of the Great Pyramid at Giza about 2600 BC, asks his sons to recount tales of wonders wrought by magicians of the past. After hearing them, one of his sons, Hardedef, informs his father that he is acquainted with a living magician called Dedi and can bring him to the court to show his skills.

Dedi is a townsman living in the south at Dedsnefru, and is apparently one hundred and ten years old (this was the traditional lifespan of the Egyptians and may be compared with three score years and ten today). Hardedef said 'he eateth five hundred loaves, a haunch of beef in the way of meat, and drinketh one hundred jugs of beer, unto this very day. He knoweth how to put on again a head that hath been cut off, and he knoweth how to make a lion follow after him, with its leash trailing on the ground. He knoweth the number of the locks of the sanctuary of Thoth.'[5,6] This description of Dedi's prowess whetted King Cheops' appetite for a demonstration and Hardedef was despatched to bring the old man to him. Dedi travelled downstream in Hardedef's vessel, accompanied by his assistants and his books in two following ships.

When they arrived in the pillared hall of the palace Cheops asked why he had never seen Dedi before, to which the magician replied it was really Cheops' fault because he had never previously invited him to the palace! The king then asked whether it was true that he could restore a head that had been cut off. The reply being in the affirmative, his majesty then called for a prisoner to be brought from captivity in order that his punishment might be inflicted. At this Dedi demurred:

'But not on a man O King, my lord! Lo, is not such a thing rather commanded to be done to the august cattle?'

And a goose was brought unto him, and its head was cut off; and the goose was placed on the western side of the hall and its head on the

eastern side of the hall. And Dedi said his say of magic, and thereupon the goose stood up and waddled, and its head likewise. Now when one part had reached the other, the goose stood up and cackled. And he had a duck brought unto him, and there was done unto it the like. And his majesty had an ox brought unto him, and its head was made to tumble to the ground. And Dedi said his say of magic, and the ox stood up behind him, while its leash fell to the ground.

Although the feat with the lion seems to have been omitted, here is the first description of the decapitation illusion which for over four and a half thousand years has remained, in one form or another,

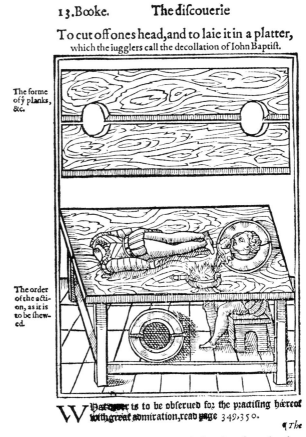

13. Booke.   The difcouerie

To cut off ones head, and to laie it in a platter,
which the iugglers call the decollation of Iohn Baptift.

The forme of y̆ planks, &c.

The order of the action, as it is to be shewed.

W̄ Hat̄ouer is to be obferued for the practifing hereof with great admiration, read page 349, 350.

¶ The

'The Decollation of John Baptist', the decapitation illusion described by Reginald Scot in THE DISCOVERIE OF WITCHCRAFT (1584). For realism he suggested: '. . . put about his necke a little dough kneeded with bul|locks bloud, which being cold will appeare like dead flesh; & being pricked with a sharpe round hollow quill, will bleed, and seeme verie strange.'

The title page of Reginald Scot's THE DISCOVERIE OF WITCHCRAFT (1584), the first book in the English language to explain the principles of legerdemain.

part of the repertoire of magicians. Perhaps few of today's wielders of the 'Head Chopper' realize its direct link with ancient Egypt! We shall see in subsequent chapters how this theme of violence and not a little horror has run like a thread through centuries of performance to fascinate audiences who, in another setting, would perhaps be jostling around the gallows or guillotine for a free spectacle with an unfortunately irreversible climax. For the historian of conjuring it is an interesting observation on the psychology of audiences that an element of violence should attract and entertain, yet in its way it is no more incongruous than that the gruesome aspects of Grimm's Fairy Tales or tales of Headless Horsemen should captivate denizens of the nursery who are equally secure in the knowledge that the story will have a guaranteed happy outcome.

The fact that Dedi was not prepared to decapitate a human being suggests that he did not have the appropriate apparatus with him, rather than the alternative suggestion that he was simply displaying his humanity.[5] The beheading of a man became part of the miracle plays and, as the 'Decollation of John Baptist', is described in Reginald Scot's *The Discoverie of Witchcraft* (1584), the first book in the English language to explain in detail how to perform sleight-of-hand tricks. (In parenthesis, we may note that the very first book in English to describe any trick preceded Scot by three years. A compilation by Thomas Hill titled *A brief and pleasant treatise* included a few simple parlour feats in company with such diverse activities as poultry keeping, fowling and killing fleas!)

Here we must explain that the application of the words 'conjuring' and 'magic' to a sleight-of-hand entertainment was not established until the later part of the eighteenth century. The first use of 'conjurer' in this sense was probably in the title of the book *The Conjurer Unmasked*, published in 1785. Prior to this time the words had supernatural connotations. A conjurer was defined as 'one who is supposed to practise the vile arts of raising spirits and conferring with the Devil',[7] while a magician was an individual who was believed to invoke spirits in order to produce marvellous effects. At a time when the belief in evil spirits and witchcraft was endemic, an entertainer who inadvertently implied that he was a conjurer or magician or, more importantly, had that accusation levelled against him, was likely to be in dire trouble. The statutes of Henry VIII against conjuration and witchcraft provided the death penalty

Matthew Hopkins, Witch-Finder General. A print by James Caulfield (1792) based on the frontispiece to Hopkins' THE DISCOVERY OF WITCHES (1647).

for such offences. Although the amending act of Elizabeth's reign limited punishment to the pillory, at least for first, less serious offences, for some two hundred years after the first Act of Parliament condemning witchcraft in England was passed in 1541 the persecution of suspected witches was vigorously enacted. Individuals such as the notorious Matthew Hopkins, the self-styled Witch-Finder General,[8] who justified his methods in *The Discovery of Witches* (1647), pursued suspects relentlessly to uphold the commandment in *Exodus* (Chapter 22, verse 18), 'Thou shalt not suffer a witch to live.'

It was, in fact, the cruelty of the proceedings revealed by witchcraft trials that led Reginald Scot, a Justice of the Peace, to write his crusading work *The Discoverie of Witchcraft*, in which he endeavoured to rebut some of the then prevalent views, although he himself was by no means the complete sceptic. The significance of this book in the history of conjuring entertainment is immense, for Scot conceived the idea that it would be a telling argument for his case if

The Cups and Balls trick in the fifteenth century. A woodcut by an unknown artist for the Block Book WIRTUNG DER PLANETEN (1470) *derived from the original* CHILDREN OF THE PLANETS *drawing by Joseph of Ulm (1404).*

he could demonstrate that feats of sleight-of-hand were produced by purely natural means and not by any diabolical intervention. At that time he possessed no knowledge of such skills, but he took lessons from a Frenchman, John Cautares, who lived at St Martin's in London, and was thus able to devote a whole section of his book to an explanation of legerdemain. As we have previously noted, it was the first book in the English language to lay bare such secrets and it is clear that Scot's conscience was thereby pricked by his action

being sorie that it falleth out to my lot, to laie open the secrets of this mysterie, to the hinderance of such poore men as live thereby: whose dooings herein are not onlie tollerable, but greatlie commendable, so they abuse not the name of God, nor make the people attribute unto them his power.

This problem of the exposure of magical secrets is one which has troubled responsible conjurers ever since Scot's day, and magical societies (a phenomenon entirely of the twentieth century) solemnly enjoin their members not to indulge in such activity. For that reason, the reader will not find in this book any explicit revelation of tricks and illusions that are currently in use, although he may perhaps discover a hint or two about some mysteries of the past!

The exponent of sleight-of-hand tricks was formerly called a juggler, initially a generic term that included also minstrels, troubadours and poets, as well as the activity that today we describe as juggling. The word was derived from the Latin *joculator* and French *jougleur*. Gradually the term became associated only with the sleight-of-hand performer, who was also referred to as a *tregetour* or *prestigiator*.[9,10] To avoid confusion, the reader should note that hereafter we shall use the terms 'juggler' and 'conjurer' interchangeably for the period during which the former name was in current use, that is almost until the end of the eighteenth century; thereafter 'conjurer' and its alternatives of 'magician', 'wizard' and even 'necromancer' (a favourite with nineteenth-century performers) will be employed solely in the sense of this type of entertainer.

While Reginald Scot did not profess to cover the whole field of legerdemain, he focused attention on the principal feats of the Art of Juggling, which he divided into three main categories—with balls, with cards and with money—and observed that 'He that is expert in these may shew much pleasure, and manie feats', stressing that by these pursuits only men's eyes and judgement are deceived. The modern sleight-of-hand performer makes excellent use of these same three items and, while techniques have improved immeasurably, some of the same tricks are still used today. One that was already ancient when Scot described it is the Cups and Balls, unquestionably the earliest of the feats of sleight-of-hand.[11] The appearance and disappearance of small cork balls beneath three metal cups in the most bewildering manner is a classic of magic. It is not surprising, therefore, that this trick, like the decapitation illusion, may be traced throughout the ages and is symbolic of the juggler. Numerous artists who have depicted conjurers at work, either as the principal figure or as incidental characters, show them performing the Cups and Balls.

Some writers have claimed that the Beni Hasan mural painting (c. 2200 BC) discovered in a tomb in

Upper Egypt is the earliest representation of the trick,[12,13] but this is almost certainly not so, the four enormous conical objects depicted defying such usage.[14] The first authenticated reference to the feat is by Seneca (3 BC–65 AD), who remarks:

Such quibbles are just as harmlessly deceptive as the juggler's cup and pebbles, in which it is the very trickery that pleases me. But show me how the trick is done, and I have lost my interest therein.

By that period it was obviously a very familiar effect. Its performers in Rome were known as *acetabularii*, a word meaning cups. The first description of the Cups and Balls from the spectator's standpoint is an interesting account by Alciphron of Athens in the second century AD.

A man came forward and placed on a three-legged table three small dishes, under which he concealed some little white round pebbles. These he placed one by one under the dishes, and then, I do not know how, he made them appear altogether under one. At other times he made them disappear from beneath the dishes, and showed them in his mouth. Next when he had swallowed them, he brought those who stood nearest him into the middle, and then pulled one stone from the nose, another from the ear, and another from the head of the man standing near him. Finally he caused the stones to vanish from the sight of everyone.

The earliest known illustration of the Cups and Balls is a coloured drawing of the *Children of the Planets, Luna* executed by Joseph of Ulm in 1404, and which is now in the Library of the University of

THE JUGGLER *by Hieronymus Bosch (c. 1460–1516).*

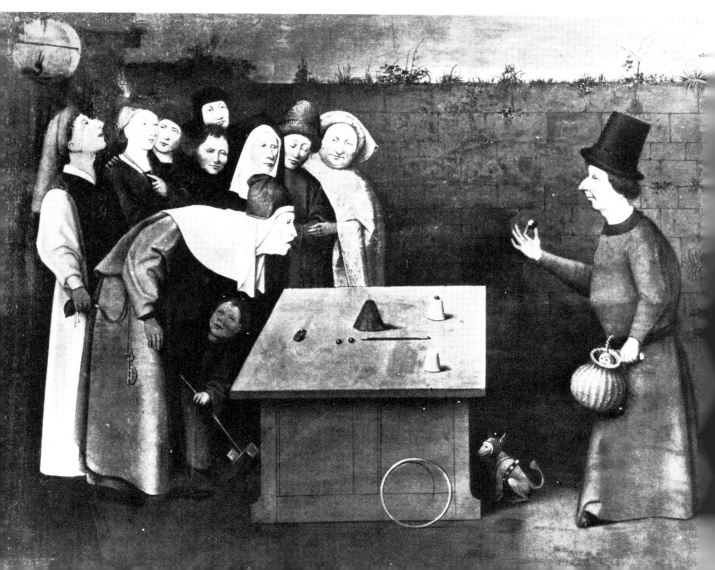

Tübingen.[15] It is an example from a Planet book, produced in the fifteenth century to show the power and influence heavenly bodies were believed to have on the children born under their aspect within a constellation. The drawing shows a juggler, with a huge feather in his hat, sitting behind a three-legged circular table, holding a goblet in each hand, and there are three balls on the table. He is one of several individuals depicted in this view of the town of Ulm and he must therefore have been a familiar figure. During the fifteenth century a whole family of similar drawings was derived from this original, and also engravings which incorporated Cups and Balls performers.

The most famous representation of a conjurer is *The Juggler* by Hieronymus Bosch (c. 1460–1516), an oil painting now in the Municipal Museum at St Germain-en-Laye. Here the performer is standing behind a table on which apparatus for the Cups and Balls is placed. He has a basket containing an owl slung from his waist. Of the watching spectators, one is a cutpurse in the act of relieving a lady, absorbed in the magic, of her money, although he is observed by a young man who endeavours to point out the misdeed to his female companion. This is the first example of a fairly recurrent theme in prints and engravings depicting conjurers, and it has been suggested that in some cases the pickpockets were accomplices of the performer.[15] It probably accounts, too, for the familiar rejoinder I frequently experience when I am introduced to someone as a conjurer—'Oh, I'd better watch my wallet'!

Many illustrations clearly show the conjurer wearing a belt with a bag or pouch attached, in which the smaller properties that he needed for his show were kept. This article of apparel, an essential part of his equipment, was virtually a badge of office. It must be remembered that clothes did not have pockets incorporated into them until the mid-sixteenth century, and therefore money and any articles needed by a trade or profession had to be carried in bags or pouches, usually slung from the belt;[16] in this respect, therefore, the conjurer was no different from the medieval medicine man carrying his medicaments or the rat-catcher his poisons. These bags were quite distinct from aprons worn for protective purposes by, for example, carpenters and stonemasons, which subsequently developed into a symbol of their trade or craft and could later be seen in specific colours; e.g., blue for gardeners and checks for barbers.[17] The earliest illustrations of con-

jurers (Ulm drawings) show the bags with ring openings, and Bosch's conjurer is even equipped with a wicker basket. Later the apron-like bag appeared, the first and virtually only reference to which in English conjuring texts occurs in *Hocus Pocus Junior* (1634) where, instructing his readers in the Cups and Balls, the author says: 'Some I have seen sit with their Cod-piece open, others play standing with a budget hanging before them.' 'Budget' was a seventeenth-century term; Moxon's *Mechanick Exercises* (1677) refers to 'A budget or pocket to hang by their sides to put their nails in.'[16] The open cod-piece is quite an interesting variation and one can only trust there was a cod-placket beneath to avert exposure of a non-magical kind.

Despite the paucity of information about this accessory in English books, the pioneer conjuring text in Spanish, which appeared in 1733, not only illustrated the apron bag but categorically stated it was the first requisite for the tyro.[18] This bag had a triangular flap which was presumably tucked inside during performances. The French term for the conjurer's bag was *gibecière* (meaning a game bag, too) and in England during the fourteenth and

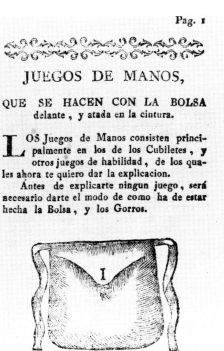

The conjurer's bag or gibecière, *illustrated in the first Spanish book of conjuring published in 1733. It was described as an essential piece of equipment.*

fifteenth centuries the *gipser* or *gipciere* was a purse or pouch. Chaucer said:

A gipser al of silke
Heng at his gurdel[19]

That the *gibecière* was synonymous with the conjurer and conjuring is evident from the work of Jacques Ozanam (1640–1717), who devoted a whole section of his *Récréations Mathématiques et Physiques* (1694) to 'Tours de Gibecière', although his instructions for the Cups and Balls do say that the balls may be put either in your pocket or in a *gibecière*.

Distinctive conjurer's dress may have been worn in some instances. Chettle in 1592 describes an itinerant juggler, William Cuckoe:

. . . an olde fellow, his bearde milke-white, his head covered with a round lowe crownd rent silke hat, on which was a band knit in many knotes, wherein stucke two round stickes after the Jugler's manner. His jerkin was of leather cut, his cloake of three coulers, his hose paind with yellow drawn out with blew, his instrument was a bagpipe, & I knew him to be William Cuckoe, better knowne than lov'd, yet some thinke, as well lov'd as he was worthy.[20]

Special dress is also indicated in 1591 by Spenser, who has one of his characters say: 'I meane me to disguize in some straunge habit . . . like a Gipsen or a Juggeler.'[21]

In the Middle Ages, legend and magic were apt to become interwoven, and some of the feats recounted by authors such as Chaucer[22] were fanciful indeed. Of the panoply of philosophers and alchemists whose names have been linked with magic we shall single out one of the most learned men of the thirteenth century, Albert Graf von Bollstadt, better known as Albertus Magnus or Albert the Great. Teacher, philosopher, theologian and scientist he undoubtedly was, but many authors have also considered him to be a magician,[23, 24, 25] although in this connexion it is rather difficult to discern precisely where fact gives way to fiction. Certainly there is little evidence to suggest that he practised legerdemain in the accepted sense although, as we shall see, the use of at least one device dear to the heart of the modern conjurer has been attributed to him.

Albert, the eldest son of the Count of Bollstadt, was born at Lauingen in Swabia, Bavaria, in 1193. About 1223 he joined the Dominican Order at Padua and a few years later he taught in Cologne and then successively was Lector at Hildesheim (1233), Freiburg, Ratisbon and Strasburg. In 1245 he was sent to the University of Paris where he graduated as master in the theological faculty and acquired great fame on account of his theological and philosophical works. Albert returned to Cologne in 1248 and there Thomas Aquinas was his chief disciple until he too was sent to Paris, in 1252. A little later (1254–7) Albert was Provincial of Teutonia, the German province of the Dominicans.

By order of Pope Alexander IV he became, in 1260, Bishop of Regensburg but resigned in 1261 following the Pope's death. In 1270 he finally settled in Cologne and, although he still travelled and apparently attended the Council of Lyons in 1274, it was in Cologne that he remained and it was there that he died, on 15 November 1280. He was proclaimed a saint in 1662 and canonized on 16 December 1931.

Albert's fame was such that even his contemporary English rival Roger Bacon acknowledged him as the most noted of Christian scholars. He was a prolific author, and there is no question that he holds a pre-eminent place in the history of science. What then of his association with magic? His pupil and contemporary Ulrich Engelbert of Strasburg referred to him as 'expert in magic' and the *Histoire Littéraire de la France* stated: 'He is an alchemist, he is an astrologer, he believes in enchantments, he delights like most savants of his age in explaining all phenomena that surprise him by supernatural causes.' The nearest that we can get to conjuring is the statement by Thorndike, discussing Albert's works:

Albert had no doubts either in his scientific or religious writings that marvels can be worked by magic. It is true that one of its departments *praestigia*, has to do with illusions and juggleries in which things are made to appear to exist which have no reality. But it also performs actual transformations. But even the actual performances of magic are deceptive in that demons by their means lead human souls astray, which is far worse than merely to deceive the eye.[25]

William Godwin records one of the best known legends concerning Albert's magical prowess.[24] It is claimed that he spent thirty years in fabricating a man entirely in brass, that the man would answer all sorts of questions and served his master in the capacity of servant. This automaton became at length so garrulous that Thomas Aquinas, at that time Albert's pupil, was perpetually disturbed in his abstrusest speculations by the machine's loquacity and, in a rage, took a hammer and smashed it completely. Bishop John Wilkins is a little less charitable towards Aquinas and comments 'that statue in the framing of which Albertus bestowed thirty years, broken by Aquinas, who came to see it, purposely that he might boast, how in one minute he had ruined the labour of so many years'.[26] Albert's automaton, like Roger Bacon's speaking head, has often been regarded as an early form of ventriloquial figure. The Duke of Wellington was similarly minded in 1846 when he visited Professor Faber's Euphonia, a speaking figure then being exhibited in London. However, in this case it was genuine enough, as the Duke soon convinced himself (page 148). Albert was credited also with the construction of a wooden mechanical horse, a swan automaton and a parachute.[27]

Albert Garreau, author of *Saint Albert*, has strongly emphasized that some of the accounts of Albert's magic are but legends and the myth has been created particularly in chapbooks and hawker's pamphlets.[28] He lays the blame squarely on popular literature and the astute editors who have used the celebrated name of a monk long dead to facilitate the sales of their works—or rubbish as the case may be!

In contrast, however, Scheeben commented:

The power of Albert over the secret forces of nature has been depicted in many of the 'legends'. First of all, mention must be made of the celebrated enchanted goblet which is preserved at Cologne. If Albert had himself made this goblet it was not for the purpose of black magic, but this goblet has the effect of conferring emetic properties on water. The explanation is simple. Inside the goblet, between two thin layers of white metal, a little antimony is introduced through a hole pierced in the upper layer. This antimony gives the water or wine its emetic properties.[29]

The use of the false bottom to aid the physician in his 'magic' cures is the same principle that was later employed for some versions of an apparent transformat on of water to other liquids.

The goblet of Albertus Magnus now reposes, some six hundred years later, in the Historical Museum at Cologne.[30] The interior of the vessel, understandably, is somewhat decayed, although traces of the double bottom are clearly discernible, affording an interesting conjuring association with

The goblet of Albertus Magnus (1193–1280), which has a secret compartment into which an emetic could be introduced.

the famous medieval scientist who also practised a little white magic with his 'enchanted goblet'.

The principal juggler in the reign of Henry VIII was called Brandon and he was the first British performer of whom any precise record exists. Shrewsbury Corporation accounts for 1521 and 1535 note payments to 'Brandon the King's Juggler', and the accounts of Thetford Priory likewise enter payment to Brandon and Smith, who are termed 'Jugglers of the King.[31] One of Brandon's remarkable feats was recorded by Reginald Scot in his *Discoverie of Witchcraft*.

In the king's presence Brandon painted a dove on a wall and, pointing out a pigeon sitting on top of a house, repeatedly stabbed the picture with a knife while uttering magic spells until, suddenly, the pigeon dropped down dead. This created great astonishment and Brandon was forbidden to perform the feat again 'least he should emploie it in anie kind of murther'. Scot observes that the story was still fresh in people's minds and akin to tales of witchcraft. He then goes on to explain how it was

The whole ART of

LEGERDEMAIN:

OR

Hocus Pocus

In PERFECTION.

By which the meaneſt Capacity may perform the Whole ART without a Teacher. Together with the Uſe of all the Inſtruments belonging thereto.

To which is now added,

Abundance of New and Rare Inventions, the like never before in Print but much deſired by many.

The Seventh Edition, with large Additions and Amendments.

Written by H. DEAN.

LONDON,

Printed for L. HAWES and Co. and S. CROWDER, in *Pater-Noſter-Row,* and R. WARE and Co. on *Ludgate-Hill.* 1772.

Strange Feats are herein taught by Slight of Hand,
With which you may divert yourſelf and Friend.
The like in print was never ſeen before,
And ſo you'll ſay, when once you've read it o'er.

Henry Dean's THE WHOLE ART OF LEGERDEMAIN *(1722), and its derivatives, served as primers for aspiring conjurers for over 150 years. Dean, who based his text on Reginald Scot's* THE DISCOVERIE OF WITCH-CRAFT *(1584), is believed to have been a dealer in magical equipment who had a bookshop in Tower Hill. The frontispiece includes the familiar decapitation illusion.*

achieved. The pigeon had previously been captured from the rooftop and drugged with *nux vomica,* a poison which killed it within half an hour. The bird was returned to its perch and the juggler, with nice timing, played out his mystery. Scot, with admirable researcher's instinct, had investigated the efficacy of the poison, for a marginal note states: 'This I have prooved upon crows and pies.' (He also mentions that a juggler named Kingsfield performed the decapitation illusion at Bartholomew Fair in 1582.)

The general interest in jugglers' tricks in Elizabethan times extended to the theatre, and there is ample evidence that juggling scenes were even inserted into plays,[32] as indicated by the denial of any jugglery in the Prologue to *Summer's Last Will and Testament:*

Such odd trifles as mathematicians' experiments be artificial flies to hang in the air by themselves, dancing balls, an egg-shell that shall climb up to the top of a spear, fiery-breathing gores, *poeta noster* professeth not to make.[33]

Wright considers that the conjurer was a favourite performer with the populace, taking rank with the clown and the devil, and stressing that the uncritical crowd cared little about the dramatic requirements of the play—they wanted to see the conjurer's spectacles irrespective of whether they were extraneous or not. The same authority emphasizes the popularity of tricks of mutilation, to which we have already referred, instancing decapitations and executions as the staple fare in many plays. The well supported conclusion is that the Elizabethan dramatist utilized jugglers' tricks to a much greater extent than was formerly appreciated, either by writing them in or adapting them to the plot, or simply by introducing

extraneous performances. Either way it satisfied the popular demand for spectacular shows.

In the reign of James I (1603–25) there was a juggler who had assumed the name of Hocus Pocus. Thus Thomas Ady, who in 1655 wrote a treatise critical of the belief in witchcraft titled *A Candle in the Dark*,[34] had this to say:

I will speak of one Man more excelling in that craft than others, that went about in King James his time, and long since, who called himself The Kings Majesties most excellent Hocus Pocus, and so was he called, because that at the playing of every Trick, he used to say, '*Hocus pocus, tontus, talontus, vade celeriter jubeo*', a darke composure of words to blinde the eyes of the beholders . . .

The book has a chapter headed 'A Jugler' which describes a seventeenth-century conjuring performance, including the decapitation illusion with a boy, a magic funnel which enabled claret apparently to be withdrawn from the forehead, the transposition of a coin, and writing in red and blue with the same ink.

Although an individual juggler had obviously assumed the name Hocus Pocus, this term became a generic one in Europe during the seventeenth

Hans Weiditz of Augsburg executed this woodcut of AMUSEMENTS OF THE JESTERS *in 1520. It was an illustration for a German translation of Petrarch's* DE REMEDIIS UTRIUSQUE FORTUNAE, *ultimately published in 1532.*

century to describe both jugglers and their performances. Samuel Butler in *Hudibras* writes:

> . . . *with a slight*
> *Conveys Mens* Interest, and Right,
> *From* Stile's pocket into Nokeses;
> *As easily, as* Hocus Pocus.[35]

The words were not recorded by Scot in 1584 nor by Sa Rid in *The Art of Jugling* (1612), and their derivation has been much debated, whether from Ochus Bochus, an ancient magician invoked by Italian conjurers[36] or as a corruption of *hoc est corpus* used in the Eucharist, as suggested by Archbishop Tillotson.[37] Recent authority inclines to the view that the juggler who assumed the name derived it from the sham Latin formula he employed in his performances.[38] The expression first appears in literature with John Gee's *New Shreds of the Old Snare* (1624):

I always thought they had their rudiments from some jugling Hocas Pocas in a quart pot[39]

but quickly entered general use and was enshrined on the title page of a whole family of conjuring texts beginning in 1634 with *Hocus Pocus Junior: The Anatomie of Legerdemain*, which subsequently went through many editions: it was the first *illustrated* book devoted *solely* to conjuring in the English language.

John Ferguson, Regius Professor of Chemistry at the University of Glasgow from 1874 until 1915 and a noted bibliophile, observed that *Hocus Pocus Junior* contained only one trick that was based on a physical principle, namely to freeze water by the fireside.

The apparatus consisted of a stool, a quart-pot, snow, a little water, and a short stick. Water is poured on the stool, the pot is set in the water, snow is put in the pot, with some salt on the sly, and the mixture is churned with the stick. By and by the pot freezes to the stool. Then the author adds: 'There's a naturall reason may be given for this, which he thats a scholler need not be told, and for a common Jugler I would not have so wise as to know, therefore I omit it.' That was hardly fair to the 'common Jugler', who would have been more successful if he had known the principle involved.[40]

Almost two hundred years later, in 1814, the 'common juggler' was still held in pretty low esteem, as witness this delightful entry under the heading of 'Legerdemain' in the *Encyclopaedia Londinensis*.

The two chief branches of Legerdemain are cups and balls and tricks upon cards . . . we think it would not be much to the credit of the work or to the satisfaction of the reader to enter into such disquisitions; since the former is practised only by the lowest class of itinerants, and a dexterity in the latter is apt to lead to a habit of cheating.

While the conjurer performs his trick the pickpocket accomplice practices his own brand of legerdemain! Titled GRANDE REUSSITE EN COEUR! *by Hippolyte Bellangé (1800–66), this picture was published in Paris in 1827.*

2
THE LEARNED ANIMALS

Even in Provence, the *Enseignamens* for
joglars [*c.* 1200AD] warn their readers to
learn the art of imitating birds, leaping
through hoops, showing off performing asses
and dogs, and dangling marionettes.

E. K. Chambers, *The Mediaeval Stage* (1903)

From the earliest times jugglers have trained animals to simulate the actions of human beings, to dance, tumble and even walk the slack rope. However, the first record of an animal performing conjuring feats appears to be that of the horse Marocco (sometimes rendered as Morocco) in 1591. This celebrated animal left his hoofprints across a wide range of Elizabethan and Jacobean literature and he is, without question, the most famous learned creature of all time. He was owned by a juggler named Banks, or Bankes, who is variously stated to have been a Scotsman[1] or a Staffordshire man,[2] and who had served Robert Devereux, Earl of Essex, Master of the Horse to Queen Elizabeth and subsequently Earl Marshal of England. Essex had a provincial company of players, the Earl of Essex's Men, from 1581 to 1596,[3] and it seems possible, therefore, that Banks' earliest appearances with Marocco may have been under the banner of these players.

In a contemporary manuscript diary kept by a native of Shrewsbury, and dated September 1591, we read:

This yeare and against the assise tyme on Master Banckes, a Staffordshire gentile, brought into this towne of Salop a white horsse which wolld doe wonderfull and strange thinges.[2]

There follows a description of Marocco telling how much money was in a man's purse by tapping with his hoof, with his mouth drawing forth any named person in the company or someone wearing a coat of a chosen colour, and of going to one of the

Banks and his famous learned horse Marocco, immortalized by Shakespeare and other writers. An illustration from a contemporary tract, MAROCCUS EXTATICUS, *published in 1595.*

two Bailiffs of the town—the one who had bade Banks welcome—and bowing and curtseying to him. Our diarist goes on to opine that these were

suche strange feates for suche a beast to doe, that many people judgid that it were impossible to be don except he had a famyliar or don by the art of magicke.

As we shall see, these Shrewsbury people were not

the last to consider that Banks and his horse were in league with the devil!

There is notice of the horse in a manuscript copy of Donne's *Satires*, dated 1593, in the British Museum but such was the beast's fame that in 1595 was published a rare tract titled *Maroccus Extaticus. Or, Bankes Bay Horse in a Trance*.[4] This satirical pamphlet purports to be a dialogue between them, and contains a crude wood engraving of Marocco and his master, the horse rearing on its hind legs with a stick in its mouth and apparently counting the number of spots on a pair of dice, while Banks, stick in hand, controls the performance. The title page suggests that Banks was exhibiting Marocco at the Belsavage Inn outside Ludgate, a place where entertainments were frequent and where, according to his custom, the juggler charged twopence for admission. In 1601 the animal was described as a middle-sized bay English gelding, about fourteen years old, and there are other descriptions of it as a bay curtall; i.e., a chestnut or brown horse with a cropped tail. Since Banks claimed to be able to train any horse in a similar fashion within one year, it has been conjectured that he may have exhibited more than one animal bearing the same name.[5] This could then well account for the inconsistencies encountered in the colour of the horse, Sir William D'Avenant much later referring to a 'white oate-eater', just as in that very first mention by the Shropshire diarist.

Such was the fame of Banks and his horse that there is scarcely a humorous writer between 1590 and 1620 who does not mention them.[6] William Shakespeare immortalized the animal in *Love's Labours Lost*, when he had the page Moth say to Armado, after puzzling him with arithmetical questions, 'How easy it is . . . the dancing horse will tell you' (Act I, Scene 2). Sir Walter Raleigh also thought fit to mention them in his *History of the World* (1614), saying: 'if Banks had lived in olden times, he would have shamed all the enchanters in the world: for whosoever was most famous among them could never master or instruct any beast as he did.'[7] Sir William D'Avenant alluded to Marocco in his poem *The Long Vacation in London* (1673), wherein he says

And white oate-eater, that does dwell
In stable small at sign of Bell:
That lifts up hoofe to show the prancks,
Taught by magician, stiled Banks.[8]

Sir Kenelm Digby recorded that the horse would restore a glove to its owner after Banks had whispered the man's name in his ear; and would correctly tell the number of pence in any silver coin shown to his master by tapping with his hoof.[9] Other feats included divining the number of coins in a purse or hidden in a glove, or indicating the spots thrown on a pair of dice, as illustrated in the woodcut, and even 'discharging himself of his excrements, whensoever he bade him'.

Richard Tarlton, the famous Elizabethan jester, who died in 1588, is reputed to have had an encounter with Marocco, as recorded in *Tarlton's Jests* published in 1611.[10] In that section of the book subtitled 'Tarlton's Sound City Jests' there is 'Tarlton's greeting with Banks his horse', wherein we read that Tarlton, who was playing at the Bell in Gracious Street, went to the Cross Keys nearby, a place of popular amusement where Banks was exhibiting Marocco.

Banks, perceiving the jester in his audience, said to his horse, 'Signior, go fetch me the veryest foole in the company,' whereupon the horse went across and with his mouth drew Tarlton forth, to the great delight of the assembly.

Tarlton said nothing but 'God a mercy horse', although he was not pleased at the laughter caused. In the end he told Banks, 'Sir, had I the power of your horse, as you have, I would doe more than that.'

To please him, Banks replied, 'What ere it be, I will charge him to do it.'

'Then,' said Tarlton, 'charge him bring me the veriest whore-master in the company.'

Marocco dutifully led his master to the jester who, mollified, said: 'God a mercy horse indeed.'

And, as the author picturesquely records, 'The people had much ado to keep peace'!

Banks took Marocco to the continent in the first decade of the seventeenth century and the trip gave rise to a wealth of stories of varying veracity. Jean de Montlyard, Sieur de Meleray, in the commentary to his translation of *The Golden Ass* of Apuleius, tells of seeing Marocco in Paris at the Silver Lyon in Rue Saint Jacques and describes the performance, which concluded with the horse dancing 'the Canaries', a wild extravagant dance.[11] There is a ring of the present day about one of the tricks, in which Marocco not only told the number of francs in a crown but also knew that the crown was devalued and the exact extent of the devaluation!

When the noted female pickpocket Mary Frith, better known as Mall or Moll Cut-purse, was quite young, for a wager of £20 she rode Banks' horse Marocco from Charing Cross to Shoreditch dressed in doublet, breeches, boots and spurs and carrying a trumpet in her hand and a banner on her back.[12] For the wearing of men's clothes on this occasion, Mall was tried by the ecclesiastical court and forced to do penance at the door of St Paul's Cathedral. However, presumably having atoned for the misdemeanour perpetrated on her ride through the streets, she henceforth adopted male attire, became an expert fencer and bold rider and, in the role of highwayman, robbed General Fairfax of 200 gold jacobuses on Hounslow Heath. For this exploit she was sent to Newgate but managed to buy her release and lived comparatively luxuriously to the age of seventy-five. Caulfield is particularly censorious, labelling her as a prostitute and procuress, a fortune-teller, a pick-pocket, a thief and a receiver of stolen goods.[13] He prints an engraving of her together with various animals which, apparently, she delighted in training; it seems that, like Banks, she made money by exhibiting their tricks.

Raymond Toole Stott, in his monumental *Circus and Allied Arts*, has observed that Marocco's dancing act was undoubtedly the original of the modern *haute école*.[4]

Not least of the claims made for Marocco was his alleged feat of climbing the steeple of St Paul's and, while it has been suggested that he might have achieved this ascension by means of the steps inside, the story is certainly apocryphal because, as Altick has pointed out, the steeple was struck by lightning and burned in 1561, and it was never rebuilt.[14]

Inevitably, for many unenlightened people, the precocity of the quadruped smacked of sorcery and the machinations of the devil. Bishop Thomas Morton recorded the following story in 1609.

Which bringeth into my remembrance a story which Banks told me at Frankfort, from his own experience in France among the Capuchins, by whom he was brought into suspicion of magic, because of the strange feats which his horse Morocco played (as I take it) at Orleans, where he, to redeem his credit, promised to manifest to the world, that his horse was nothing less than a devil. To this end he commanded his horse to seek out one in the press of people who had a crucifix on his hat; which done, he bade him kneel down

unto it, and not this only, but also to rise up again and to kiss it. And now, gentlemen (quoth he), I think my horse hath acquitted both me and himself; and so his adversaries rested satisfied; conceiving (as it might seem) that the devil had no power to come near the cross.[15]

Despite the contretemps at Orleans, there is nothing to suggest that Banks did ultimately suffer the fate attributed to him in Ben Jonson's *Epigrams*:

But 'mongst these Tiberts, who do you think there
*   was?*
Old Banks, the Juggler, our Pythagoras,
Grave tutor to the learned horse; both which,
Being, beyond sea, burned for one witch,
Their spirits transmigrated to a cat.[16]

Quite the contrary, for Banks returned to England after his continental adventures and was temporarily employed by Henry, Prince of Wales, in the management of his horses, as revealed by the *Privy Purse Expenses* for 1608–9. Certain it is, too, that in later years he became a vintner in Cheapside, for there are references to a vintner Banks, who 'taught his horse to dance and shooed him with silver' and who was still alive in 1637.[1]

The first explanation of the remarkable tricks performed by Marocco was given in 1607 by Gervase Markham, a prolific author of the period, in a volume titled *Cavelarice, or the English Horseman*.[17] This compendium of eight books embraces the art of horsemanship and devotes the last of these books to 'an explanation of the excellency of a Horses understanding, and how to make him doe Tricks lyke Bankes his Curtall . . .'. Markham tells his readers that, although it may be considered unnecessary and unnatural to teach the horse to carry out actions more properly associated with dogs, apes, monkeys and baboons, nonetheless he desires to satisfy Man's delight in novelties, especially since the tricks he describes reveal the extraordinary capacities and worthy qualities of the horse. He goes on to explain how to teach one's horse to count numbers, to lie down and even 'to pisse when you woulde have him (or at least to straine and move himselfe thereunto)'.

Five years later, when the first book in the English language devoted exclusively to conjuring, *The Art of Jugling or Legerdemaine* (1612) appeared, the compiler, Sa Rid, who had leaned very heavily on Scot's *Discoverie of Witchcraft* for his material, introduced a final section on the learned horse:

And now to conclude, let us backe again with one pretty knacke, which is held to be marvellous and wonderfull. And that is to make a horse tell you how much money you have in your purse.

After telling of a learned ass that feigned death to enable his master to wager he could bring him back to life, Sa Rid goes on to describe the specific case of Marocco:

Such a one is at this day to be seene in London, his master will say, sirra, heere be divers Gentlemen, that have lost divers things, and they heare say that thou canst, prethee shew thy cunning and tell them: then hurles hee downe a handkercher or a glove that he had taken from the parties before, and bids him give it the right owner, which the horse presently doth: and many other pretty feates this horse doth, and some of those trickes as the Asse before mentioned did, which not one among a thousand perceives how they are done, nor that all the feates that this horse doth, is altogether in numbering, as for ensample, his master will aske him how many people there are in the roome: the horse will pawe with his foot so many times as there are people: and marke the eye of the horse is always upon his master, and as his master moves, so goes he or stands still, as he is brought to it at the first: as for ensample, his master will throw out three dice, and will bid his horse tell how many you or he have throwne, then the horse pawes with his foote whiles the master stands stone still: then when his master sees he hath pawes so many as the first dice showes it selfe, then he lifts up his shoulders and stirres a little: then hee bids him tell what is on the second die, and then of the third die, which the horse will doe accordingly, still pawing with his foote untill his master sees he hath pawed enough, and then stirres: which the horse marking, will stay and leave pawing. And note that the horse will pawe an hundred times together, untill he sees his master stirre: and note also that nothing can be done, but his master must first know, and then his master knowing, the horse is ruled by him by signes. This if you marke at any time you shall plainly perceive.

Thus, over 350 years ago, the perceptive Sa Rid clearly explained the principle upon which all such 'educated' animal acts are based: yet the same type of act is performed to this day and is still guaranteed to deceive the majority of the audience, although not, of course, *you*, dear reader!

In this context, it is perhaps worth recalling that only fifty years ago Dr Joseph Banks Rhine, the prominent researcher on extrasensory perception, investigated Lady Wonder, a Virginian-educated horse.[18] In the winter of 1927–8 Rhine, then aged thirty-three, and his wife tested the powers of this three-year-old filly which spelled out the answers to questions by touching her nose to alphabetical and numbered blocks. They published the results of their tests in 1929 in the *Journal of Abnormal and Social Psychology* in an article titled 'An Investigation of a "Mind-Reading" Horse'.[19] Rhine had correctly observed that the horse could read his mind only when her owner, Mrs Claudia Fonda, was standing nearby but, instead of concluding that she was cueing Lady in the standard fashion of such acts, he believed that Lady was receiving the information telepathically. This belief stemmed from the observation that Mrs Fonda could not see what he (Rhine) wrote on the pad provided for him and, obviously being ignorant of the technique known as 'pencil reading', he attached no significance to the additional fact that when. he wrote the number down behind Mrs Fonda's back the horse failed completely to 'read his mind'. The critical experiments which would have settled the issue beyond dispute were not performed and Lady, the Wonder Horse of Virginia, was launched happily on her mind-reading career. It was left to Milbourne Christopher, the noted professional magician and author, to carry out the crucial tests in 1956 on an elderly Lady who was now operating on a mechanical 'typewriter', which pushed up letters in response to pressure of the mare's nose on individual levers.[20] Christopher proved conclusively that Mrs Fonda was pencil reading and signalling the horse with a rod similar to a riding crop, as Lady moved her head slowly across the 'keyboard'.

Marocco was the first of a long line of famous and not-so-famous learned horses that have spanned the last three-and-a-half centuries. In the reign of Queen Anne (1702–1714) 'the finest taught horse in the world' was exhibited at the Ship upon Great Tower Hill. According to a show-bill in the Harleian Library,[21] this equine performer 'fetches and carries like a spaniel dog. If you hide a glove, a handkerchief, a door key, a pewter bason, or so small a thing as a silver two-pence, he will seek about the room till he has found it; and then he will bring it to his master. He will also tell the number of spots on a card, and leap through a hoop; with a variety of other

THE WONDERFUL PIG OF KNOWLEDGE. *This print, of the creature which created a sensation in London during 1784–5, was published by Carrington Bowles on 13 April 1785, one day after a similar representation of the animal by Thomas Rowlandson.*

curious performances.' Later in the same century came Philip Astley's Billy, the Little Learned Military Horse, and there were many others, some of them being recorded by Christopher.[20]

Animal celebrities have seemingly always eclipsed their human counterparts. When, today, the reader is beguiled by the latest sensation in the popular press let him reflect on Robert Southey's evaluation of the Learned Pig which was the rage of fashionable London in 1785. This creature, wrote Southey, was in his day 'a far greater object of admiration to the English nation than ever was Sir Isaac Newton'.[22] The antecedents of this particular pig are not known with certainty, although it was exhibited in Yorkshire during the summer of 1794. It is possible that it was the same pig that the famous animal trainer Bisset had in his possession when he died in Chester in 1783, *en route* from Dublin to London, where he was intend-

ing to exhibit his latest animal marvel which, according to Frost, 'performed all the tricks since exhibited by the learned grunters' successors at all the fairs in the kingdom'.[23] These feats we shall shortly survey.

Thomas Rowlandson caricatured *The Wonderful Pig* in an engraving published in April 1785, and there were several subsequent representations of learned porkers. This first of the line figured in the conversations of Dr Samuel Johnson who opined: 'Had he been illiterate he had long since been smoked into hams. . . . Now he is visited by the philosopher and the politician . . . and gratified with the murmur of applause.'[24] Johnson died on 13 December 1784, shortly before the learned pig made his London debut at 55 Charing Cross. Barely four months after the Doctor's death, there appeared in the *Public Advertiser* for 6 April 1785 the following stanzas:

ON THE LEARNED PIG

Though Johnson, learned Bear, is gone,
Let us no longer mourn our loss,
For lo, a learned Hog is come,
And wisdom grunts at Charing Cross.

Happy for Johnson—that he died
Before this wonder came to town,
Else had it blasted all his pride
Another *brute should gain renown.*

Strutt, writing in 1801, refers to a learned pig which had lately attracted much attention 'at the polite end of the town'. It was, he said, a large un-wieldy hog, which had been taught to pick up letters printed on cards and to arrange them at command. The animal apparently gave great satisfaction to all who saw him and 'filled his tormentor's pocket with money'. However, the training process was arduous: the showman confessed that he had lost three very promising pigs in the course of training, and that the phenomenon currently being exhibited had frequently caused him to despair of success.[21]

Where pioneer pigs led, a legion of imitators followed. The learned pig Toby, who made his initial appearance at Bartholomew Fair in 1817, was exhibited by a showman named Hoare.[23] This porker seems to have been the first of a succession of educated beasts bearing the same name. In 1825 William Hone visited the Fair and recorded the presence of Toby, the Swinish Philosopher and Ladies' Fortune Teller, an animal not only claimed to be endowed with the natural sense of the human race but obviously a charmer in his own right—'the most beautiful of his race; in symmetry the most perfect; in temper the most docile'.[25] This paragon of porcine perfection had a complete knowledge of the alphabet, understood arithmetic, spelled and cast accounts, told the points of the globe, the dice box and the hour of anyone's watch. Toby was put through his paces by a show-woman, for whom he spelled words by pushing lettered cards with his nose and did simple addition sums. Then, at the behest of his mistress, he indicated those of the assembled throng who were in love or addicted to John Barleycorn, and grunted his conviction that a stout gentleman 'loved good eating, and a pipe, and

Signor Castelli and his poodle Munito performing an arithmetical feat (c. 1820).

Mrs Midnight's Animal Comedians, a company of performing dogs and monkeys that captivated London in 1753. On the left THE SIEGE *is enacted with canine soldiers storming the battlements of Simian Town while on the right a ballet dance, quasi-equestrian performances and card tricks are represented.*

a jug of ale better than the sight of the Living Skeleton'.

Toby was at the Fair again in 1833, exhibited by James Burchall in conjunction, perhaps not inappropriately, with the proprietor's monstrously fat child.[23] If he was the same pig, then he had changed his nationality for he was now the 'Unrivalled Chinese Swinish Philosopher, Toby the Real Learned Pig.' In addition to the feats previously recounted, he would kneel at command, perform blindfold with twenty handkerchiefs over his eyes, tell the hour to the minute by the watch, tell a card and give the age of any party. But he had a rival this year, for James Fawkes, at the George Inn, was showing the 'Amazing Pig of Knowledge' which could tell the number of pence in a shilling, the shillings in a pound, count the spectators, divine their thoughts, distinguish colours and, as if this were not enough, 'do many other wonderful things'.

On the other side of the Atlantic, William Frederick Pinchbeck, an Englishman, and descendant of the Pinchbeck who partnered Isaac Fawkes at Bartholomew Fair, exhibited the Pig of Knowledge in the closing years of the eighteenth and in the early nineteenth century.[26] He claimed to have paid a thousand dollars for his star performer. Eventually he gave up exhibiting his pig and made literary history by authoring the first original book on conjuring to be published in the United States. Fittingly *The Expositor: or Many Mysteries Unravelled*, which was published in Boston in 1805, not only explained how you could train a pig to pick up cards in response to appropriate signals but was suitably embellished with a frontispiece of the Pig of Knowledge putting these precepts to the test.

Cats are usually considered to be so independent that training them is a very difficult procedure. However, Bisset, who died *en route* for London with his learned pig, had previously succeeded in teaching three cats to play the dulcimer and squawl to the notes. The resulting Cat's Opera attracted crowds and the Scotsman cleared a thousand pounds in a few days.[27] The following century an Italian conjurer, Capelli, augmented his legerdemain with a company of cats at Bartholomew Fair in 1832. These felines beat a drum, played the organ, turned a spit, ground knives, hammered upon an anvil, ground coffee, and rang a bell. One of the cats understood French as well as Italian and responded to instructions in both languages.

There were learned dogs, too. These animals

Such was Munito's fame that plates were sold bearing his likeness.

followed in the wake of remarkable theatrical performances by troupes of dogs in the eighteenth century. At Mrs Midnight's Oratory in the Haymarket were exhibited the Animal Comedians,[28] a company of performing dogs and monkeys brought from Italy in 1752 by a man named Ballard.[29] Some thirty years later, in 1784, came the canine entertainment that broke all records and netted a profit of over £7,000—Scalioni's troupe of performing dogs.[24, 30] Under their leader, a dog called Moustache, they acted *The Deserter* at Sadlers Wells. Dressed in soldier's uniforms with helmets and muskets and wearing little boots, they scaled ladders and stormed forts.

In the nineteenth century another Italian, Signor Castelli, arrived in England with his dog Munito, a poodle which, it was claimed, was proficient in the sciences of geography, botany and natural history. Munito was exhibited at No 23 New Bond Street in 1817 and a sixpenny explanatory booklet titled *Historical Account of the Life of the Learned Dog 'Munito'*, by 'A Friend to Beasts', was sold at the Exhibition Room.

Castelli and his dog returned to the continent but later came back to England, for an undated broadside proclaimed that Munito, having been abroad for some time to finish his education, was now At Home at No 1 Leicester Square. Besides such accomplishments, Munito had also been awarded a medal by the Humane Society for having saved the life of a lady 'in the most extraordinary manner'. For one shilling spectators could witness the poodle solving simple sums with numbered cards, spelling out the answers to questions they posed, distinguishing colours, playing dominoes and finding selected cards.

The London Season of 1875 was crowned by the appearances of a brown Maltese poodle called Minos, exhibited by a Madame Hagar of Innsbruck. Minos and his mistress met the Royal Family at Osborne House on the Isle of Wight on 14 August, and Queen Victoria expressed herself as being extremely pleased with the exhibition. So, too, were most of Society, for, although Minos was merely the latest in the long line of learned dogs, apparently he created great excitement and admiration wherever he appeared. His repertoire was fairly standard— spelling words by means of alphabet cards, simple arithmetic by numbered cards, pointing out times as indicated by any watch shown to him and, at request, selecting from a variety of photographs placed before him that of any of the currently great person- alities of Europe. Finally, while his head was covered with a handkerchief, three cards were selected by members of the audience and returned to the pack, which was then spread out on the surface of a table. Minos had his eyes unveiled and successfully located each card in turn. In the words of the reporter of the *Spectator* (17 June 1875) 'the little dog, with unabated gravity and gentleness, received the personal congratulatoins of the audience, who after- wards had the pleasure of seeing him running about on the croquet lawn, sniffing at the balls, inspecting the mallets, and inspiring all observers with the conviction that he could croquet everybody, if he only gave his very superior mind to it'.

Breslaw in 1789 leavened his conjuring perfor- mances with a truly remarkable exhibition of performing birds, a show that proved so popular that he initially had no difficulty in charging five shillings for admission, although subsequently it was reduced to half-a-crown and then to a shilling. Strutt visited the entertainment and gave a first-hand description.[31]

A number of little birds, to the amount, I believe, of twelve or fourteen, being taken from different cages, were placed upon a table in the presence of the spectators; and there they formed themselves into ranks like a company of soldiers: small cones of paper bearing some resemblance to grenadiers' caps were put upon their heads, and diminutive imitations of muskets made with wood, secured under their left wings. Thus equipped, they marched to and fro several times; when a single bird was brought forward, supposed to be a deserter, and set between six of the musketeers, three in a row, who conducted him from the top to the bottom of the table, on the middle of which a small brass cannon charged with a little gun- powder had been previously placed, and the deserter was situated in the front part of the cannon; his guards then divided, three retiring on one side, and three on the other, and he was left standing by himself. Another bird was immediately produced; and a lighted match being put into one of his claws, he hopped boldly on the other to the tail of the cannon, and, applying the match to the priming, discharged the piece without the least appearance of fear or agitation. The moment the explosion took place, the deserter fell down, and lay, apparently motionless, like a dead bird; but, at the command of his tutor he rose again; and the cages being brought, the feathered soldiers were stripped of their ornaments, and returned into them in perfect order.

Strutt subsequently makes it clear that it was not Breslaw himself who was the trainer of the birds but a man who later assumed the name of Rossignol (i.e., nightingale) and appeared at Covent Garden Theatre with bird imitations, at which he excelled. He was engaged by Philip Astley for his 'Fire-Side Amusements', presented during the winter of 1778–9. Rossignol also did an imitation of a concerto using a stringless violin and a small truncheon as the bow, producing the sounds with his voice. After attaining considerable success and a horde of copiers his popularity waned suddenly when it was discovered that the sounds were produced by a small instrument concealed in his mouth. Shorn of their mystery, all wonders cease to charm!

BAGS, BUBBLES AND BOTTLES

A Credulous Man
He finds most delight in believing strange
things, and the stranger they are the easier
they pass with him: but never regards those
that are plain and feasible, for every man
can believe such.

Samuel Butler, *Characters* (1667/9)

The eighteenth century is a key one in magical history, for until that period our knowledge of conjurers is fragmentary. The crucial factor was the lapsing of the Licensing Act for periodicals in 1695, coupled with the establishment of postal services, which led to a spate of newspapers called *Postmen* and *Postboys*, and the appearance of the first English daily paper, *The Daily Courant*, on 2 March 1702, just three days after Queen Anne had ascended the throne.[1]

With these newspapers came the dissemination of information and the gradual growth of advertising. Happily for the historian of magic, the conjurers of the day were quick to seize upon this new medium to announce their performances and, from such primary sources, we can for the first time piece together the careers of those purveyors of legerdemain who were sufficiently affluent to advertise, and who were in the public eye.

Of the magical luminaries of the eighteenth century, Isaac Fawkes was one of the most respected, accomplished and successful of his kind, his performances being attended by nobleman and commoner alike, and furnishing all the elements of

Isaac Fawkes, exhibiting his 'surprising and incomparable dexterity of hand'. In this print by James Caulfield he is seen with his amazing bag from which eggs, gold, silver and wild fowl were produced in profusion. Beneath are his contortionists or posture masters.

entertainment that promote good showbusiness. Nothing is known of the early years of Fawkes (also Fawks and Faux), although it seems likely he was a Londoner. The information about him and his show

F A W K E S ,
(Slight of Hand-man.)

derives principally from advertisements and paragraphs in the newspapers of the day.

In this respect we owe a great deal to Harry Houdini who, having acquired much valuable material from a venerable English conjurer and magic collector called Henry Evanion shortly before the old man died in 1905, enshrined much of it in his historical work *The Unmasking of Robert-Houdin*, including a series of news cuttings relating to Fawkes.[2] The indefatigable Houdini pursued the trail of Fawkes assiduously and to him we owe the knowledge of the performer's first name, Isaac, for Fawkes never used it in his advertisements: in 1904, aided by Mr R. Bennett, the clerk of St Martin's-in-the-Fields Parish Church, he found the burial record with the name.

The earliest records of Fawkes relate to 1720 when he had a booth at Bartholomew Fair, where, from two to eight each day, he presented his 'surprising and incomparable dexterity of hand'. Evidently he was already at the height of his popularity, and patronized by royalty:

On Thursday Night last his Royal Highness the Prince, and several Noblemen and Gentlemen, went to see the famous Mr Fawks in the Haymarket, who were extremely pleas'd with his extraordinary performance; as also with the two Boys.[3]

The two boys were posture-masters or contortionists who accompanied the show.

Fawkes spent the winter and spring of 1723 in the Fore-Room at the French Theatre, over against the Opera House in the Haymarket; in May he removed to a Great Booth in Upper Moorfields and in the summer appeared at the Fairs. In the autumn he had a booth on Tower Hill. Then, on 18 December, he was performing in the same building as the Swiss impresario Heidegger, Handel and his Italian opera, and in the same room as the masquerades. His advertisements announced his times of performance as 'beginning every Evening precisely at Five, excepting Tuesday and Saturday, being the Opera Nights, when there will be no Performance at all'. In 1723 the *London Journal* observed:

The Famous Mr Fawks, as he modestly stiles himself, has since Bartholomew and Southwark-Fairs, put seven hundred Pounds into the Bank: He may certainly challenge any Conjurer of the Age to do the like.[4]

An advertisement for 7 February 1724 relates:

In the Long Room, over the Piazza's at the Opera House in the Haymarket, the famous FAWKES performs his most surprizing Tricks by Dexterity of Hand, with several Curiosities of that Kind, being entirely new and different to what has been shown by any other person.[5]

Of particular interest is the statement:

Likewise he designs to follow this Business no longer than this Season; so that he purposes to learn any Gentlemen and Ladies his Fancies by Dexterity of Hand for their own Diversion.

The *Daily Post* had already announced that it was likely that this would be Fawkes' final season, he 'being already so much encouraged, as to be able to live privately in a handsome Manner'.[6] In the event, he did not retire but continued performing up to the time of his death in 1731. However, this announcement does lend support to the contention that Fawkes was well into his prime as a performer.

In 1725 an advertisement for Fawkes' performances at the Cock and Half-Moon Tavern in Chancery Lane near Temple Bar is noteworthy because it includes the earliest illustration of the juggler in action.

The famous Mr FAWKS performs his most surprizing Tricks by Dexterity of Hand, with his Cards, Eggs, curious India Birds, Mice and Money. Which curiosities no person in the Kingdom can pretend to show like himself.

Fawkes' stress on 'dexterity of hand' in his advertisements is interesting and could possibly reflect a lingering concern that some members of his audience might still attribute to him a supernatural ability: although the legal persecution of witches had long since ceased, the witchcraft Acts of James I and Mary of Scotland were not in fact to be repealed until 1736.

The following year (1726) he teamed up with Powell and his puppet show at the Old Tennis Court[7] in James Street near the Hay Market and the advertisement reveals also that Fawkes had now acquired 'The Musical Clock, that plays Variety of

Christopher Pinchbeck, Senior (1670?–1732), the famous clock and musical automaton maker, who exhibited with the conjurer Isaac Fawkes during the period 1727–31. An engraved portrait by I. Faber after a painting by Isaac Whood.

Tunes, on Organ, Flute and Flagelet; with birds whistling and singing as Natural as Life itself', for this indicates his first association with Christopher Pinchbeck Senior, the famous clock and automaton maker.

Pinchbeck, who was born in Clerkenwell about 1670, invented and made the famous astronomico-musical clock which became his sign at the premises he first occupied in 1720 in Fleet Street, near the Leg Tavern.[8] Besides clocks he made musical automata such as singing birds, and barrel organs for churches. Pinchbeck exhibited collections of his automata at fairs, and it seems reasonably certain that it was in this way that he first came into contact with Fawkes. Pinchbeck's exhibitions were grandiosely titled The Temple of the Muses, Grand Theatre of the Muses or Multum in Parvo. He was the inventor of the copper/zinc alloy that bears his name; its gold-like appearance for many years led to 'pinchbeck' being used as a synonym for the cheap and tawdry, although we have now come full circle and pinchbeck is today quite avidly collected.

In 1726 Fawkes appeared at Bartholomew Fair, and his advertisement on this occasion gives a valuable account of his show.

This is to give notice that the famous Mr Fawks, at his Booth in West Smithfield, performs the following most surprizing tricks after a new Method, viz: He takes an empty bag, lays it on the table and turns it several times inside out, then commands 100 Eggs out of it, and several showers of real Gold and Silver; then the Bag beginning to swell several sorts of wild fowl run out of it upon the Table. He throws up a Pack of Cards, and causes them to be living birds flying about the room. He causes living Beasts, Birds and other Creatures to appear upon the Table. He blows the Spots of the Cards off or on, and changes them to any pictures.[2]

Fawkes was exhibiting again in association with Pinchbeck in 1727, an arrangement which seems to have endured until Fawkes' death in 1731, when Pinchbeck went into partnership with Fawkes' son and, indeed, himself performed some dexterity of hand. Pinchbeck did not, however, long survive Fawkes Senior, dying on 18 November 1732; he was buried at St Dunstan's Church in Fleet Street.[8] One of Pinchbeck's sons then went into partnership with the Junior Fawkes.

The famous *Gentleman's Magazine* commenced publication in 1731 with the pseudonym Sylvanus Urban, Gent., covering the identity of the editor Edward Cove, who daringly published lengthy reports of Parliament from 1736 onwards, despite prohibition of such reporting. Its first volume recorded that on 15 February 1731 the Aglerian Ambassadors visited Fawkes' show and that, at their request, he showed them 'a prospect of Algiers and

Fawkes, flanked by his two posture masters, is seen here with cards and India birds and the bag trick with which he was always associated.

rais'd up an apple tree, which bore ripe apples in less than a minute's time, which several of the company tasted of'.[9] This was the fruit of Pinchbeck's invention. On the same page was noted the performance of 'the famous French bitch'—canine species presumed, and therefore a forerunner of Munito, whom we have already mentioned (page 33).

Unhappily, some months later, the *Gentleman's Magazine* carried the news of Fawkes' death, which occurred on 25 May 1731; he was said to leave a fortune of £10,000.[10] Fawkes was buried at St Martin's-in-the-Fields. Over sixty years later Caulfield stated

His death was noticed, in the papers of his time, in the following terms:—May 25, 1731, died Mr Fawkes, famous for his dexterity of hand; by which he had honestly acquired a fortune of above

ten thousand pounds, being no more than he really deserved for his great ingenuity, by which he had surpassed all that ever pretended to that art.[11]

The estate of £10,000, an enormous sum for those days, has been a matter of some controversy among historians of magic, stemming principally from a press cutting in which the punctuation indicated that the estate concerned was of the individual adjacent to Fawkes in the obituary list.[12] We have already noted that Fawkes was reputed to have cleared £700 at Bartholomew and Southwark Fairs in 1723; further, it is on record that another eighteenth-century showman, Flockton, 'the prince of puppet showmen', left £5,000.[13] That Fawkes was a man of some substance, and a religious man, is borne out by his will, made on his deathbed.

In the name of God Amen
I, Isaac Fawkes, of the Parish of St Martin's-in-the-Fields, of the Liberty of Westminster, being sick and weak in body but of sound mind and memory, thanks be given to Almighty God for the

MASQUERADES AND OPERAS, BURLINGTON GATE *by William Hogarth, published in 1724, satirizing the tastes of the town. Faux's Dexterity of Hand was incorporated as an attraction at the Long Room.*

BARTHOLOMEW FAIR, *1721, a fan leaf published by J. F. Setchel of Covent Garden in 1824. It was based on a painting by Thomas Loggon, the dwarf fan painter, about 1740; Setchel's attributed date is definitely in error. Fawkes and his booth are clearly in evidence.*

same, and calling to mind and duly considering the uncertainty of this mortal life and that it is appointed unto all men once to die, do make and ordain this to be my Last Will and Testament. First and principally I commit my soul into the hands of my Dear Redeemer and my body to the earth to be decently buried according to the discretion of my Executrix hereinafter named and as the worldly estate wherewith it hath pleased God to bless me I give and bequeath the same in manner and form following. In premise I give and bequeath unto my truly and well beloved wife, Alice Fawkes, all and every my goods, chattels, plate, jewels, bills, notes, bonds, together with all movables and all my estate both real and personal and I do also constitute and appoint her, my said wife, whole and sole Executrix of this my Last Will and Testament and I do utterly revoke and disannul all former Wills by me made ratifying and confirming this to be my Last Will and Testament in witness whereof I have here unto set my hand and seal this 25th day of May 1731, the mark of Isaac Fawkes signed, sealed, and declared this and no other to be my Last Will and Testament in the presence of us, William Peterson, George Campbell, Ditus Bagnalle.

Probate was granted to his widow on the following day, 26 May 1731, in what seems to have been considerable haste.

A somewhat jaundiced view of the juggler is taken by Professor Ronald Paulson, who considers that Fawkes emerges 'as a symbol of distorted values, another illustration of misdirected patronage and degenerating standards of aristocratic taste'.[14] What price Queen Victoria's extensive patronage of conjurers at a later date! The balance is restored by the accolade accorded Fawkes by William Hogarth (1697–1764), the great painter, engraver and satirist. As a delineator of current events, fierce critic and moralist, Hogarth used Fawkes in two of his engravings. The first of these, *Masquerades and Operas*, published early in February 1724, represents Hogarth's first independent venture. It sold rapidly and was widely pirated, but a second set of verses was engraved and these referred directly to Fawkes thus:

> O how refin'd how elegant we're grown!
> What noble Entertainments Charm the Town!
> Whether to hear the Dragon's roar we go,
> Or gaze surpriz'd on Fawks's matchless Show.[15]

Hogarth subtitled this print *The Taste of the Town*, for he depicted Londoners rushing to see Fawkes' show in the Long Room, to pantomimes at the theatre, to the Italian Opera and to the midnight masquerades organized by the Swiss impressario John James Heidegger (1659–1749), who subsequently became Master of the Revels to George II. Heidegger is seen leaning out of the window, and in a wheelbarrow the serious plays of 'Congrav, Dryden, Otway, Shakespere, Addison and Ben Jonson' are being hauled away as 'Waste paper for shops'.

The second of Hogarth's engravings to feature Fawkes is *Southwark Fair*, which was painted in the latter part of 1733 with an engraving also produced by the end of the year.[16] Southwark Fair, second in importance to Bartholomew Fair, was held on 7, 8 and 9 September. Its focal point was Borough Street near St George's Church and it overflowed into nearby alleys, courts and bowling greens, and was eventually extended from three days to fourteen. As with all fairs, it began as a cloth, agricultural and general market, became a place of amusement and was finally abolished in 1762 because of the increasing vice and violence which occurred, especially after dark.

There is a wealth of material in the scene, in which Hogarth used features from Bartholomew Fair as well as Southwark Fair. Signor Violante, the slack rope performer, and Isaac Fawkes' booth, with its showcloth advertising 'Fawx^S Dexterity of Hand' and showing his contortionists, are depicted. Fawkes himself stands in front of his booth, arms outstretched, dice box in one hand and one of his famous India Birds in the other. As Fawkes died in 1731, Hogarth's engraving is a posthumous representation of the conjurer.

The best known portrait of Fawkes is that published by James Caulfield (1764–1826) in his *Portraits, Memoirs and Characters of Remarkable Persons* and accompanied by some interesting text under the heading 'Fawkes, A Juggler'.

Fawkes, whose christian name (if ever he had any) has not been handed down to posterity, made a distinguished figure in the reign of George the First, and, by his slight of hand, and other ingenious devices, contrived to ease as many fools as he could find, or make, of their pence . . . The portrait of Fawkes is engraved from a very curious and highly finished drawing of Bartholomew-fair, in the early part of the reign of George the First;

copied for this work, by permission of the proprietor Mr Setchell, of King Street, Covent-garden.[11]

The drawing referred to was in fact a painted fan leaf showing Bartholomew Fair. John Frederick Setchel was a bookseller, printseller and publisher of King Street, Covent Garden, and it was only later, in 1824, that he published an aquatint of the fan in his possession, to which he added a label with descriptive letterpress referring to Bartholomew Fair in 1721.[17] This date is certainly wrong because *The Siege of Gibraltar*, one of the peepshow attractions, did not occur until 1727[18] and, anyway, on the internal evidence of the costume, the seventeen-forties would be a nearer estimate.[19]

The original fan painting, which is now in the British Museum, is attributed on stylistic grounds to Thomas Loggon, a dwarf fan painter who was born

Thomas Loggon, the dwarf fan painter. A self-portrait included in his drawing of characters at the Pantiles, Tunbridge Wells, in 1748, purchased by the novelist Samuel Richardson (1689–1761).

at Great Grimsby in Lincolnshire on Christmas Day 1706. At the age of twenty-two, only 4ft 1in in stature, he was living 'at the sine of the Fann in queen Street Near Montague House'.[20] His name is frequently rendered as Loggan but it should be noted that there is apparently no connexion between Thomas Loggon and David Loggan (1635–93), the much better known portrait draughtsman.

During the seventeen-thirties Loggon established himself in both the fashionable watering places of Bath and Tunbridge Wells where he painted topographical fans and views, often portraying well known visitors, presumably both commissioned and sold as souvenirs. For a period Loggon was dwarf to the Prince and Princess of Wales (Frederick Louis and Augusta of Saxe-Gotha), at a time when royalty maintained dwarfs and midgets in their entourages.[21]

Samuel Richardson (1689–1761), the novelist, purchased one of Loggon's drawings of characters at the Pantiles at Tunbridge Wells in 1748, and reproduced it as the frontispiece to the third volume of Richardson's *Correspondence*.[22] Fortunately, Loggon included himself in the picture, the only known representation of this little man who painted the original of Fawkes on the Bartholomew Fair fan. It seems that fan painting eventually became an insufficient source of livelihood since he had to diversify his interests into bookselling, bookbinding, the sale of chocolate and a circulating library at Bristol Hot Wells. The precise date of his death is unknown, but it was before 1780.

Setchel's label on the fan leaf states that the distinguished-looking visitor wearing the Order of the Garter is Sir Robert Walpole (1676–1745) who was effectively Prime Minister from 1721 to 1739. However, bearing in mind Loggon's former association, it is more likely to be the Prince of Wales, who in 1740 'visited the Fair in a sort of semi-state, and wearing his blue ribbon, star and garter' with the Manager, John Rich, 'introducing his royal guest to all the entertainments of the place'.[23] The attribution of an approximate date in the seventeen-forties for the fan would thus also accord with this interpretation. Consequently, it is clear that the fan painting is anachronistic and the portrait of Fawkes a posthumous one—indeed, the only representation that appeared in his lifetime was the cut he used for his advertisements.

Shrouded in mystery though Fawkes' origins may have been, we have now seen how the last eleven years of his life were sufficiently chronicled for us to gain a reasonably clear impression of a highly successful conjurer presenting a 'matchless show' for royalty and commoner alike, acquiring a fame that has survived his lifespan as the only identifiable conjurer portrayed by a famous artist, and a fortune that eclipsed those of all other conjurers of his day.

For a valuable description of an early eighteenth century conjuring performance we are indebted to the poet John Gay (1685–1732), who is perhaps best known to posterity as the author of *The Beggars' Opera* which, making its debut in 1728, is still performed to the present day. This satire of the corruptions of society was the work of a perceptive observer who published many other pieces in which contemporary activities were brought into sharp focus. It is scarcely surprising, therefore, at a time when such performers as Isaac Fawkes and Matthew Buchinger were household names, that practitioners of the magic art should have attracted Gay's attention. His *Fables*, published in 1727,[24] included the following poem titled 'The Jugglers' (Fable XLII), which furnishes a detailed account of a contemporary magical performance.

THE JUGGLERS

A Juggler long through all the town
Had rais'd his fortune and renown;
You'd think (so far his art transcends)
The devil at his finger's ends.

Vice heard his fame, she read his bill;
Convinc'd of his inferior skill,
She sought his booth, and from the croud
Defy'd the man of art aloud.

Is this then he so fam'd for slight,
Can this slow bungler cheat your sight,
Dares he with me dispute the prize?
I leave it to impartial eyes.

Provok'd, the Juggler cry'd, 'tis done.
In science I submit to none.

Thus said. The cups and balls he play'd;
By turns, this here, that there, convey'd:
The cards, obedient to his words,
Are by a fillip turn'd to birds;
His little boxes change the grain,
Trick after trick deludes the train.
He shakes his bag he shows all fair,
His fingers spread, and nothing there,
Then bids it rain with showers of gold,

And now his iv'ry eggs are told,
But when from thence the hen he draws,
Amaz'd spectators hum applause.

Vice now stept forth and took the place
With all the forms of his grimace.

This magick looking-glass, she cries,
(There, hand it round) will charm your eyes:
Each eager eye the sight desir'd,
And ev'ry man himself admir'd.

Next, to a Senator addressing;
See this Bank-note; observe the blessing:
Breathe on the bill. Heigh, pass! 'Tis gone.
Upon his lips a padlock shone.
A second puff the magick broke,
The padlock vanish'd, and he spoke.

Twelve bottles rang'd upon the board,
All full, with heady liquor stor'd,
By clean conveyance disappear,
And now two bloody swords are there.

A purse she to a thief expos'd;
At once his ready fingers clos'd:
He opes his fist, the treasure's fled,
He sees a halter in its stead.

She bids Ambition hold a wand,
He grasps a hatchet in his hand.

A box of charity she shows:
Blow here; and a church-warden blows,
'Tis vanish'd with conveyance neat,
And on the table smoaks a treat.

She shakes the dice, the board she knocks,
And from all pockets fills her box.

She next a meagre rake addrest;
This picture see: her shape, her breast!
What youth, and what inviting eyes!
Hold her, and have her. With surprise,
His hand expos'd a box of pills;
And a loud laugh proclaim'd his ills.

A counter, in a miser's hand,
Grew twenty guineas at command;
She bids his heir the sum retain,
And 'tis a counter now again.

A guinea with her touch you see
Take ev'ry shape but Charity;
And not one thing, you saw, or drew,
But chang'd from what was first in view.

The Juggler now, in grief of heart,
With his submission own'd her art.
Can I such matchless sight withstand?
How practice hath improv'd your hand!
But now and then I cheat the throng;
You ev'ry day, and all day long.

An illustration of John Gay's fable THE JUGGLERS *by Audinet for Stockdale's edition of* FABLES *(1793). First published in 1727, the original version was designed by William Kent (1684–1748) and engraved by P. Fourdrinier.*

Of particular interest is the accompanying wood-cut depicting the contest of magic between Vice and the Juggler which forms the theme of this Fable. It was designed by William Kent (1684–1748), the architect, sculptor and landscape gardener who, among other activities, laid out Kew Gardens and built the Horse Guards and Treasury buildings in London. The scene is a booth with Vice seated at a small table under which may be seen the face and arms of a boy. Presumably the youth is a confederate, although Gay's description does not reveal his rôle. On the table are the classic Cups and Balls,

and Vice is holding up the banknote to the Senator, on whose lips we may discern (with difficulty) the padlock. The Juggler is in a harlequin costume and plumed hat, wearing a mask.

Gay's *Fables* proved to be an extremely popular work; to date it has passed through some 150 editions. According to the *Gentleman's Magazine* for May 1824, the *Fables* and *The Beggar's Opera* were assigned to Tonson and Watts on 6 February 1728, for ninety guineas. In the light of history these publishers were undoubtedly onto a good thing!

The illustration for 'The Jugglers' underwent various changes over the years, but all the earlier

plates were based on Kent's original design, occasionally as a mirror image. A particularly fine example is the Audinet version in the John Stockdale edition of 1793; here the padlock on the Senator's lips is clearly visible, as is not the case with the original woodcut. This trick, depending upon a special lock, was a development of the deceit recorded in Scot's *The Discoverie of Witchcraft*, 'To put a ring through your cheeke'. It was first described and illustrated in *Hocus Pocus Junior* in 1634 where the reader was told 'How to put a Lock upon ones mouth'; almost a century later it was clearly a standard feat in the juggler's repertoire.

Robert Southey said of Gay: 'few poets seem to have possessed so quick and observing an eye', and nowhere can his acuteness of observation be appreciated to better advantage than in *Trivia*. This work, subtitled *The Art of Walking the Streets of London*, was published in 1716 and in its three books imparts an incredible wealth of detail concerning London and its street activities in the early eighteenth century. Not least, in the present context, are the episodes of magical interest.

Book Two of *Trivia* records 'Of walking the Streets by Day' and here we find:

Careful Observers, studious of the town,
Shun the Misfortunes that disgrace the Clown.
Untempted, they contemn the Jugler's Feats,
Pass by the Meuse, nor try the Thimble's Cheats.

Gay appended a footnote to elucidate the Thimble's Cheats and we read 'A Cheat commonly practis'd in the Streets with three Thimbles and a little Ball'. Here, then, was an example of a street performer thimble rigging; a small pea or ball was placed under one of the three thimbles or small cups, which were then moved around and the spectator invited to bet on the pea's whereabouts, sleight-of-hand ensuring that he was right only if the operator so wished.

In Book Three, 'Of walking the Streets by Night', Gay recounts various cheats that were formerly in vogue.

Who can the various City Frauds recite,
With all the petty Rapines of the Night?
Who now the Guinea-Dropper's Bait regards,
Trick'd by the Sharper's Dice, or Juggler's Cards?

ARLEQUYN ACTIONIST (*1720*), *an engraving which satirized the follies of the South Sea Bubble, shows a conjurer in the foreground with his cards and apparatus.*

His familiarity with cheating is revealed also in other poems. In Volume Two of *Fables* (1738), in 'Pan and Fortune (To a Young Heir)', Fortune asks Pan

Is't I who cog or palm the dice?
Did I the shuffling art reveal,
To mark the cards, or range the deal?
In all employments men pursue,
I mind the least what gamesters do.

These trust alone their fingers' ends,
And not one stake, on me, depends,
When'er the gaming board is set.

Cogging was the loading of dice with pellets of lead to ensure that a particular number was thrown: the artifice lay in the subtle switching of the loaded dice for genuine ones.

John Gay was a substantial stockholder in the South Sea Company, and he was brought to despair and misery when the company collapsed in 1720; the disaster was all the more poignant because he had on various occasions disregarded the advice of friends who had urged him to sell his stock.[25]

Both the Mississippi Bubble and the South Sea Bubble financial disasters generated an extensive array of books, pamphlets and even playing cards.[26] One of the most fascinating of these publications, which appeared not in the countries concerned but in Holland, is of considerable interest to the historian of magic and the playing-card collector on account of some of the plates therein. This Dutch work of 1720, titled *Het Groote Tafereel der Dwaascheid* or *The Great Mirror of Folly*, is made up principally of satirical plates, although the text does contain the charters of important companies which were floated in Dutch cities during the period of the Bubble mania.[27]

The engraving 'Arlequyn actionist' (Harlequin stockholder) is the frontispiece to a comedy of the same name and depicts the stage of a theatre with Arlequyn or Bombario and Scaramouche respectively at the sides, holding back the curtains to reveal the scene of the Rue Quincampoix in Paris, the street of the stockbrokers where the Mississippi Bubble was finally pricked. The shop for the sale of shares is in the background, and three men on the pedestal are pouring coins through a victim *via* a funnel while he delivers from his bare posterior a paper inscribed with his name 'Laaun' (John Law of Laurieston, the Scots financier and gambler who played such an important rôle in the Mississippi scheme). In the foreground is 'Mercury imprisoned' in a large bird cage, weeping and saying 'Oh deliver me' while another man pumps wind into the cage. Mercury is apparently the prisoner of the conjurer who displays his cards, dice and apparatus on the ground while appealing to the crowd with 'Who will gain?'. An ape squats before him with bags of coins, and near Scaramouche is written 'One fool makes many fools'.

The *Tafereel* also included engravings of playing cards intended for separation and pasting onto cardboard for use. These cards carried various designs, including mountebanks teaching a performing dog to go through its feats, with a man rushing forward to take one of the pieces of paper the mountebank holds before the dog.

The mania that the South Sea Bubble generated is an illuminating example of public hysteria. It highlights one of the traits that both conjurer and confidence trickster trade upon—the gullibility of the masses and an almost pathological compulsion to be deluded.

The credulity of the public for advertised conjuring shows must surely have reached its peak in the eighteenth century. It was sufficient to have attracted the satirical attention of Jonathan Swift who, around the seventeen-thirties, issued what purported to be an advertisement for a performance in Dublin by a wholly fictitious conjurer called Schoritz.[28]

THE WONDER OF ALL THE WONDERS
THAT EVER THE WORLD WONDERED AT.

For all Persons of Quality and Others.

Newly arrived in this city of Dublin, the famous artist John Emanuel Schoritz, who, to the great surprise and satisfaction of all spectators, is ready to do the following wonderful performances; the like before never seen in this Kingdom.

He will heat a bar of iron red hot, and thrust it into a barrel of gunpowder before all the company, and yet it shall not take fire.

He lets any gentleman charge a blunderbuss with the same gunpowder and twelve leaden bullets, which blunderbuss the said artist discharges full in the face of the said company without the least hurt, the bullets sticking in the wall behind them.

He takes any gentleman's own sword, and runs it through the said gentleman's body, so that the point appears bloody at the back to all the spectators; then he takes out the sword, wipes it clean and returns it to the owner, who receives no manner of hurt.

He takes a pot of scalding oil, and throws it by great ladlefuls directly at the ladies, without spoiling their clothes or burning their skins.

He gives any gentleman leave to drive forty twelvepenny nails up to the head in a porter's backside, and then places the said porter in a loadstone chair, which draws out every nail, and the porter feels no pain.

He likewise draws the teeth of half a dozen gentlemen, mixes them and jumbles them in a hat, gives any person leave to blindfold him, and returns each their own, and fixes them as well as ever.

With many other wonderful programmes of art, too tedious here to mention.

The said artist has performed before most Kings and Princes in Europe with great applause.

He performs every day (except Sundays) from 10 o'clock to 1 in the forenoon: and from 4 till 7 in the evening, at the New Inn in Smithfield.

The first seat a British crown, the second a British half-crown, and the lowest a British shilling.

N.B. The best bands in town are to play at the said show.

As we mention elsewhere (page 96), it seems exceedingly likely that the famous German physicist Lichtenberg used this piece as a model for his own broadside ridiculing Philadelphia's performance at Göttingen. Further, later in the century, Katterfelto (page 61) frequently prefaced his advertisements with 'Wonders! Wonders! Wonders!', possibly borrowing from the same source.

Gullibility unsurpassed occurred, however, in 1749 when, for a wager to test public credulity, John, second Duke of Montagu (*c.* 1688–1749), perpetrated an amazing hoax. On 11 January in *The General Advertiser* appeared an announcement that on the evening of 16 January at the Theatre in the Haymarket a performer would

play on a common walking-cane the music of every instrument now used, to surprising perfection; and he would, on the stage, get into a tavern quart bottle, without equivocation; and, while there, sing several songs, and suffer any spectator to handle the bottle; that if any spectator should come mask'd, he would, if requested, declare who they were; that in a private room, he would produce the representation of any person dead, with which the party requesting it should converse some minutes as if alive, &c. to begin at half after 6.

The prices were by no means cheap—Stage 7s 6d, Boxes 5s, Pit 3s and Gallery 2s—but this only served to emphasize the joke.

On the appointed day a great crowd of people packed the theatre and waited good humouredly until seven o'clock when they became, not unreasonably, impatient and noisy. Someone came forward to assure them that if the conjurer did not turn up their money would be refunded. At this juncture some wag in the audience called out 'For double the prices the conjurer will go into a pint bottle'. The realization that they had been duped

dawned and a tumult began. A spectator in one of the boxes threw a lighted candle on the stage while the majority of the audience hastily made their way to the exits. But a mob which had been waiting outside, unable to get in for the 'performance', now broke into the theatre, tore down the inside of the house and burnt it in the street, making a flag of the curtain which was placed on a pole in the middle of the bonfire. During this fracas, the takings, which had been secured in a box according to a contract with the theatre owner, was carried off. It was also recorded that 'Several persons of high rank being present, the

AN APOLOGY TO THE TOWN, FOR HIMSELF AND THE BOTTLE *by J. Nick-all published on 16 January 1749. A print satirizing the Bottle Conjurer hoax with Harlequin striving to enter a quart bottle* via *a funnel.*

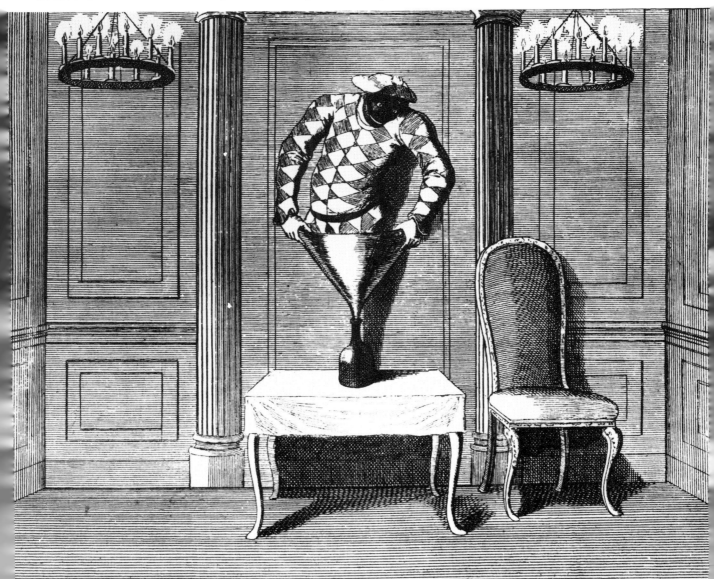

The Bottle Conjurers ARMS.

pick pockets made a good booty, and a great general's rich sword was lost, for the recovery of which a reward of 30 guineas was advertised'.[29] The 'great general' was none other than the 'Butcher' Duke of Cumberland, and his embarrassment was not assuaged by an engraving titled *The Magician, or Bottle Conjurer* published on 5 March 1749 which depicted him as one of the dupes.

Suspicion fell on Mr John Potter, the proprietor of the Theatre, but he wrote to the editor of *The General Advertiser* disclaiming any responsibility for the acts of the person who took his theatre.[30] Samuel Foote, the actor, was also suspected and he, too, wrote to protest his innocence.[31]

The Bottle Conjurer hoax generated a crop of contemporary prints and cartoons with accompanying letterpress,[32] as well as skits in periodicals. Thus a notice appeared that there had

Lately arrived from Italy, Sig. Capitello Jumpedo, a surprizing dwarf, no taller than a common tavern tobacco pipe; who can perform many wonderful equilibres, on the slack or tight rope; ... and after he had diverted the spectators two hours and a half, he will open his mouth wide, and jump down his own throat. He being the most wonderfull'st wonder of wonders as ever the world wonder'd at, would be willing to join in performance with that surprizing musician on Monday next at the Haymarket.[33]

Elsewhere the bill announced that

The Great Zammanpoango, Occultist & Body Surgeon to the Emperor Monoemungi would invite spectators to pull out his eyes, pass them round the audience and replace them in their sockets. No money need be paid until the performance is over.[34, 35]

Hawkers in the streets sold toys in the form of a bottle with a man's head and shoulders in place of a cork, and the escape of Harlequin into a quart bottle was added as a scene to pantomimes. One of the contemporary engravings *The Bottle Conjurer, from Head to Foot, without Equivocation*, dated 24 January 1749, carried the following lines:

When Conjurers ye Quality can bubble
And get their Gold wth very little trouble
By putting giddy Lyes in publick Papers—
And jumping in Quart Bottles—such like Vapours
And further yet, if we the matter strain
Woud pipe a Tune upon a Walking-Cane;
Nay more surprizing Trick! he swore hed show,
Granums who dy'd a hundred Years ago.—
Tis whimsical enough, What think ye Sirs
The Quality can ne'er be Conjurers
The De'el a Bit; no let me speak in brief
The Audience Fools, the Conjurer a Thief.

The Bottle Conjurer provided a recurrent theme for folly and appeared as an incidental embellishment in many other prints and engravings, even years later as witness its use in Gillray's *The Theatrical Bubble* in 1805 and Ackermann's *Britannia—Blowing up the Corsican Bottle Conjurer* in 1803.

Over half-a-century after the Bottle Conjurer hoax the theme was still being used for political satire, as in The Bottle Conjurers' Arms, published in Dublin.

4
THE PHENOMENA

Blows fire out of his mouth like a jugler,
as the Roman slave did when he set all
Sicily on a flame.

Samuel Butler, *Characters* (1667/9)

The triumphs of dexterity and determination over appalling physical deformity were embodied in Matthew Buchinger, 'the Little Man of Nuremberg', who was the most extraordinary conjurer of all time. Born at Anspach in 1674, the last of a family of nine children, he had neither hands nor legs, and in place of arms was endowed with two fin-like appendages. He was but twenty-nine inches high. Incredible as it may seem, so single-mindedly did he apply himself that he became a most accomplished player of the flute, dulcimer and trumpet, and even mastered the bagpipes. He also developed penmanship and draughtsmanship of a very high order, executing a beautiful script, drawing coats of arms, portrait sketches and landscapes in Indian ink. He could produce mirror writing and also sign his name upside down. As if these accomplishments were not enough, Nature compensated further for his deformities by endowing him with remarkable skill as a conjurer.

While it is not chronicled that Buchinger's parents ever exhibited him for gain, as a man he made his living, as so many others before and since have done, by trading on the misfortune of his genes. Yet, unlike the exhibits of so many nineteenth and twentieth century freak shows, who have been content to allow a morbid and curious public simply to gaze at their malformed bodies, Buchinger gave them their money's worth with action. He could play at skittles and nine-pins with considerable skill, shave himself unaided, and play games of cards and dice. Souvenirs in the form of samples of his calli-

graphy, or of engravings of himself likewise suitably embellished, were sold to the audiences and usually dated. From this source we know that he survived much longer than Caulfield's[1] date of 1722 and was still performing on 20 October 1734 at Ludlow.[2] We are told that the late Mr Herbert, of Cheshunt, editor

Matthew Buchinger (1674–1735?), 'the little Man of Nuremberg', born without hands and legs, yet who performed the Cups and Balls and other feats of dexterity.

of *Ames' History of Printing*, had many curious specimens of Buchinger's writing and drawing, the most extraordinary of which was a self-portrait on vellum, in which he had ingeniously inserted in the flowing curls of the wig the 27th, 121st 128th, 140th and 150th Psalms, together with the Lord's Prayer!

A delightful engraving by Lorenz Beger of Buchinger surrounded by thirteen illustrations of him engaging in various activities appeared in both German and English versions, differing in three illustrations as well as in the captions, which were apparently altered on the same plate. They included him making a pen, writing, drawing pictures with a pen, playing at dice, cards, threading a needle, playing on a dulcimer, charging a gun, playing skittles, performing the Cups and Balls, producing live birds from under the cups, playing the hautboy and blowing a trumpet.

His conjuring performances thus included that classic of magic, the Cups and Balls, with the climax of live birds being produced from beneath the cups. In modern times Galli Galli featured the production of live chicks in this same effect.

It is believed that Buchinger arrived in Britain in the early part of the eighteenth century, when he was patronized by George I and by Robert Harley, Earl of Oxford. The Harleian manuscripts in the British Museum include a hand-written bill for his appearance in London in 1716.

By Authority. Lately arriv'd, and to be seen at the Globe, and Duke of Marlborough's H—, in Fleet Street, a German born withoht [*sic*] hands, feet, or thighs (that never was in this kingdom before) who does such miraculous actions as none else can do with hands and feet. He has had the honour to perform before most kings and princes, particularly several times before King George. He makes a pen, and writes several hands as quick and as well as any writing-master, and will write with any for a wager; he draws faces to the life, and coats of armes, pictures, flowers, &c., with a pen, very curiously. He threads a fine needle very quick; shuffles a pack of cards, and deals them very swift. He plays upon a dulcimer as well as any musician; he does many surprizing things with cups and balls, and gives the curious great satisfaction thereby; he plays at skittles several ways very well; shaves himself very dexterously; and many other things, too tedious to insert.

This is written by Matthew Buchinger at

London, 1716/7 born without hands and feet at Anspack, 1674, the 3 Jan^y.[3]

He also performed in many other taverns and rooms in London and travelled widely in England and in Scotland. In 1723, next door to the Two Blackamoor's Heads in Holborn, near Southampton Street, he was exhibiting punctually at the hours of 10, 12, 2, 4, 6 and 8, which must have been an exceedingly arduous day for the little man. The influence of his Scottish travels was revealed when his programme was broadened to include a hornpipe in Highland dress danced 'as well as any man' although, perhaps significantly, the performance was now only twice nightly!

Buchinger was married four times and fully virile, for he had eleven children. However, the novelty and popularity of his show obviously waned for it is recorded that, on these grounds, he petitioned the Palatine Commissioners to grant him King's Bounty, on the strength of having married Anna Elizabeth Tyse, a Palatine, by whom he had two children. He stated: 'your petitioner's expenses and great charges in travelling and keeping servants, who must support the entertainment with musick and other employments, eats out, wastes, and consumes much the greater part of the profit; so that now your petitioner despairs of getting any more'.[3] It was similar unfavourable economics of transportation and employment of personnel that precipitated the demise of the large full evening illusion show in the years following the Second World War—history does repeat itself!

Caulfield, writing in 1819, mentioned that one of Buchinger's wives was in the habit of ill-treating him, frequently beating and in other ways insulting him, which he tolerated patiently for a long time. But once his anger was so much aroused that he sprang upon her in fury and battered her severely with his stumps; apparently thereafter she prudently mended her ways to avoid further thrashings.

Among the Harleian manuscripts is a very beautiful ornamental letter by Buchinger, addressed to the Earl of Oxford, concerning a fan mount which had occupied him fifteen months in its execution. The letter, written at Chelmsford and dated 14 April 1733, quaintly runs as follows:

My Lord,—I hope your goodness will excus my not writing sooner to your Lordship; I was prevented by an ague and feavour, which have hindered me from doing anything for a long time. I

An example of Matthew Buchinger's calligraphy showing upside-down and mirror writing and, incidentally, furnishing evidence that he was still alive in October 1734.

have finish'd a curious fan, of my own drawing, which I had not an opportunity till lately, I have send it to your Lord^p with my wife, and there not being such another piece of my work and I dispair of ever performing the like again, I was feiffteen months a drawing of it, and if your Lord^p have a fance for it, as for the price I leave to your Lord^p', if your Lord^p shall please to favour me with a line, I shal take it as the greatest honour, that can be confer'd on, my Lord, your Lordships obedient & most humble servant regnihcuB wehtaM [written backwards].
Chelmsford, April the 14, 1733.
P.S. My Lord, I make bold to let your Lord^p know, that we shall go from hence to Colchester.
To the Right Honourable the Eaerl of Oxford, London.[3]

The precise date of Buchinger's death is unknown but, as we have seen, he was still performing at the age of 60 in 1734. He travelled to Ireland and some of his children settled there with their maternal grandmother. A son named John Adam Buchinger, who was born at Strasbourg on 30 December 1715, settled at Dartford, Kent, where he worked as a brazier until his death in 1781; he left a son and three daughters.[4] Caulfield reported that one of Buchinger's grandsons kept a music shop in the Strand and was acknowledged as the best performer on the lute in England.

Jonathan Swift, under his nom-de-plume of B. M. Drapier, published in Dublin *Drapier's Miscellany* a long punning elegy and epitaph on Buchinger.[3] A small portion of it follows:

Poor Buchinger at last is dead and gone,
A lifeless Trunk, who was a living One:
TRUNK, did I say, wherein all Virtues met?
I shou'd ha' call'd him a rich CABINET.
No wonder in Life's Warfare he shou'd die,
Who wanted Hands to fight, or Feet to fly.
Nature to form so great a Life to come,
Wisely took care to maim him in the Womb.

He play'd all Games with Skill, but was most nice,
Tho' without Slight of Hand, at Cards and Dice;
And tho' he won at Play, yet no one can
Say, that he made a Hand of any Man.
One poor Escutcheon is his Due,
Who, when alive, so many drew.
Give him but this, and then he'll have
Arms and Supporters to his Grave.

Buchinger's fame was traded upon by the printers of the chapbooks and pamphlets that were sold in profusion to satisfy the curiosity and, perhaps, even the aspirations of the populace during the years between 1730 and 1760. *The Whole Art of Legerdemain or Hocus Pocus in Perfection*, printed and sold at the Printing Office in Bow-Church Yard, was one of these undated trifles, sporting a long, rambling title page. It offered hope for 'any person of the meanest capacity' to 'perform the whole Art without a Teacher, as performed by the best Artist in the World' and, as a bonus, added 'Several Tricks of Cups and Balls &c., as performed by the little Man without Hands or Feet'. And, if that were not enough to whet the appetite, there was more to come—the wonderful Art of Fire Eating! This was presumably a good selling point, for invulnerability to fire is almost as mysterious today as it was centuries ago, and the individual who can consume flames without apparent harm commands both wonder and awe.

Fire-eating is an ancient art known to have been practised by the Greek jugglers at public spectacles in the third century BC, while a Syrian called Eunos excited much notice by his exhibitions in Sicily around 135 BC, claiming that he owed his immunity to the favours of the Gods.[5] However, a sceptical writer, Florus, attributed Eunos' dragon's breath rather to the very materialistic use of nutshells containing burning material which were secreted in his mouth! As with conjurers, detailed accounts of fire-eaters are not available until the seventeenth century, when the diarist John Evelyn faithfully records the performance of Richardson, a renowned exponent of the art, who was very much in vogue with the savants and upper classes. On 8 October 1672 Evelyn had dinner with Lady Sunderland at Leicester House and afterwards she sent for Richardson.

He devoured brimstone on glowing coals before us, chewing and swallowing them; he melted a beer-glass and eat it quite up; then taking a live coal on his tongue he put on it a raw oyster; the coal was blown with bellows till it flamed and sparkled in his mouth, and so remained until the oyster gaped and was quite boiled: then he melted pitch and wax with sulphur which he drank down as it flamed: I saw it flaming in his mouth a good while; he also took up a thick piece of iron, such as laundresses use to put in their smoothing boxes, when it was fiery hot, held it between his teeth,

then in his hand, and threw it about like a stone, but this I observ'd he cared not to hold it very long; then he stood on a small pot, and bending his body, took a glowing iron with his mouth from between his feet, without touching the pot or the ground with his hands; with divers other prodigious feats.

Evelyn's account gives a good impression of the then stock-in-trade of the fire-eater which had probably flourished in a similar form for hundreds of years. But quickening scientific interest in such apparent defiance of heat and fire led to Sir Hans Sloane and several Fellows of the Royal Society presenting Robert Powell, a famous eighteenth century salamander, with a purse of gold and a silver medal for submitting himself to investigation in 1751. Powell had a long period before the public,

THE FIRE-EATER, *an engraving perhaps erroneously attributed to William Hogarth, was published in Thomas Clerk's edition of Hogarth's works in 1810.*

from 1718 until 1780, with a repertoire which did not differ in its essentials from that of Richardson although he did offer an additional service to the public

He displaces teeth or stumps so easily as scarce be felt. He sells a chymical liquid which discharges inflammation, scalds and burns, in a short time, and is necessary to be kept in all families.[6]

Whether the customers believed that someone impervious to heat and pain himself could remove offending molars so expeditiously is an interesting conjecture.

When Thomas Clerk put out a new edition of Hogarth's works in 1810 he included an engraving titled 'The Fire-Eater' which he claimed had never before been published, the original having been in the collection of 'the late Mr Deuchar, seal engraver (of Edinburgh) . . . Mr D. was fully persuaded that it was an undoubted original of Hogarth's'.[7] Apparently this persuasion did not extend to Paulson, whose recent authoritative treatment excluded this item even from the list of prints questionably attributed to Hogarth.[8] Clerk felt it necessary to enlighten his readers about Richardson's methods, quoting the *Journal des Sçavans* for 1680. The secret (so it was claimed) consisted in rubbing pure spirit of sulphur on the exposed parts; this burned and cauterized the epidermis and so rendered it resistant to the flame. Ambrose Paré had tried the art and, after washing the hands in urine and *unguentum aureum*, declared that anyone might safely dip them in molten lead! Paré further vouchsafed that, by washing his hands in the juice of onions, he could bear a hot shovel on them while it melted lead.[7]

A predilection for fire was by no means an exclusively male trait for in 1814 John Richardson, whose shows dominated the fairs during the first half of the nineteenth century, introduced to a marvelling public at Portsmouth Signora Josephine Girardelli—the Great Phenomenon of Nature.[9] She quickly graduated to the London scene where, in Mr Laxton's Rooms at 23 New Bond Street, she daily demonstrated her resistance to heat.

She will, without the least symptoms of pain, put

Signora Josephine Girardelli, the female salamander, who drew the crowds in London from 1814 onwards by demonstrating her invulnerability to fire. This engraving was published by R. S. Kirby on 16 March 1819.

boiling melted lead in her mouth, and emit the same with the imprint of her teeth thereon; red-hot irons will be passed over various parts of her body; she will walk over a bar of red-hot iron with her naked feet; will wash her hands in aquafortis; put boiling oil in her mouth!

Admission was pricey at three shillings but sceptics, if not satisfied, could witness the performance *gratis!* She subsequently toured the provinces and obviously did very well indeed. Although she claimed originally to be 'The Fireproof Female from Germany',[10] Signora Girardelli was of Italian birth.[11]

The most intriguing and controversial of fire-eaters was Ivan Ivanitz Chabert (1792–1859), a Frenchman and soldier in the Napoleonic Wars who subsequently found it profitable to demonstrate his incombustibility. Chabert arrived in London in 1818 and, according to his handbills, in addition to all the standard marvels of the fireproof brigade, poured vitriol, oil and arsenic into a fire and held his head in the flames, inhaling the vapours and, as his *pièce de résistance*, had a brilliant display of fireworks play upon him until his shirt was burned from his back.[12] *The Times* noted that he did not actually inhale the vapours[13] but, eight years later, when Chabert was appearing at White Conduit Gardens in London, he received a very comprehensive and flattering report from the same paper.

In the first instance, he refreshed himself with a hearty meal of phosphorus . . . he washed down this infernal fare with solutions of arsenic and oxalic acid . . . he next swallowed with great *gout* several spoonsful of boiling oil and, as a desert to this delicate repast, helped himself with his naked hand to a considerable quantity of molten lead . . . the exhibitor offered to swallow Prussic acid, perhaps the most powerful of known poisons, if any good-natured person could furnish him with a quantity of it.[14]

The medical profession, altruistically rather than good naturedly, subsequently entered the arena when the prussic acid swallowing feat came to their notice. Dr Thomas Wakley, editor of *The Lancet*, maintained that if Chabert were in possession of an antidote to such a lethal poison he should, in the interests of humanity, divulge it. Wakley took his own prussic acid to one of the shows at the Argyll Rooms, Regent Street, and challenged Chabert to swallow it; the Fire King declined, asserting that he had claimed he would administer poison to his two

MONSIEUR CHABERT THE FIRE KING

Ivan Ivanitz Chabert (1792–1859), the Fire King, emerging from his oven. He is flanked by two well known conjurers: Breslaw, who has performed the decapitation illusion, and Gyngell. This was the delightful hand-coloured folding frontispiece to FAIRBURN'S NEW LONDON CONJURER *published in the eighteen-twenties.*

dogs, one of which would die and the other of which, given his antidote, would survive. This considerably angered the audience and the performance ended in disorder.[15] However, in March 1830 he did appear before an audience of critical doctors and prussic acid was administered to one dog which quickly succumbed. The other dog, similarly treated but given Chabert's nostrum, survived.[16] Chabert did not vindicate his position with the medical men, however, and he certainly overstepped the mark with the animal experiments. Perhaps, as a foreigner, he might be excused for under-estimating the British love of animals, especially at a time when man's inhumanity to man could daily be observed in the slums and stews of London, but his popularity undeniably waned after this episode and he left the shores of Britain in 1832 for the USA.

One other feat which captured the imagination of the populace of London was Chabert's entry to an oven, about six feet by seven feet, heated to 220°F (104.5°C), and remaining there, conversing with the audience *via* a tin tube, while a rump steak and a leg of lamb cooked. The performer's chicanery in endeavouring to make the feat appear even more impressive, by secretly putting the bulb of the thermometer in the fire embers and displaying triumphantly 595°F (330°C), was readily detected as being unworthy of 'the best of all fire eaters we have yet seen'.[17] Here, however, scientists were ahead of

the showman for in 1774 Dr Charles Blagden FRS had participated in experiments with various colleagues, including Mr (later Sir) Joseph Banks, at the invitation of Dr George Fordyce, to observe how the human body could withstand temperatures much higher than had previously been realised. The scientists occupied a heated chamber for varying periods and noted how, in the dry heat, they could readily tolerate temperatures in the range 198–211°F.

In the USA Chabert continued his career as a fire-eater, but the initial success that attended his efforts in New York did not accompany him on tour and, in dire financial straits, he retired from the stage and duly emerged as J. Xavier Chabert MD with a drug store on Grand Street, New York. The instantly qualified quack peddled elixirs, which were alleged to cure consumption, and made a 'Chinese Lotion'. Apparently he could produce a remarkable array of paper 'qualification'—diplomas and certificates as well as medals—to bolster his claim to the healing arts.[18] His elixir proved of no personal avail, alas, for

Blaise de Manfre, a famous Maltese water spouter and juggler, who flourished in Europe during the seventeenth century.

Floram Marchand of Tours, a pupil of Manfre, who came to Britain in 1650. His methods were exposed in a tract titled THE FALACIE OF THE GREAT WATER-DRINKER DISCOVERED (1650).

Chabert died on 28 August 1859 of tuberculosis. An appreciation held little brief:

Dr C. has 'gone to that bourne whence no traveller returns', and we fervently trust and hope that the disembodied spirits of the tens of thousands whom he has treated in this sphere will treat him with the same science with which he treated them while in this wicked world.[18]

From consuming fire to spouting water might perhaps seem a logical progression for a conjurer, the one activity complementing the other, yet there is no record of a performer combining these two astounding feats. Blaise Manfre or Manfrede was a Maltese entertainer who flourished around the middle of the seventeenth century. He drank copious draughts of water which was then ejected from his mouth as wine. Manfre called for a bucket of warm water, rinsed his mouth and gargled, to disprove the presence of any concealed materials. Then he drank further glasses of water, immediately returning them from his stomach apparently as red wine or as beer. Taking further glasses of water, these were consumed and vomited as rose water, orange-flower water and brandy. Spectators would throw handkerchiefs and gloves on the stage to be moistened with the water he produced and have them returned duly perfumed. Finally, he swallowed thirty to forty glasses of water and then, throwing back his head, spouted out the liquid like a fountain to the great delight of the audience.[19]

Cardinal Mazarin (1602–61) suspected that Manfre had diabolical assistance, and the only way the juggler could save his life was by explaining his methods to the prelate.

Manfre taught the act also to Floram Marchand, and his French pupil arrived in London from Tours in 1650 accompanied by two English promoters, Thomas Peedle and Thomas Cozbie. Unfortunately their partnership did not long survive and the erstwhile promoters became exposers, publishing a four-leaved pamphlet titled *The Falacie of the Great Water-Drinker Discovered* (1650).[20] They explained that Marchand prepared for his performance by swallowing a pill the size of a hazel nut 'confected with the gall of an heifer and wheat flour baked'. A concentrated extract of red dye was prepared from the leguminous plant *Caesalpinia brasiliensis* (Brazil wood) and half a pint swallowed before appearing in public. Some of the glasses used were secretly treated by rinsing with white-wine vinegar. Then, by drinking from a series of untreated glasses, the ingested water would mix with the dye and be regurgitated as glasses of claret. When the vinegar-treated glasses were used, the action of the acid on the dye changed the colour to brown and beer apparently resulted. The perfumed rose and orange-flower waters and brandy were produced by the substitution of glasses hidden behind the water bucket and already containing a portion of each liquid. For the final effect, a metal instrument with three orifices was inserted in his mouth which enabled him to discharge his three-jet fountain.

All these performers who employed the fiery and watery elements comprise, together with other 'phenomena' such as stone-eaters, sword-swallowers, memory men and lightning calculators, practitioners of the arts allied to conjuring and magic. We shall meet up with some others of these arts in another chapter.

5
THE CONJURING QUACKS

*The Mountebank now treads the stage, and sells
His pills, his balsams, and his ague spells.*

John Gay, *The Shepherd's Week* (1714).
Saturday; or, The Flights.

In the last two decades of the eighteenth century, Londoners, and subsequently their country cousins, were beguiled by the activities of one Gustavus Katterfelto, the son of a Prussian colonel of hussars who, after travelling on the continent for sixteen years as a conjurer, descended on the metropolis in 1781 with a new style of entertainment.[1] He was an early exponent of the combination of the marvels of science with conjuring, thereby initiating a trend which continued well into the nineteenth century. Katterfelto commenced his entertainments with a philosophical lecture which lasted for about an hour, and then devoted the rest of the evening to experiments, demonstrations and finally a conjuring performance.

The principal scientific feature of his show was the solar microscope, which made use of direct sunlight for microprojection, a popular form of microscopy at that time. Usually the microscope was mounted in a shutter of a darkened room in such a way that the adjustable mirror caught the rays of the sun outside the window and reflected the light through the horizontal tube of the microscope. The image was projected onto the screen; the engraving of Katterfelto that appeared in the *European Magazine* of June 1783 fancifully depicted some of the minute creatures he exhibited in this way.[2] Living organisms in a drop of stagnant water, maggots, insects and caterpillars were all paraded across his screen for the enlightenment of the audiences who paid one, two or three shillings for their education. (Although Katterfelto implied that he had invented, or at least improved, the solar microscope, such was not the case; the

inventor was Johannes Lieberkühn, who had exhibited the apparatus to the Royal Society as early as 1739.)

A great advertiser, modesty was certainly not one of Katterfelto's failings, as witness his description of himself as 'the greatest philosopher in this kingdom since Sir Isaac Newton'. In the London *Morning Post and Daily Advertiser* he proclaimed:-

KATTERFELTO
As a DIVINE and MORAL PHILOSOPHER
BEGS leave to say, that all persons on earth live
in darkness, if they are able to see, but won't see,
that wonderful Exhibition on the Solar Microscope.
There will be seen in a drop of water, the size
of a pin's head, above 5,000 insects; the same
in beer, milk, vinegar, blood, flour, cheese,
Marechalle powder, and 200 other uncommon
objects.

However, even the magician was dependent on the whims of the weather for the operation of his solar microscope, and he found it necessary to add: 'If the sun does not appear this day, he will show them by the Compound Microscope, with his New Occult Secrets.'

Katterfelto's lectures were broad in their scope, and on twelve different evenings he promised a selection from philosophical, mathematical, optical, magnetical, electrical, physical, chymical, pneumatic, hydraulic or hydrostatic topics, not to mention proetic, stenographic, balensical and caprimantic delights! It was only after their 'enlightenment' in this manner that his audiences were then to be

entertained, for

after his Lecture, Mr Katterfelto will shew and discover several new Deceptions on, Dice, Cards, Billiards, Tennis, Letters, Money, Watches, Caskets, Silver and Gold, Boxes, Medals, Pyramidical Glasses, Mechanical Clocks.

Another of his advertisements tells of 'a gentleman of the faculty belonging to Oxford University, who, finding it likely to prove a fine day, set out for London purposely to see those great wonders that are advertised so much by that famous philosopher, Mr Katterfelto'. This erudite academic declared 'if he had come three hundred miles on purpose, the knowledge he had then received would amply reward him; and that he should not wonder that some of the nobility should come from the remotest part of Scotland to hear Mr Katterfelto, as people of that country in particular are always searching for knowledge'.

The showman's flair for advertising was to be matched only by Anderson, the Wizard of the North, in the nineteenth century. Many of his advertising puffs were prefaced by the proclamation of 'Wonders, Wonders, Wonders', apparently drawing upon Swift's satirical squib on the mythical Schoritz (page 48).

Katterfelto was described as a rather tall, thin man who wore a long black cloak and a square velvet cap for his performances. Capitalizing on his foreign accent and poor command of English—as so many of the conjuring profession have subsequently done, either legitimately or by assumption of a fictitious continental origin—he clothed his exhibitions with mysterious patter which cartoonists quickly appropriated. 'Dere you was see de Vonders of the Vorld'— and doubtless his audiences thought they did!

Associated with Katterfelto's shows was a black cat to which, evidently with tongue in cheek, he gave the impression of attributing powers essential for the performance of his wonders. The cat accompanied him about and was the subject of much comment, the pair of them being jokingly alluded to by the press as the Black Devils, although undoubtedly the less sophisticated were apt to take the assessment at its face value. Katterfelto made great

'Colonel' Gustavus Katterfelto, empiric and conjurer, who, when sunlight permitted, exhibited his solar microscope during his performances. He was very popular in London during the period 1781–4 and peddled nostrums during the great influenza epidemic of 1782.

play of this circumstance in his advertisements, as witness:

KATTERFELTO is sorry to find that the writers in the newspapers have several times, and particularly within the last fortnight, asserted that he and his BLACK CAT were DEVILS. On the contrary, Katterfelto professes himself to be nothing more than a Moral and Divine Philosopher, a Teacher in Mathematics, and Natural Philosophy; . . . that the idea of him and his Black Cat being Devils arises merely from the astonishing performances of Katterfelto and his said Cat, which both in the day's and at the night's exhibition, are such as to induce all the spectators to believe them both Devils indeed!—the Black Cat appearing at one instant with a tail, and the next without any, and which has occasioned many thousands of pounds to be lost on wagers on this incomprehensible subject.[3]

Besides the black cat, the conjurer was assisted by two black servants.

LE CHARLATAN *by Borel (1784) conveys the atmosphere of an eighteenth-century French street fair with the wonder-worker peddling nostrums as well as performing the Cups and Balls. (A section of a larger engraving.)*

Nov 18. 1782.

Great **WONDERS! WONDERS! WONDERS! WON-**
DERS! and WONDERS! are now to be feen in a very
warm Room, at No. 22, Piccadilly, This and every day this
week, from eleven in the morning till four in the afternoon, and precifely at feven clock, every evening this week,

MR. KATTERFELTO will fhow a variety
of new furprifing Experiments in Natural and Experimental Philofophy and Mathematics, and his whole regular
Courfe of Philofophical Lectures are deliver'd in Twelve
different times, a different Lecture and Experiment every
day, and every evening at 7 o'clock. His various Experiments are as follow, viz.

PHILOSOPHICAL,	PNEUMATIC,
MATHEMATICAL,	HYDRAULIC,
OPTICAL,	HYDROSTATIC,
MAGNETICAL,	PROETIC,
ELECTRICAL,	STENOGRAPHIC,
PHYSICAL,	BLENCICAL,
CHYMICAL,	CAPRIMANTIC ART.

By his new-improved SOLAR MICROSCOPE,
Will be feen many furprifing infects in different waters, beer,
milk, vinegar, and blood; and other curious objects.

Mr. K A T T E R F E L T O

Has, in his travels for thefe eighteen years paft, had the honour to exhibit with great applaufe before the Emprefs of
Ruffia, the Queen of Hungary, the King of Pruffia, Denmark, Sweden, and Polland, and before many other
Princes.

And after his Lecture, Mr. Katterfelto will fhow and dif-
cover feveral NEW DECEPTIONS, on

DICE, CARDS,	SILVER and GOLD,
BILLIARDS, TENNIS,	BOXES, MEDALS,
LETTERS, MONEY,	PYRAMIDICAL GLASES
WATCHES, CASKETS,	MECHANICAL CLOCKS

Admittance, front feats 3s. fecond feats 2s. back feats
1s. for fervants only.

Newspaper advertisement for Katterfelto's Wonders in 1782.

At various times Katterfelto styled himself as Doctor or Colonel, again initiating a fashion which persisted among nineteenth-century conjurers, who additionally adopted the title of Professor to dignify their exhibitions. He was also the first to include an exposé of conjurers' and gamblers' secrets as part of his public performances. Thus an advertisement for his appearance at Cox's Museum in Spring Gardens, London, in the Spring of 1781, stated:

As many ladies and gentlemen lose their fortunes by cards and dice, and the public in general is imposed upon by a person who shows a variety of tricks in dexterity of hand by confederacy, Mr Katterfelto will, after his philosophical lecture, discover and lay open those various impositions, for the benefit and satisfaction of the public.

In the rôle of public benefactors many subsequent generations of conjurers have justified similar exposures of techniques and methods, but not always without engendering the wrath of their fellow practitioners.

Credit has been given to Katterfelto by some writers for the innovation of the famous Gun Trick, which we consider elsewhere (page 169), and certainly his first London advertisement of March 1781 announced that he would demonstrate the 'Art of Gunnery'. 'Any gentleman may load his gun with powder and ball, and he will fire at a glass bottle and will cause the balls to drop in the bottle or before it, without breaking the glass.' Although clearly one of the earlier exhibitors of this feat, he was not the first—nor was his contemporary Philip Astley, founder of the circus, who made similar claims in his book *Natural Magic*, published in 1785.

Katterfelto moved in 1782 to 22 Piccadilly, declaring there was insufficient light in Spring Gardens for the exhibition of his solar microscope, and then to 24 Piccadilly early in the following year, where he remained until embarking upon his tour of the provinces in 1785. In July 1784 he gave a Command Performance for King George III at Windsor, in order that the King's children might see his show. Even so, his fortunes were apparently already fluctuating, for late in 1783 he had advertised that all his 'philosophical and mathematical apparatus' was for sale at the bargain price of £2,500 (he claimed it was worth £4,000) and 'would be very valuable to a school like Harrow or Winchester as many young gentlemen would reap very great advantages from them'. The opportunity to equip themselves was evidently spurned by these and other educational establishments, for Katterfelto continued in business, albeit with declining prosperity.

Katterfelto's claim to fame—or notoriety, as the case may be—stems not only from his conjuring and scientific activities but also from his rôle as an empiric and quack doctor. The great influenza epidemic which swept London in 1782 gave him the opportunity to peddle nostrums, and his exhibition room was open daily from 10am to 5pm for this purpose; it seems probable that this activity occupied him entirely for several weeks. His later advertisements advised that 'Mr Katterfelto likewise makes and sells Dr Bato's medicines at 5s a bottle, which cured many thousand persons of the late Influenza'. Katterfelto himself came through the epidemic unscathed and thereafter capitalized on his experiences, which led him into direct competition with other empirics at a time when popular interest was being stimulated by discoveries in mesmerism and so-called electro-biology.

His greatest rival in quackery was a Scot, Dr James Graham (1745–94), who had studied medicine at Edinburgh University.[4] After settling in Pontefract and marrying, Graham travelled as a doctor in the USA and spent two years in Philadelphia, where he became acquainted with Benjamin Franklin's electrical experiments. He returned to England in 1784, and a year later set up an establishment in Pall Mall which quickly became fashionable, aided not a little by the fact that one of his first, enthusiastic patients was the redoubtable Mrs Catherine Macaulay, historian and author.[5] This controversial figure, regarded by Mary Wollstonecraft in her *Vindication of the Rights of Women* as 'the woman of the greatest abilities that this country has ever produced', subsequently married Graham's younger brother, William, at Leicester in 1788; the tongues wagged yet again, for she was forty-seven and he but twenty-one.

For suitable fees Graham's patients were placed on a 'magnetic throne' or in a bath through which electric currents could be passed, furnished with aetherial balsams and generally subjected to dubious treatments. Then, as now, the greater the denunciation as quackery the more fashionable did Graham's practice become so that, in 1779, he was able to open his palatial Temple of Health in the Royal Terrace, Adelphi, overlooking the Thames. This remarkable establishment with its equipment was reputed to have cost £10,000 and comprised rooms where the electrical apparatus was housed and medicines sold, a lecture hall and the Great Apollo Apartment—'a magnificent temple, sacred to health and dedicated to Apollo'. To stimulate custom, a beautiful Goddess of Health was to be seen at the temple and in 1781 it is alleged that Emma Lyon, the future Lady Emma Hamilton, played this star rôle. He also employed two gigantic porters. Patients and visitors alike could gaze at these marvels, provided they paid the exorbitant prices. Horace Walpole wrote on 23 August 1780 to the Countess of Ossory that it was 'the most impudent puppet-show of imposition I ever saw, and the mountebank himself the dullest of his profession, except that he makes the spectators pay a crown apiece'. However, Graham was certainly a consummate showman, for Walpole records that 'the apothecary' came up through a trapdoor, which was a novelty, although he adds critically that 'he might as well come up stairs'![6]

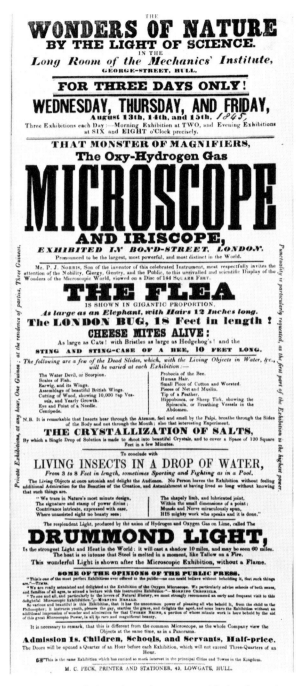

The demise of the solar microscope with its dependence on sunlight came in the nineteenth century when illumination by the Drummond or lime light was introduced. Showmen again embraced the new discovery, as witness this Hull bill for 1845 extolling the marvels that the Oxy-Hydrogen Gas Microscope would reveal, including 'Cheese mites as large as cats'!

The Wonderful most Wonderful D.ʳ Kate-he-felt-ho, having pack'd up his Alls is trudging away with his Family & all his little necessary Appendices to his own Dear Country — Weep England, Weep, Oh! ...31 March 1783 by H. Humphrey ...New Bond Str

THE WONDERFUL, MOST WONDERFUL DR KATE-HE-FELT-HO, *a cartoon published by W. Humphrey on 31 March 1783, which depicts the conjurer's wife and children as devils.*

The high costs of running such an elaborate establishment took their toll and, with falling attendances, Graham had perforce to move in 1781 to less expensive surroundings at Schomberg House, Pall Mall, which became the Temple of Health and Hymen. Graham's new establishment in Pall Mall was used also for gaming, and the EO tables there were broken by the Westminster justices on 1 August 1782, two days after a raid on the premises by two constables had revealed some three hundred people indulging in the prohibited game (EO was a game of chance, rather resembling roulette, in which the ball located in niches on the table marked with the letters E and O). It is noteworthy that Katterfelto

included in his explanatory demonstrations an exposure of the means by which persons lost their fortunes at the EO tables. The same year Graham's property was seized for debt and thereafter his affairs suffered considerably.

One of Graham's most fanciful yet lucrative enterprises was the Celestial Bed, a georgeous piece of furniture which was claimed to cure sterility—any childless couples who slept in it would be assured of heirs, provided they could pay the fee of £100 per night (subsequently reduced to £50 at Schomberg House). This amazing piece of furniture was said to have cost £12,000.[7] It was 'beautifully carved and gilt, covered with silk damask, supported by twenty-eight glass pillars each surmounted by a richly carved and gilt canopy from which crimson silk curtains with fringe and tassels were suspended'. The bedclothes and pillows were impregnated with Arabian perfumes and tubes were connected to a cylinder which provided quantities of 'celestial fire', presumably to fuel the flames of love required to achieve its purpose, while its occupants were admonished by the commandment at the head to 'BE FRUITFUL, MULTIPLY AND REPLENISH THE EARTH'. Graham stated that

The chief principle of my Celestial Bed is produced by artificial loadstones. About 15cwt of compound magnets are continually pouring forth in an ever flowing circle.

In such opulent and diverting surroundings the barren couple must have experienced not a little difficulty in concentrating on the more important matter of procreation.

Interestingly, the bed was made by a certain Thomas Denton, who was executed on 1 July 1789 as a member of a gang of counterfeiters and whose place in the literature of conjuring is assured on account of the three editions of *The Conjurer Unmasked* for which he was responsible. We shall have more to say about Denton later.

Thus Katterfelto entered the London scene at the time of Graham's triumphs and the rivalry between the two became intense. The Scot labelled Katterfelto 'a German Maggot Killer', and the focus of the public eye on this pair of expert advertisers was such that political cartoonists were not slow to feature them.[8] A few of these cartoons are worthy of mention and a particularly fine example was published by H. Humphrey of 51 New Bond Street on 31 March 1783. The caption of the engraving reads

The Wonderful most Wonderful Dr Kate-he-felt-ho, having pack'd up his Alls is trudging away with his Family and all his little necessary Appendices to his own Dear Countrey—Weep England! Weep! Oh!

As can be seen from the illustration, carrying his solar microscope on his back, Katterfelto wears a military uniform and a hat decorated with the skull and crossbones of the Death's Head Hussars and also bearing a curious addition depicting the sciences of geography, optics and astronomy. An enormous sabre, its scabbard inscribed '100000000000 Caterpillars slain in one year', hangs at his side and his left hand clutches a bag containing 5,000 English guineas, apparently mulcted from his audiences. In his right hand he carries a strange electrical implement termed 'Gentle Restorer'. He is uttering the words: 'Galante Show, here be de Death of Philosophy and de Glory of Legerdemain, here be de

Vonders of all the Kings in Europe, Asia, Africa and America.'

His wife and children are endowed with short horns and cloven feet and the youngsters ask: 'Aynt my Daddy a Cunning Man, Mammy?', 'Aynt de Englishmen great Fools, Mammy?' and 'Is my Daddy a Devil, Mammy?'

Another cartoon, titled *The Quacks*, was published on 17 March 1783 by W. Humphrey of 227 Strand, and this featured both Katterfelto and Graham, pitting their marvels one against the other, each standing on a stage. Katterfelto's stage is flimsy, supported on thin planks, with cross planks, one decorated with skull and crossbones and the other with insects. The conjurer crouches over a cylindrical conductor supported on a pillar and inscribed 'Positively charg'd'. His feet rest on the base of the pillar and a trident on its other end touches a grindstone which is being turned by the Devil who declares: 'Away with it my Dear Son, I'll find fire eternally for you'. Sparks issue from Katterfelto's finger and thumb, and also from his chin, dropping to the touch hole of a small cannon which is directed at Graham. The conjurer is saying: 'Dare you was see de Vonders of the Varld, which make de hair Stand on tiptoe, Dare you was see mine Tumb and mine findgar, Fire from mine findger and Feaders on mine Tumb—dare you was see de Gun Fire viddout Ball or powder, dare you was see de Devil at mine A – e – O. Vonders! Vonders! Vonderfull Vonders!'

Graham is on a stage shaped like an EO table astride a cylinder inscribed: 'Prime conductor Gentle restorer Largest in the World.' He points at Katterfelto, saying: 'That round Vigour! that full-toned juvenile Virility which speaks so cordially and so Effectually home to the Female Heart, Conciliating its Favour and Friendship, rivetting its Intensest Affections away thou German Maggot killer, thy Fame is not to be Compar'd to mine.' And at his feet stands a duck, ballooning from its beak the entirely appropriate comment: 'Quack. Quack. Quack.'

Both Katterfelto and Graham were targets of theatrical burlesques. As Dr Caterpillar, Katterfelto was lampooned at the Haymarket in *None are so Blind as Those Who Won't See*, while Graham was the 'Emperor of the Quacks' in George Colman the elder's *Genius of Nonsense* at the same theatre. They were astute enough to turn these attacks to their own advantage in their advertisements and so further enhanced their reputations as 'puffers'. Indeed, they were the subject of a song, *The West Country Puffing*

The QUACKS.

THE QUACKS, *a cartoon satirizing Dr James Graham and Katterfelto, published by W. Humphrey on 17 March 1783. The two empirics are engaged in a contest with their respective marvels.*

Family, 'dedicated to those *Princes of Puffs*, who exist at their *Wholesale Puff* a de *Puff Warehouses*, the Sign of the *Devil* and *Black Cat*, Piccadilly; the *Temple of Health, Pall Mall*', the last verse of which was

> *Thus Puffing's become now the Trade,*
> *Of* Katerfelto* *and* Graham* *well known,*
> *Whose Mouths confessedly are made,*
> *For nought else but* Puffing *alone.*
> **Two Travelling Philosophers.*

to be sung to the tune of *An Old Woman Cloathed in Grey*.

Contemporary with Katterfelto's London successes was the remarkable achievement of Montgolfier's balloon ascents, and so the *Rambler's Magazine* in January 1784 carried an engraving titled *The New Mail Carriers, or Montgolfier and Katterfelto taking an airing in Balloons*, in which the pair face one

another in balloons. Katterfelto says: 'Monsieur Montgolfier let us be reconciled' while that worthy replies: 'Let us fly up to de Sun Mr Katerfelto'; on the top of the conjurer's balloon is his black cat, surrounded by kittens.

Katterfelto added the new discovery to his entertainments, and the demonstration of fire balloons subsequently led to his imprisonment in Yorkshire when a balloon descended upon and ignited a hayrick and the hapless conjurer did not have the necessary funds to compensate the aggrieved farmer.

It would seem that Katterfelto took his exhibition on the road around 1785 and thereafter toured the provinces with varying but generally decreasing success. It is recorded that he frequently visited Whitby, where he was well received, one of his most popular tricks being to raise his daughter to the ceiling by means of a huge magnet, after she had put on a massive steel helmet held in position by leather straps under her armpits. He probably favoured this part of the Yorkshire coast for there he could secure the exhibits of fossils, ammonites and agates required for the geological display which comprised part of his travelling museum.[4]

A writer to the *London Mirror* in 1831 recalled a

boyhood encounter with Katterfelto and his family when he appeared in Durham City in 1790 or 1791, and it is evident that the showman was then in poor circumstances.[3] The family travelled in an old coach pulled by a pair of sorry hacks and were attended by two black servants who announced Katterfelto's appearances by blowing trumpets and distributing handbills around the town. The correspondent's recollections indicate that the format of the show was unchanged but, on the first advertised night, as he was the sole member of the audience, no performance took place and he was invited by Katterfelto's wife backstage, when he met the great man, enveloped in an old green, greasy roquelaure and wearing his familiar black velvet cap. The dress of the wife and daughter was, as he puts it, 'equally ancient and uncleanly'.

On the next night there was a reasonable audience and the show went ahead as planned. In its course a clergyman became the butt of Katterfelto's legerdemain. When a chosen card vanished from the pack and could not be found, the performer suggested that someone must have removed it and invited the cleric to turn out his pockets. Indignantly, that worthy initially refused but, finally persuaded, did so and was surprised to find the offending card. He did not appreciate the amusement afforded the audience by his discomfit, however, and when a similar episode occurred with money he stormed out threatening the conjurer with vengeance in a manner quite unbecoming a man of the cloth.

Katterfelto's later years represent a sorry tale of misfortune, and the glory of his London seasons faded into the insignificance of an itinerant performer barely eking out an existence. He was imprisoned at Shrewsbury as a vagrant and imposter and died at Bedale in Yorkshire on 25 November 1799. *The Gentleman's Magazine* carried a simple notice:

At Bedale, co. York, the eccentric Dr Katterfelto, whose advertisements of himself and his black cat used generally to be ushered in with the word 'Wonders!' three times repeated.[9]

His former antagonist, Dr Graham, whose final years were consumed by a religious mania, had died in 1794.

Katterfelto's links with Whitby were maintained after his death when his widow remarried a publican of that town, John Carter, who was instrumental in the revival of the manufacture of jet around 1800.

Despite the inglorious end to his career Katter-

felto's fame in the annals of conjuring is secure and it is sufficient to recall that his impact on contemporary London society was such that not only did the cartoonists make him their subject but also that the unhappy poet William Cowper (1731–1800) mentioned him in his poem 'The Task', which he wrote at his summer house at Olney in 1785:

> *And Katterfelto, with his hair on end*
> *At his own wonders, wondering for his bread.*

These likeable charlatans were, in a sense, successors to the itinerant conjurers of the fifteenth and sixteenth centuries, who were frequently classed together with rogues and vagabonds—and possibly not a few deserved such labelling! The general opprobrium expressed by William Alley in 1565 regarding the influence of the stage and entertainers on the people is perhaps a reflection of what others thought too:

Alas, are not almost al places in these daies replenished with juglers, scoffers, jesters, plaiers, which may say and do what they lust, be it never so fleshly and filthy? and yet suffred and heard with laughing and clapping of handes.[10]

While the law did not take kindly to itinerants, pursuing them with vigour, there is no record of a conjurer having reached an untimely end until the eighteenth century when, with all the majesty of law, one Thomas Denton went to the scaffold before Newgate Prison on 1 July 1789. Denton was sufficiently noteworthy to warrant an entry in the *Dictionary of National Biography*[11] and the essential features of his career were recorded by the contemporary journals.[12, 13]

He was a Yorkshireman who started life as a tinman or metalworker but, through a taste for literature, then kept a bookshop in York for a period before moving to London about 1780 where, in Holborn, he continued in business as a bookseller. But Denton's interests diversified when he saw in 1784 a Speaking Figure exhibited by a Frenchman at Bury Street in London; it was in the form of a doll, suspended by cords or ribbons, which answered questions.[14] He quickly copied it and was soon exhibiting in opposition at Coventry Street and subsequently in the provinces, before selling it to a printer.

The enterprising bookseller was also a proficient amateur chemist and he combined the plating of coach harness with his book business which expanded also into toyman. Mathematical and scientific instrument manufacture, including pentagraphs, a Writing Figure, Graham's Celestial Bed (page 66) and other automata—all testify to Denton's abilities which ultimately led to his downfall.

An interest in books, conjuring and mechanical devices undoubtedly fostered Denton's publication in 1785 of a translation of Henri Decremps' new book, *La Magie Blanche Dévoilée* (1784), as *The Conjurer Unmasked*. The second edition of 1788 incorporated 'Large Additions and Alterations by T. Denton, Proprietor of the Mechanical Exhibition lately exhibited in London, Edinburgh, Newcastle, York etc.', the addendum comprising five new tricks, while the third edition of 1790, published after Denton's execution, made no reference to its French provenance.[15]

Denton formed an association with a well known coiner named John Jones and together they were arrested in 1789. After a trial lasting seven hours Denton was acquitted of counterfeiting but con-victed of possessing coining implements and sentenced to death. On 24 June the Recorder of London confirmed the sentence which was duly carried out on 1 July. *The Gentleman's Magazine* reported that Jones and Denton 'died professed infidels and while under sentence of death in Newgate behaved infamously, which conduct Denton continued until the last', which seems a little at variance with the tenor of the letter Denton wrote to his parents before he was brought forth for execution:[16]

Hon. father and mother
When you receive this, I shall be gone to the country from whence no traveller returns. Don't cast any reflections on my wife; she has been the best of wives, the best of mothers, and the best of women; and if ever woman went to heaven, she will. If I had taken her advice, I should not have been in this situation. God bless my poor Dick. The bell is tolling. Adieu.

Tho. Denton.[12]

A German stock magic poster depicting various illusions, including the Floating Lady and Sawing through a Woman. Individual performers purchased these lithographs from the printer and then added their own names and billing matter.

6
#

Said Syntax, "I have often heard
Philosophers of high regard
Speak of this nitrous inhalation
And of its gay exhilaration."

Doctor Syntax in Paris (1820)

In the year of Katterfelto's death a brilliant young Cornishman, Humphry Davy (1778–1829), who was the Superintendent at Dr Thomas Beddoes' Pneumatic Institution in Bristol, was carrying out some experiments which were subsequently to have enormous repercussions in the world of medicine and less importantly, although perhaps more divertingly, immediate effects on early nineteenth-century conjuring entertainment.

Nitrous oxide gas was isolated in 1772 by the famous English chemist Joseph Priestley, but its interesting physiological properties were not recognized until 1799, when the 20-year-old Davy recorded the pleasurable and exhilarating sensations that its inhalation produced.

The objects around me became dazzling and my hearing more acute. Towards the last inspirations, the thrilling ceased, the sense of muscular power became greater, and at last an irresistible propensity to action was indulged in; I recollect but indefinitely what followed; I know my motions were various and violent.[1]

I now had a great disposition to laugh, luminous points seemed frequently to pass before my eyes, my hearing was certainly more acute and I felt a pleasant lightness and power of exertion in my muscles.[2]

Davy's work attracted much attention. The poet Robert Southey participated in the early experiments at Beddoes' Institute and conjectured that the gas must constitute the atmosphere of 'the highest of all possible heavens'. Samuel Taylor Coleridge also inhaled the gas and Beddoes reported that he had a propensity to laugh which, however, he restrained.[3] In 1779 Coleridge was already taking, although not yet addicted to, opium, and the vivid imagery of his *Kubla Khan* stems directly from this source, while the thesis that parts of *The Rime of the Ancient Mariner* and other poems could be attributed to opium dreams has also been advanced.[4, 5] Consequently Coleridge was in a position to compare the effects of nitrous oxide with those of laudanum, and it is evident from his correspondence that he was greatly interested in pain and its alleviation.

In 1800 Davy published his classic text *Researches, Chemical and Philosophical; chiefly concerning nitrous oxide, or dephlogisticated air, and its respiration*, in the pages of which he made the prophetic observation:

As nitrous oxide in its extensive operation appears capable of destroying physical pain, it may probably be used with advantage during surgical operations in which no great effusion of blood takes place.

In the event, over forty years elapsed before the gas was adopted for anaesthesia.

Davy moved from Bristol in 1801 to the newly established Royal Institution in Albemarle Street, London, founded by Count Rumford (Sir Benjamin Thompson, 1753–1814) with the object of combining the dissemination of useful knowledge with the amusement and instruction of 'the higher ranks'. There his lectures quickly became the centre of

SCIENTIFIC RESEARCHES!—NEW DISCOVERIES IN PNEU-
MATICS. *James Gillray's rather scurrilous cartoon of the
demonstration of the properties of nitrous oxide
(laughing gas) at the Royal Institution in 1802. Young
Humphry Davy holds the bellows while Sir John Coxe
Hippisley is the victim of an explosion in his breeches.
On the right Count Rumford keeps a watching brief.*

attraction for brilliant and fashionable audiences.
Indeed, one critic commented that the audience was
assembled merely by the influence of fashion.[6]
Davy's meteoric success marked also the turning
point in the financial affairs of the Institute, which
were at a low ebb when he first joined its staff. A few
months after his arrival there he gave a course of

lectures on pneumatic chemistry which concluded
with one on respiration, after which an opportunity
was given, to those who wished, to breathe some
nitrous oxide. On 23 June 1801 a select party met at
the Institution to sample the gas and it was undoubtedly the publicity attendant on this and subsequent demonstrations that popularized the subject
and led to James Gillray's famous coloured cartoon
published on 23 May 1802. Titled *Scientific Researches!—New Discoveries in Pneumaticks!—or—an
Experimental Lecture on the Powers of Air*, the
caricature depicts Professor Thomas Young, physician, physicist and Egyptologist, administering the
gas to Sir John Coxe Hippisley, who was manager of
the Royal Institution. Holding him by the nose, he

has inserted into his mouth a tube connected to a series of retorts in which a gas has been prepared. The results are spectacular, an explosion of flame and smoke from Hippisley's breeches! (In subsequent more delicate days it was sometimes reproduced in carefully censored form.[7] Undoubtedly it reflects the rather coarse and boisterous humour of the time but it is nonetheless a very important landmark in the history of chemistry.)

The youthful Davy is holding the bellows and assisting Young while Count Rumford, wearing the decoration of the Polish Order of the White Eagle, stands to the right of the lecture bench and presides benevolently over the proceedings, much as Sir George Porter does today in the televised pro-

MR HENRY'S CONVERSAZIONE. *This print gives a good impression of Henry's stage setting and some of his equipment, including the mechanical peacock and inn. He has just broken a wine bottle to produce a dove.*

grammes from the Royal Institution. Gillray also portrayed several other readily identified luminaries in the caricature, including Isaac D'Israeli, Lord Gower, Lord Stanhope and Sir Harry Englefield, holding notebook and pencil. The thin elderly lady who is also taking notes was probably Mrs Frederica Locke, one of the best known blue-stockings in England.[8]

On account of its singular effects, nitrous oxide was soon popularly known as Laughing Gas and its preparation and properties were described in textbooks of chemistry, the first of which was Thomson's *A System of Chemistry in Four Volumes* in 1804. Thus information concerning the gas became freely available and the showmen of the early nineteenth century, never slow to seize upon the latest scientific discoveries that could be turned to an honest penny, were soon advertising exhibitions of Laughing Gas as part of their programmes.

The earliest documented entertainment in Britain employing Laughing Gas was that of Mr Henry, conjurer and ventriloquist, at the Adelphi Theatre in the Strand, London, in 1824. It is believed that Henry's real name was Galbraith and that he was of Scottish birth, probably being the same Henry who, billed as a Professor of Natural Magic, had appeared at the Lyceum Theatre and at Astley's Theatre in 1788. He claimed to have invented parlour fireworks and travelled widely with a show that included conjuring, ventriloquism, dissolving views and mechanical novelties. The British Museum has a collection of his playbills dating from 1817 from which his appearances at Stourbridge, Chelmsford, Witham, Colchester, Ipswich, Lynn and Leicester can be followed to the early part of 1824.[9] Then, on 5 March 1824, he started a season at the Adelphi Theatre in the Strand which was to become the first of a series of six consecutive annual seasons in London.

On 7 and 9 April, 1824 his bill announced:

LAUGHING GAS

(So denominated from the pleasurable sensations attendant upon inhaling it) having been received on Wednesday last with unequivocal Marks of Approbation by a crowded and brilliant Audience, will be repeated. Gentlemen intending to take the Gas are requested to address a line to M.H. at the Theatre, previous to the Day, in order to prevent any Disappointment arising from his not being provided with a sufficient Quantity.

The bill also enjoined:

Let those Laugh now, who have never laughed before,
And those who always Laugh, now Laugh the more.

Laughing Gas became an established feature of Henry's programme; and later in April he announced that, to render his performances more completely worthy of the distinguished patronage they had received, he had engaged a Quintett Band. A critic in

Egan's Paper considered that the risible effects produced by the Gas were better than a pantomime.

Henry's 1824 season at the Adelphi ended on Saturday 5 June, and the bill for this occasion was headed:

THE NITROUS OXIDE, or
LAUGHING GAS
Will continue to be administered to any of
the Audience who may chuse to inhale it:
The WONDERS of which were first experienced by
SIR HUMPHREY [*sic*] DAVY,
and the exhilarating Effects it produced, as
described by this Gentleman, have been fully
evinced during the Period of its Exhibition
by M.H.

A reviewer writing in the *Globe and Traveller* on 1 April 1824 commented that Henry's exhibition was not to be placed in the same rank as the Gyngells and Inglebys of former days, but considered that Henry possessed an easy and gentlemanly delivery and that, 'notwithstanding the occasionally obstreperous ebullition of the gods', he could safely recommend the entertainment to the most fastidious of his readers.

For the most detailed contemporary description of Laughing Gas entertainment we have to turn to a German naturalist, C. F. Schoenbein, who in 1825 became a teacher at Epsom and remained in England for two years thereafter; while he may have been in England as early as 1824, the earliest entry recorded in his *Journal* is from 1826.[10] Although Schoenbein's account does not mention Henry by name, the fact that he witnessed the performance at the Adelphi Theatre makes it virtually certain that Henry was the performer concerned.

In some of the smaller theatres, physical and chemical experiments are sometimes made, more for the entertainment than for the edification of the audience, and I once saw such a performance. It was at the Adelphi Theatre and they wanted to demonstrate the very odd properties and the physiological effects of the laughing gas.

When the curtain was raised, you could see on the stage, in a wide semicircle, a dozen or more large caoutchouc bladders with shining metal taps, filled with the laughing gas. The 'Experimentator' appeared in a simple dress suit, and made a short opening speech in which he described the properties of the gas, and its preparation, in a way which would have done credit to a professor of chemistry.

Playbill issued during Mr Henry's first season at the Adelphi Theatre in the Strand in 1824. The 'Splendid spectacle' of laughing gas featured prominently in his programme.

Mr Henry, whose conjuring performances at the Adelphi Theatre during the period 1824–9 included demonstrations of laughing gas.

At the end of his lecture he asked for someone from the audience to come on the stage and to inhale from one of the bladders. A tall daring fellow jumped over the orchestra and on to the stage, and grabbed one of the bladders. But the audience didn't like him and greeted him with cries of 'Off! Off!' At first he did not comply, but when the cries grew louder he went away. A second candidate appeared, but he too was shouted off. When the third met with the same undignified reception, the 'Experimentator' interceded and asked the audience firmly but politely not to be so fickle and to let the show go on. This appeal had the desired effect and they proceeded. The volunteer—sitting in a chair—put the tap to his

mouth, compressed his nose, and inhaled the laughing gas while the 'Experimentator' held the bladder. The tap was then closed while the subject breathed out through the nose. The tap was opened again, the nose compressed, and some more gas inhaled through the mouth. He continued in this way until the bag was emptied. Now the 'Experimentator' retired; but the 'luft-trunken' man remained sitting in his chair for a few minutes, while he stared straight ahead, holding his nose. You can imagine how this comical posture sent the audience into roars of laughter which increased when the intoxicated man leapt smartly from his chair and then made astonishing bounds all over the stage.

When the audience had had its fill and the man had sobered up, a voice called out: 'All nonsense and humbug!' 'All nonsense and humbug!' echoed immediately from hundreds of throats. 'No! No!' came the emphatic reply. When the protests continued, the 'Experimentator' appeared and shouted at the top of his voice: 'Ladies and Gentlemen'. When he obtained a hearing he assured the audience that the experiment was genuine, and he invited the man who had first voiced his doubts to try the experiment himself. The man responded with alacrity and displayed his incredulity by demanding to empty the largest bladder. His request was immediately complied with, and the effect of the gas upon the disbeliever was so great that he beat around him like a madman and assaulted the 'Experimentator'. This performance confirmed the sceptics in their doubts and brought forth fresh demonstrations of disbelief.

The sceptical reactions of the audience recorded by Schoenbein are particularly interesting because it would be reasonable to have supposed that the effects of inhaling the gas were widely known at that time and, indeed, Fiévée, in his *Lettres sur l'Angleterre*, condemned the practice as a national vice of the English![7] Schoenbein continued with a description which supports Fiévée's contention:

My chemical readers may be interested to know that this gas is nowhere inhaled more often than in England, because its marvellous effects were first discovered in this country by Sir Humphry Davy. Once when I stayed in the country with a friend, who was an amateur chemical experimenter, we discussed laughing gas and decided to make a good supply of it ourselves. One fine afternoon, a large party met in the garden to inhale the intoxicating gas in the open air. Some young men inhaled it first, and they all showed undoubted signs of wellbeing and pleasure. When another man of more mature age had his doubts, he decided to take a large quantity of the gas for himself. After breathing a lot of gas, he began to dance and devastate the adjoining flower-bed in his ecstacy to the delight of his audience. Maybe it will become the custom for us to inhale laughing gas at the end of the dinner party, instead of drinking champagne, and in that event there would be no shortage of gas factories.

Happily, Schoenbein's prediction was only half-fulfilled and, while there is currently no shortage of gas factories for the production of nitrous oxide for anaesthetic purposes, the pre- or post-prandial imbiber has not had his champagne usurped by nitrous oxide from a gas cylinder.

Laughing Gas continued to be a featured item in Henry's programmes after his first London season and it was toured to Margate, Coventry and Lynn before his second season opened at the Adelphi in 1825. Although the frequency of the demonstration in his programmes declined, he was still using the Gas at the Adelphi Theatre and in Belfast in 1829, the last records we have of this performer. However, eight years later, another conjurer, Mons. Buck, was advertising Laughing Gas at the New Strand Theatre in March 1837, so that a span of some thirteen years of its use for popular entertainment can be documented.

Mr Henry's performances at the Adelphi and Haymarket Theatres were obviously very popular and, like Anderson later in the nineteenth century, he issued several audience booklets which undoubtedly sold in great numbers at the time but which are now exceedingly difficult to find. The undated *Edward Duncombe's ONLY Correct Edition* of

M. HENRY'S NEW ENTERTAINMENT;
Now performing at the Haymarket Theatre
Written by D.W.J. Esq.

suggests that pirated copies were also in circulation. This 24-page booklet, with folding coloured frontis-piece, sold for a modest sixpence and contained 'Novel Experiments, Laughing Gas, &c.' wherein we read

'I now proceed' said Mr Henry, 'to administer to any of the audience disposed to inhale it, the Laughing Gas, or Nitrous Oxyde. It is so called from the pleasurable sensations produced by inhaling it. I am surprised that it is not used by medical men, as from the exhiliration it creates, it might be of great use to those who labor under hypochondriasis, mental dispondency, and nervous irritability. Sir Humphrey [*sic*] Davy states that when he made use of it, it produced a pleasurable sensation in the chest and extremities, and incited to strong muscular energy. He further states that when tortured with a head-ache, the use of a small quantity completely cured him of the infliction.'

At Mr Henry's call, three persons jumped on the stage; and having inhaled the gas, the nose being stopped in order to prevent the admission of atmospheric air through the nostrils—and from the writhings and contortions of the body of these individuals, we have no doubt that its effect fully verified the description of the highly gifted chemist.

Other booklets were titled *Conversazione or Mirth and Marvels* and *Table Talk or Shreds and Patches*, which had a striking portrait of Henry as frontis-piece. As these titles indicate, Mr Henry's conjuring performances were liberally endowed with patter and his amusing and whimsical conversation was a feature of the show, as exemplified in 1826 when his appearances at the Adelphi Theatre were heralded as 'Odd Sayings and Queer Doings'.

Mr Henry opened his programme of conjuring by changing wine to water and water into wine—'at pleasure', as he charmingly put it, although the latter of these transformations presumably evoked the greater delight. A dove placed in a box on one side of the stage was then produced from a box on the other side. Coffee and rice, contained in two vases, were transposed, and Mr Henry then intro-duced 'a curious mechanical trick'. From a model inn the automaton hostess emerged to take orders; having received them she returned into the inn and brought forth the various liquors called for by the audience, waited payment and then went back inside and shut the door. This piece was a version of the Winstanley Dairy House and Balducci's Druggist of the eighteenth century. The first part of Henry's show was closed by another mechanical item, a chest of drawers and bookcase into which a pack of cards, containing several cards selected by members of the audience, was placed. The chosen pasteboards were

The old Adelphi Theatre in the Strand, scene of Mr Henry's annual appearances in London. Allegedly one of the worst constructed, badly ventilated and uncomfortable theatres in the capital,[18] it finally closed on 2 June 1858.

made to appear in every drawer and finally in the bookcase itself.

Part two of the entertainment commenced with Mr Henry borrowing a wedding ring, loading it into a pistol and firing it. The ring was found suspended from the neck of a canary 'taken out from the blossom of a full blown rose'. The ring was returned to its owner none the worse for its adventure and the bird given to a lady to hold—in whose hands it appeared to die. The corpse was placed in a magic sepulchre and restored to life at the wishes of the lady. Now it was the turn of a borrowed watch to be wrapped in a handkerchief and placed in an empty silver urn, from which wine was immediately drawn. A bottle of wine was introduced and the borrowed watch in its handkerchief commanded to pass from the urn into the bottle; the bottle was broken and, sure enough, the watch and handkerchief were found within.

Two borrowed half-crowns were dropped into a glass vase and made to strike on the glass the number of pips on any card drawn from the pack by the audience; the coins then danced in the glass and beat time to the music of the orchestra. A mechanical, plumaged peacock was introduced, spread its tail on command, ate and drank, and told the pips on various cards selected by the audience. It was claimed that 'it's caw is exceedingly natural, and altogether a very clever mechanical performance'.

The final part of Mr Henry's Conversazione comprised the musical glasses, dissolving scenes, a theatrical picture gallery and a 'laughable and grotesque ballet entitled Monkeyana!', which was produced by a combination of optical and mechanical effects and was claimed to be a truly whimsical spectacle in which several hundred figures performed intricate manoevres.[11] Into this programme format Henry would introduce his Laughing Gas demonstrations as occasion dictated.

The popularity of nitrous oxide as a form of entertainment was reflected by the appearance of a comic song written by W. H. Freeman and bearing the title 'Laughing Gas'. Although undated it seems reasonable to suppose that it first appeared in the period 1825–1830. The eleven verses of the song tell the tale of Jeremy Jones, a professional mourner whose activities have had such a grievous effect on his appearance and well-being that a wag persuades him to swallow a bladder of laughing gas.

> *Poor Jeremy Jones, long sought for relief*
> *For of Mourners, he really was the Chief;*
> *His nerves were shook he was thin as a leaf*
> *His flesh was worn from his bones with grief.*
> *Ha ha ho ho he he too ral ral loo ral loo.*
>
> *A wag, who heard of poor Jeremy's case,*
> *Told him, He'd very soon alter his face,*
> *Invited him home and while there, alas!*
> *He swallowed a bladder of Laughing Gas!*
> *Ha ha ho ho he he too ral ral loo ral loo.*

Jeremy's subsequent adventures are told in the remaining nine verses of doggerel and are depicted in part on the music cover. A variant of the cover additionally records that the song was 'Sung with unbounded Applause by Mr W. Smith of the Royal Surrey Theatre'.

(Dr Denis Smith, Reader in Anaesthesiology at the University of Leeds, who has carried out exten-

sive researches on the history of nitrous-oxide anaesthesia,[12] arranged, in connexion with a paper he presented at the World Congress of Anaesthesiologists held in London in 1968, for a short film to be made of a music hall artiste singing the song. The British Film Institute took care of the filming and Peter Honri was engaged to sing parts of the song. It was filmed at the City of Varieties, Leeds.[13])

An amusing illustration of the effects of nitrous-oxide inhalation was provided by George Cruikshank for the book *Chemistry No Mystery; or a Lecturer's Bequest*, published in 1839. The caption reads

Some jumped over the tables and chairs; some were bent upon making speeches; some were very much inclined to fight; and one young gentleman persisted in an attempt to kiss the ladies.

In the USA, too, the wonders of laughing gas were exhibited, principally by showmen who toured the country from the early eighteen-thirties lecturing and demonstrating. One of the most picturesque of these travelling lecturers was Samuel Colt (1814–62) of Hartford, Connecticut, perhaps better known as the designer of the first revolver that was mass-produced.[14,15] In 1832, as a youth of eighteen, he toured the east coast between Maryland and Canada with home-made apparatus carried on a handcart. With this equipment he would prepare nitrous oxide and demonstrate its effect on himself and those members of his audience who volunteered to sample the gas. Young Colt posed as 'Dr S. Coult of New York, London and Calcutta', and a typical advertisement for one of his demonstrations is that used at Portland on 13 October 1832:

NITROUS OXIDE GAS FOR LADIES AND GENTLEMEN Dr S. Coult respectfully informs the Ladies and Gentlemen of Portland and vicinity, that he will administer the NITROUS OXIDE or Exhilarating Gas, on Monday evening at the City Hall. The peculiar effects of this singular compound upon the animal system was first noticed by the English Chemist, Sir Humphry Davy. He observed that when inhaled into the lungs it produced the most astonishing effects upon the nervous system: some individuals were disposed to laugh, sing and dance; others, to recitation, and that the greater number had an irresistible propensity to muscular exertion such as wrestling, boxing, etc., with numerous fantastic feats. In short, the sensations

George Cruikshank's frontispiece to CHEMISTRY NO
MYSTERY *(1839) gave prominence to some of the
diverting physiological properties of laughing gas.*

produced by it are highly pleasurable, and are not
followed by debility . . . Dr C. has exhibited the
extraordinary powers of the gas in many cities of
the United States, to audiences composed of
Ladies and Gentlemen of the first respectability—
and many Ladies have inhaled the gas at select
Exhibitions. Those Ladies who may be anxious of
witnessing the Exhibition, in this city, may be
assured, that the City Hall embraces every
accommodation for their comfort, and that not a
shadow of impropriety attends the Exhibition, to
shock the most modest. He will attend, on
reasonable terms, to any applications for private
Exhibitions to select parties of Ladies and
Gentlemen . . .

It was the money raised by such exhibitions that
enabled him to take out the patents in the USA and
Canada on his revolver, and so bring him fame and
fortune with the Colt's Patent Firearms Manufactur-
ing Co. at Hartford. He was at one time in the
eighteen-thirties part-owner of the Penny Museum
in Cincinnati, where he also gave nitrous oxide
demonstrations, one of which involved six Red
Indians as a special feature. However, when he
administered the gas to the Indians they all subsided
into sound sleep, leaving the embarrassed showman
without the lively spectacle he had anticipated for his
audience. Fortunately a blacksmith, who then
volunteered his services, was made of sterner stuff
and promptly chased Colt all round the stage. The
intriguing feature of this occasion was the fact that
the astute inventor had failed to appreciate the
remarkable phenomenon of the complete anaesthesia
he had produced in his Indians. In the event, it was
almost ten years later, in 1844, that the use of
nitrous oxide for anaesthesia was properly appreciated.

Another of these early American showmen was
Gardner Quincey Colton (1814–98) who, at the age
of twenty-eight, entered the College of Physicians
and Surgeons, New York, and studied under the
famous Dr Willard Parker. After two years, shortage
of money necessitated his withdrawal, and for a
livelihood he assumed the mantle of a lecturer on
popular scientific subjects, including breathing
nitrous oxide, the properties of which he had learned
from Parker.[16] On 10 December 1844 Colton
appeared at Hartford on what proved to be an
historic occasion, for among the volunteers was a
Hartford dentist, Dr Horace Wells, who observed
that when another of the volunteers, a young man
named Samuel A. Cooley, cavorted about the stage
while under the influence of the gas and badly
bruised his legs by crashing into some furniture, he
apparently was unaware of the injury. This observation led next day to Colton visiting Wells' surgery,
where the crucial experiment on nitrous oxide
anaesthesia was carried out. A colleague, Dr Riggs,
extracted an aching tooth from Wells, who had
inhaled the gas: Wells felt no pain and, when he
recovered, he exclaimed: 'A new era in tooth
pulling!' and there must have followed countless
millions who echoed, thankfully, this sentiment.

These then were the US laughing-gas showmen
who followed in the wake of Mr Henry, of Adelphi
Theatre fame, in the use of a scientific discovery for

Robert-Houdin's LA SUSPENSION ÉTHÉRÉENE, *introduced in 1847, which purported to demonstrate how inhalation of ether could enable one to defy gravity. The
subject was the illusionist's young son.*

entertainment purposes, a discovery which was to
have far greater consequences for the benefit of
humanity than any then realized.

The use of nitrous oxide for anaesthesia was
eclipsed by the introduction of ether in the USA by
C. W. Long and W. T. G. Morton between 1842
and 1846, and by the use of chloroform by J. Y.
Simpson in Edinburgh in 1847. The impact of these
discoveries on three of the leading conjurers of the
day was immediate.

The French maestro Robert-Houdin in 1847
introduced 'La Suspension Ethéréene', in which he
claimed that he had discovered a new, truly marvellous property of ether.[17] When ether was at its

highest concentration, if inspired by a living being, it
would quickly render the body of the patient as light
as a balloon! To demonstrate his claim he had
cleverly adapted a suspension illusion which was
already a feature of his show. In the new version
three stools were placed on a wooden plank which
was raised by two trestles. His son stood on the
centre stool and extended his arms; beneath them
were placed canes which rested on the outer stools. A
flask purporting to contain ether was then held
beneath his son's nose until the boy apparently fell
asleep; the smell of ether pervaded the theatre but,
unbeknown to the audience, it was generated by
assistants backstage who poured ether onto hot
shovels! The boy's feet were seen to rise above the
stool which was then removed leaving him suspended
on the two canes. Then one of the canes and its
supporting stool were taken away and, to the great
surprise of the audience, he remained suspended from

SUSPENSION ÉTHÉRÉENNE.

the single cane. An even greater surprise was in store when Robert-Houdin lifted his son to a horizontal position with his little finger, defying gravity in the most remarkable manner. Finally he removed one of the trestles and lowered that end of the plank to the floor with the boy still suspended in mid-air.

Compars Herrmann, who was appearing at the Theatre Royal in the Haymarket, London, in 1848 also featured the suspension illusion as Le Suspension Ethéréenne (or Suspension by Ether), while Robert-Houdin's great rival Anderson, the Wizard of the North, gave allegiance to his native Scotland by calling his version Suspension Chloroforeene. His son, Master John Henry Anderson, apparently inhaled sufficient chloroform to send him to sleep. The Wizard then displayed what he chose to call the extraordinary effect of the drug which had 'baffled the whole of the medical profession of Russia, Prussia, Germany and every country which Professor Anderson has recently visited', Master Anderson sleeping in the air with a walking stick as his only support.

Science and medicine thus made distinctive contributions both to the composition of the programmes of nineteenth-century wizards and to their styles of presentation, and in the process gave a new lease of life to an ageing yet baffling illusion, and one, let it be noted, that is still amazing audiences today.

Compars Herrmann featured the SUSPENSION ÉTHÉRÉENE *during his appearances at the Theatre Royal in the Haymarket, London, in 1848.*

7
PHANTASMAGORIC PROFESSORS

Jugglers, indeed, seldom exhibit any thing that
can appear wonderful to those acquainted with
natural philosophy and mathematics; but these
even often find satisfaction in seeing truths
already known to them applied in a new manner.

J. Beckmann, *A History of Inventions
and Discoveries* (1797)

At the time of the French Revolution, there arrived
in Paris a thirty-year-old Belgian, Etienne-Gaspard
Robert, later called Robertson, who was a teacher of
physics in his native town of Liège. The son of a
wealthy merchant, he had studied natural science in
Paris under Brisson and Jacques Alexander Cesar
Charles (1746–1823), of Charles's Law fame, the
latter being the young physicist at the Academy who
pioneered the hydrogen balloon: Charles's interest in
the undertaking, however, was apparently confined
to one ascent!

Robertson had applied his knowledge of optics to
construct a mirror which would emulate the mirror
that Archimedes had used to burn the ships of the
besiegers at Syracuse.[1] Essentially it was a mechanical
device to concentrate the Sun's rays on one focal
point from a large number of reflectors. The military
potential of such an apparatus might seem to have
been patent (with especial application towards the
British fleets blockading the French ports) but,
despite recommendations and submission to the
National Institute in Paris, the invention was never
embraced by the authorities. It was then that
Robertson turned his attention to the more lucrative
venture of producing spectres, and embarked upon
his highly successful career as a showman and
entertainer.

A French journalist provided a contemporary
account of Robertson's show in 1798 at the Pavilion
de l'Echiquier.[2] Robertson having assured his
audience that he could bring the dead to life, the
candles were extinguished and he threw onto a

brazier containing lighted coals, blood, vitriol and
aqua fortis and, almost immediately, in the smoke
above the brazier were seen phantoms that were
recognized by spectators as Marat, Voltaire, Mira-
beau, Danton and Jean-Jacques Rousseau, as well
as a dear departed wife whose appearance caused
the widower to flee from the pavilion, apparently
apprehensive that what he saw was not a phantom!

With a stroke of genius Robertson moved his now
popular show to an abandoned chapel of the Capucin
Convent near the Place Vendôme and there, in this
sepulchral setting, surrounded by tombs, he achieved
unparalleled success. The formula of charging people
good money to be, in many cases, frightened out of
their wits is a sure and certain one, and Robertson
may be regarded as the legitimate forerunner of all
the Midnight Ghost Shows that gave vicarious thrills
to cinema audiences in the USA during the nineteen-
forties and -fifties. The chapel was draped in black
and the sound effects were convincing and calculated
to create the appropriate atmosphere—wind and
rain, thunder and lightning, and the tolling of a
church bell. The ghost of Robespierre rose from a
tomb and a flash of lightning struck the spectre,
which sank back into the ground. Finally, Robertson
would remark that he had shown the citizens of the
Republic every species of phantom but one, the most
terrible—the spectre of the fate which awaited them
all. Whereupon there appeared a skeleton armed with
a scythe which grew to a colossal size before fading
away.

The impact was tremendous, and it was no un-

FANTASMAGORIE, *the spectacular ghost show staged by E. G. Robertson in the Capucin Convent, Paris, in 1797.*

usual thing for some members of the audience to be carried away in a fainting state. Parisians flocked in their thousands to Robertson's exhibitions and he realized a nice fortune from his activities which enabled him to indulge in other pursuits, including ballooning. One of his imitators in both ballooning and ghost-raising, Andrew Oehler,[3] was less fortunate, losing his money with the former and being jailed in 1806 by the superstitious Mexicans for sorcery with the latter.

The Phantasmagoria entertainment reached Britain in 1802 when Monsieur Philipsthal exhibited a show similar to that of Robertson in Edinburgh and London. To the familiar accompaniment of thunder and flashes of lightning, ghosts, skeletons and identifiable individuals were paraded in eerie surroundings, and the head of Dr Benjamin Franklin was gradually transformed into a skull. Particularly impressive was the way in which these spectres advanced, increasing in size to tower above the spectators, and then receded; in other cases they approached and suddenly vanished, apparently being swallowed up by the ground. Sir David Brewster (1781–1868), Professor of Natural Philosophy in the University of Edinburgh, who devoted several pages of his *Letters on Natural Magic* (1832) to a description and explanation of Phantasmagoria, commented that the audience were not only surprised but

agitated, and many of them believed they could have touched the figures.[4]

All of these seemingly supernatural effects were achieved by the astute use of the magic lantern. This optical instrument was invented by a Jesuit priest, Father Athanasius Kircher, who described the principles in his book *Ars Magna Lucis et Umbrae* (1645). Kircher appears to have been a successor to the sorcerer-priests of the ancient temples, for he used his lantern to produce images of figures of varying sizes on a gauze screen, the glass slides being opaque apart from the figures so that no stray light was visible to spoil the illusion for his audiences. This crude forerunner of the modern slide projector thus provided the itinerant conjurer with a device for conjuring up ghosts at will, although it took the genius of Robertson to invest the performance with a showmanship that ensured it became a box-office attraction.

The Phantasmagoria entertainment depended upon a screen being interposed between the lantern and the spectators—i.e., what is now referred to as 'back projection'—and the lantern being concealed

Another example of the Phantasmagoria ghost show illustrated in Robertson's MEMOIRES, *which he published in 1831–3.*

so that they were unaware of its existence. By using a transparent gauze instead of an opaque white screen, the spectral effect of the images could be enhanced and, as with Robertson's show, by focusing the image on billowing smoke above a brazier, movement would be imparted to the figures. Mouth and eye movements were additionally secured by ingeniously superimposing glass sliders; quite surprising movements could be effected in this way. In those days, well over a century before the advent of the zoom lens, the only way in which the size of the image could be changed was by altering the distance between the lantern and the screen. To produce the effect of approaching and receding spectral visitations, Robertson and Philipsthal mounted their magic lanterns on rails so that they could be moved back and forth smoothly.

The art of painting lantern slides was an exacting one, for any imperfections were greatly magnified on the screen. It generated a breed of experts, one of whom, Henry Langdon Childe (1781–1874), invented the 'dissolving views', a metal shutter device which enabled one slide to be changed for another without the audience being made aware of the movement, although a brief interval of darkness intervened.[5]

Phantasmagoria shows subsequently became popular at the fairs and were still commonly encountered during the eighteen-thirties. However, the term phantasmagoria was gradually adopted for general magic-lantern exhibitions, as opposed to its specific use for ghost shows, and it is now frequently applied in relation to illusionary and perceptive experiences.

Some writers have been so carried away by their enthusiasm for phantasmagoria entertainments that they have attributed the fanciful lithographs of later nineteenth-century magicians, depicting ghosts,

THE GHOST OF BANQUO

PROFESSOR PEPPER

THE METEMPSYCHOSIS

Professor John Henry Pepper (1821–1900) and his Ghosts—Banquo and Metempsychosis—as seen after his arrival in Australia in 1879.

skeletons and demons, to these shows, where such was certainly not the case.[6] This style of poster can be traced to the influence of the Davenport Brothers from the USA, who took the literati and public of London by storm in 1864. Securely roped hand and foot and placed in a wardrobe-like cabinet with a guitar, violin and bells between them, they created music with the instruments and caused ghostly hands to appear. These effects were claimed to be a manifestation of spirit activity and not conjuring feats. Thereby Ira Erastus and William Henry Davenport profoundly influenced the course that magic was to take for the next twenty-five years, simply because many of the conjurers of the day were incensed by the imposture and introduced similar feats into their own programmes, often with exposures of methods, in order to demonstrate the materialistic nature of the deception. Consequently, it became fashionable for magicians to adorn their

The Spirit Cabinet. A splendid example of imaginative poster design which attributed the 'manifestations' of the séance to spirit aids and demons but had no connexion with the Phantasmagoria type of entertainment. This was a stock poster which magicians could purchase and then add their own name and details.

posters with their own assortment of 'spirit aids'— but these had no connexion whatever with phantasmagoria shows.

The ghost shows proved a source of inspiration for the topical cartoonists. At the height of Philipsthal's success James Gillray (1756–1815) took the theme to belabour the government over the uneasy peace of Amiens negotiated on 27 March 1802. On 5 January the following year he put out *A Phantasmagoria; —Scene—Conjuring-up an Armed Skeleton* depicting Addington, Hawkesbury and Fox as Macbeth's witches raising the spectre of Britannia from the cauldron.[7]

Although interest in phantasmagoria exhibitions waned, interest in ghosts did not and around 1847 Henri Robin, 'The French Wizard', presented 'The Living Phantasmagoria' in France, Italy and Germany. Robin's exhibition in the Boulevard du Temple in 1847 drew all Paris to see him conjure up spectres, pierce them with swords, fire bullets through them and make them appear and disappear at will.

This illusion was undoubtedly the precursor of the much more famous ghost illusion which captivated London in 1862—Pepper's Ghost. John Henry Pepper (1821–1900) was appointed as an assistant chemistry lecturer at the Granger School of Medicine when only nineteen years of age. In 1848 he moved to become analytical chemist and lecturer at the Royal Polytechnic Institution in Regent Street, and four

The principle of the Pepper's Ghost illusion or 'How to produce Spectres', as explained in Marion's WONDERS OF OPTICS *(1868) in relation to Robin's entertainment.*

years later became its Honorary Director.[8] Thomas W. Tobin was the Secretary of the Institution and together they were responsible for some fascinating presentations including the famous Sphinx illusion (page 153). Pepper gave courses of lectures at the Polytechnic and delighted both juvenile and adult audiences with his popular expositions of science, optical illusions and magic-lantern entertainments, which he delivered in a fluent, conversational manner. Pepper was accorded the privilege of Royal performances and, on one of these occasions, clearly conscious of his responsibilities, he reputedly prefaced an experiment with the observation that 'the oxygen and the hydrogen will now have the honour of combining before your Majesty'.[9] No doubt Queen Victoria was both amused *and* instructed.

The Board of the Institution conferred upon Pepper the title of Professor, and it is a reflection on the contemporary misappropriation of that designation that he felt constrained to inform his audiences he was neither a hairdresser nor a dancing master! But showman he certainly was, for he had quickly

perceived the potential of an apparatus for providing spectral optical illusions devised by a civil engineer, Henry Dircks,[10, 11] and communicated to the British Association at their meeting in Leeds in 1858.

Pepper carried out some modifications to Dircks' apparatus which enabled it to be used at the Polytechnic and, after a private showing, it was exhibited as a Christmas attraction on 24 December 1862 in illustration of Dickens' *Haunted Man*. This dramatic representation of a man conversing with the ghost of his other self on Christmas Eve proved highly successful and had an enormous vogue. Dircks and Pepper patented the apparatus on 5 February 1863.

The principle of this now well known illusion is best illustrated by the familiar experience of being in a brightly illuminated room (especially at night) and seeing one's transparent image 'through' the window, apparently as far beyond the pane as one is situated before it. If the intensity of illumination in the room decreases the image fades. The ghost illusion demands that the actor playing the part of the ghost be unseen by the audience although he can be illuminated as required. To meet these limitations the arrangement illustrated is set up with the sheet of plate glass angled to the audience and the illuminated actor in front of it but below the level of the stage and out of sight of the spectators. By cutting off the light the ghost disappears. Alternatively, it is possible to site the ghost-actor in the wings and have the plate glass vertical to the stage and angled accordingly. The actor on stage cannot, of course, see the ghost and therefore his movements have to be carefully rehearsed with the aid of markings on the stage, in order that he may engage in ethereal combat or otherwise encounter the ghost.

Unfortunately, the enormous success of the illusion at the Polytechnic and its inevitable association with the name of Pepper to the exclusion of that of Dircks led to a rift between the patentees, and the engineer who had devised the original apparatus published a full account of the history, construction and various adaptations of the illusion in 1863 to establish his rôle in 'Pepper's Ghost'.[12]

The popularity of the effect led to its appropriation by other theatrical entrepreneurs, but Pepper vigorously pursued these miscreants by litigation and, in Britain, it was firmly established that licences had to be taken out if the illusion was staged. In France, however, Robin's prior presentation of essentially the same effect prevented Pepper and Dircks from securing any royalties.

That indefatigable theatregoer the Reverend Benjamin Armstrong did not miss the new attraction and his diary for 21 July 1863 records:

London. To the R.A. Exhibition—In the evening took the boys to the Polytechnic to see 'Pepper's Ghost' a most extraordinary optical illusion of a misty transparent nature, dying out by degrees, dissolving into thin air and yet moving and conversing.[16]

Pepper's Ghost represents an important landmark in the history of conjuring for it established the tremendous possibilities for the production of magical illusions that the use of glass—either plain or, as subsequently introduced, silvered—created. From that time onwards the mirror principle became an important weapon in the armoury of the magician.

In 1872 Pepper exhibited the ghost at the Egyptian Hall and subsequently toured the provinces with it and other illusions. He appeared in Hull during January 1878 when, on the last night of his engagement, he introduced the phantom of a beautiful dancing girl 'distinctly visible on the stage and ONLY TWELVE INCHES HIGH, after which the Ghost will come out of the coffin and dine with its late occupant'.[13] The ghost illusion itself ultimately foundered when familiarity with the principle spread and small boys were wont to throw paper balls on to the stage to see them bounce off the invisible sheet of glass.

Pepper went to Australia in 1879 at the invitation of a newly formed Lecture Association and at St George's Hall in Melbourne fascinated audiences with both his scientific expositions and the ghost. (During his programmes there the Hall was first illuminated by electric light.)

One of the Professor's most marvellous illusions, 'Metempsychosis', was incorporated into a dramatic sketch titled 'The Artist's Dream', which made a sensational impact on the Melbourne audiences.[14] The curtain went up to reveal an artist's studio with a large easel to one side, near the front of the stage. Up-stage on the same side was a wooden table bearing a lamp to illuminate the studio and, at the centre back, a small chamber raised about three feet above the stage was reached by a short flight of stairs. In this alcove was an armchair. The plot called for an artist's lay figure to be brought to the studio and assembled on stage. The artist falls asleep while reading the paper and suddenly, out of thin air, an imp appears and makes passes over the lay figure, which becomes imbued with life, advances to the easel and there draws a caricature of the artist before sitting down on a chair. The imp then makes passes over the artist who, somnambulistically, progresses to the armchair in the recess from whence he is carried forward by the imp and lay figure, only to discover he is now a dummy figure! They put the dummy back in the armchair and after further mystic passes it rises and walks back to the original chair. The lay figure now moves to the recess and the imp, standing in front of it, gradually dissolves from view, while the artist wakes up in a fright. His shout brings servants who pull the lay figure to pieces and the curtain descends, leaving an audience completely mystified as to how these changes were effected.

The Professor remained in Australia for ten years and became a public analyst at Brisbane before returning to Britain in 1890. His attempt to stage a revival of the ghost failed and so, instead, he withdrew into private life and wrote *The True History of Pepper's Ghost* (1890). He died on 29 March 1900.

Pepper's rôle as a pioneer of science education is widely acknowledged.[9] He wrote several successful books including *The Boy's Playbook of Science* (1860), *The Playbook of Metals* (1861) and *Cyclo-*

paedic Science (1869), which did much to stimulate youthful interest, and he was also a visiting lecturer to secondary schools. The emphasis in his books and lectures was always on entertainment and utility, combining amusement with instruction, in which respect they differed from conventional presentations which were more rigidly structured to the particular scientific discipline. Consequently, while his books fired the imagination and captured interest, they did not meet the requirements of mental training that featured prominently in the institutions of formal education. Nonetheless, Pepper's presentation of science to his Victorian audiences was not only highly commendable but also enjoyable.

Another scientist who became a showman was Hungary's greatest magician, Professor Joseph Vanek, who appeared before Queen Victoria and her family on 15 April 1854.[15] Unlike so many of his contemporary conjuring 'Professors' Vanek had a legitimate claim on the title for he was a former Professor of Physics at the Pester Seminary in Budapest. Born on 31 July 1818, in the Hungarian capital, he was the son of a military bandmaster. At university he studied chemistry, physics, mathematics and philosophy and became assistant to his Professor of Physics, A. Jedlik. He spent some time at the chemical works in Warmbrunn, Germany, before returning in 1843 as Professor to the Pester Seminary where his scientific achievements were recognized by the award of the Silver Médaille de l'Industrie.

Vanek had been interested in mechanical toys and conjuring from his boyhood and, during his student days, had combined demonstrations of scientific experiments with magic. The events which resulted in the conversion of the professional scientist into the professional magician were political. Vanek was a personal friend of Louis Kossuth, the Minister of Finance, who led the Hungarian War of Independence in 1848 and virtually took over the government himself. Vanek was appointed Superintendent of the State Printing Office of the Hungarian Treasury. Kossuth's triumph was short-lived and in 1849 he and his followers, including Vanek, had to flee to Turkey where they were interned for a period.

In Constantinople the penniless Vanek conceived the idea of becoming a professional magician, despite the loss of all his apparatus in the flight from Hungary. With the help of friends at home, who furnished essential funds, he overcame considerable difficulties to construct within a period of five months all the necessary electrical and magical equipment. It included a 'Grand Optical Cyclorama' which had three lenses for producing dissolving views. He took his show on the road in Turkey until he had overcome the inevitable teething difficulties that beset any such venture. Then, through the good offices of an Hungarian official, he sought and secured an entree to Sultan Abdul Mecid. Vanek's performance so delighted the Sultan that he received not only the customary diamond-studded gold watch but also 25,000 piastres and a diploma. Indeed he became such a firm favourite of the Turkish court that he was appointed Court Magician.

He then travelled in the southern states of Europe, thence to Greece and France with performances for the Greek king and Louis Napoleon III, before arriving in England in 1854. The following year he was able to return, at long last, to his native Hungary, an amnesty having been declared for the conspirators of 1848. There his triumphal magic shows were greatly admired and there he spent the next three years. He was, however, simultaneously working on the improvement of a magical classic which was to become synonymous with his name.

Vanek's masterpiece was his version of the famous decapitation illusion, originally described by Reginald Scot in 1584. This sensational presentation stunned by its awful realism, and many spectators fainted with horror. It had taken Vanek two years to perfect. His son, Joseph Vanek junior, was for many years his daily victim. Without any covering the boy's head was apparently severed with a scimitar and placed, dripping with blood, upon a tray; it was carried thus into the audience for inspection. Anyone who so desired could touch the warm skin and feel the hair, including members of medical committees who were equally baffled. The artificial head used was a perfect copy and the secret of its daily preparation, which convinced the spectators that it was real flesh and blood, was carried by Vanek to his grave.

Vanek returned to Constantinople in October 1859 to show the Sultan his latest marvel; that worthy was so delighted that he decided that his wives, too, would enjoy the gory spectacle. Accordingly, there followed the remarkable distinction of a show before the Imperial Harem, the inevitable and

Josef Vanek (1818–89), a Professor of Physics at the University of Budapest, whose interest in magnetic and electrical experiments led him to desert academia for the career of a highly successful magician.

acceptable 25,000 piastres, and a letter of recommendation to the Viceroy of Egypt together with travelling expenses and the use of a private yacht. There followed tours of Asia Minor, the Balkans, Greece, France and Spain, with Vanek the whole time planning to fulfil his great ambition, a tour of the Far East. It was 1867 before this desire could be satisfied but thereafter Vanek became one of the most widely travelled magicians of the nineteenth century, visiting even countries where transport difficulties were legendary—Hong Kong, India, the Dutch East Indies, islands of the Pacific, China, Japan, Indo-China, Burma and Siam; almost five years elapsed before he returned to Hungary.

The wanderlust continued unabated, however, and on 13 October 1872 he opened at the German Stadt Theatre, New York, at the start of a tour that embraced the North American States and ended on 21 November 1873 at San Francisco. From there he crossed the Pacific to Japan and commenced another pilgrimage in the Far East and India, finally closing his world tour in Madras on 21 March 1878 and sailing for home.

The time had come for the travel-weary magician to lay down his wand, but first he gave his farewell performance at an exclusive club in Budapest on 12 October 1878.

In retirement Vanek was far from idle. He built an elegant Coffee House on one of the capital's finest thoroughfares, continued to exhibit his famous Dissolving Views, and founded a business for importing Chinese and Japanese commodities which he ran successfully until his death on 11 December 1889.

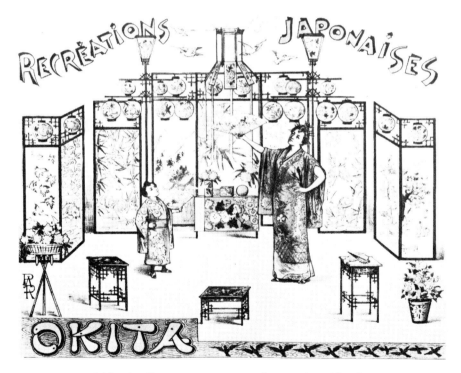

Okita (Julia Ferret, 1852-1916) was the wife of an expatriate English conjurer (H. S. G. Williams, 1843-1931) who ran a famous magic dealer's business in Paris under the name of Charles De Vere. She presented a pleasing Japanese act which was first seen in Brussels in 1877. Okita was the mother of Ionia, whose illusion act enchanted audiences in the second decade of this century.

8
THE JEWISH CONNEXION

This is the head of JONAS, or the card-playing
conjuring Jew. He could make matadores with
a snap of his fingers, command four aces with
a whistle, and get odd tricks.

G. A. Stevens, *A Lecture on Heads* (1785)

Jacob Philadelphia is the earliest known conjurer to
have been born in North America and yet is one who,
paradoxically, never performed on that continent. He
is equally important in the chronicles of North
American Judaism since his birthdate is the earliest
record of a child born to a resident Jewish family in
Pennsylvania [1]—even allowing for uncertainties in
the exact date, which has been variously quoted as
1720, 1721 and 1735.[2, 3] His real name was Jacob
Meyer and he was born at Philadelphia, subsequently
taking the name of his native city when he sailed for
England. He occasionally used also the name Meyer
Philadelphia on his advertising matter.

Philadelphia had a fair education and displayed a
penchant for mathematics, physics and 'the speculations of the Cabbala'. He went into seclusion for
several years to study higher mathematics, the
mechanic arts and metaphysics, and it is believed that
his mentor was Dr Christopher Witt, a Rosicrucian
mystic and survivor of a community of German
Pietists which was formed in the Province of Penn in
1694. By all accounts Witt was an expert mechanician, horologist, botanist and astronomer, and well
versed in occult sciences and Cabbalistic lore. He also
practised astrology. Successful students were granted
what seem to be the earliest known US medical
diplomas, testifying that the individual concerned

Hath Lived with me a Considerable time, as a
Disciple, to learn the Arts and Mysteries of
Chymistry, Physick & the Astral Sciences, whereby
to make a more perfect Discovery of the Hidden
causes of more occult and uncommon Diseases, not

so easily discovered by the Vulgar Practice . . .

There is little wonder, then, that Jacob Meyer
subsequently made pretensions to the occult in his
performances! When he had secured his diploma he
set sail for England—around the mid-seventeen-
fifties—armed with a letter of introduction to
William Augustus, Duke of Cumberland, furnished
by Dr Witt, who was one of the Duke's corres-
pondents. William Augustus was the famous
military commander in the Netherlands and 'The
Butcher' of the Rising of '45; under his patronage
Jacob spent some time on the ducal estates carrying
out mechanical experiments and further studies in the
mathematical sciences. After the death of his patron
in 1765, the American embarked upon a series of
public lectures on the mechanic arts in various towns
throughout England, including also conjuring
exhibitions. These proved extremely popular, and
Philadelphia then proceeded to Portugal and other
European countries, visiting seats of learning and
leading cities where he repeated his lectures and
performances with equal success. However, it is to
Germany that we must turn for the best documentary
evidence of Philadelphia's activities.[4, 5]

It is recorded that in Germany Philadelphia's five
main tricks were based on mathematics and physics,
which prompted the learned mathematician Johan
Gottlieb Schmidt in Schulpforte, Saxony, to endeavour to explain all of his repertoire in this way,
although Philadelphia would concede to such an
explanation for only three.[6] It was his custom to sign
himself in his letters as a 'mathematical artist'.

Jacob Philadelphia

Jacob Philadelphia was born in America but became famous as a conjurer in Europe during the second half of the eighteenth century.

However, he performed sleight-of-hand feats in addition to apparatus effects, the latter including a figure of Bacchus holding a barrel of water, which changed to wine when the tap was turned, and a magic inkstand which yielded inks of various colours as desired by the user. He also raised ghosts by means of a magic lantern projected on to smoke, the 'phantasmagoria' subsequently perfected by Robertson, which called forth the comment that Philadelphia often conjured up the souls of people not present and, as it were, called forth souls from their nerve tissue.'[4]

He was at Lauchstadt near Halle in the summer of 1775, and a contemporary chronicle[7] relates:

The greatest conjurer Philadelphia who has astounded all three continents with his magic feats, recently appeared with great success in Lauchstadt, in the presence of the Elector, his wife and his mother. The naval hero Orlow, the Russian cavalryman, was also present, and Philadelphia was royally rewarded.

A footnote was added:

Comus and Philadelphia have taken things so far in the mathematical, the mysterious, the mesmeric and in all conjuring feats that one hundred years ago, and even today in * * * *, they would have been burnt as the most despicable wizards. I have seen both of them, and most of what I saw is still incomprehensible to me.

Philadelphia's reputation as a wizard was undoubtedly enhanced by such stories as his departure by carriage from Berlin simultaneously through each of the four gates of the city: whether this was purely legend or whether the astute showman employed doubles is unrecorded. The impact that he made on his audiences is testified also by Ludwig Boclo[8] in a letter written on 25 September 1813:

I could tell you of a second Appolonius of Tiana, or, if you prefer, Philadelphia, the man who cut off heads and presented them on a plate before an astounded public and then healed them again just as rapidly. I could tell you how the miraculous man, before my very eyes, healed the head of a dove which I had cut off with my own hand so that the warm blood ran through my fingers. I held its trembling body so tightly there was no possibility of exchanging it for another, living one; yet afterwards the creature looked around as brightly as before.

Here then were the decapitation illusions recorded in the Westcar papyrus and in Scot's *The Discoverie of Witchcraft*, Boclo appended a note:

The beheading of the two boys was an illusion, as I convinced myself the next evening, but the resuscitation of the dove, whose body I held in my hand whilst the head was passed round the assembled company, remains to this day an unsolvable mystery.

Proclaiming that he would show 'fifty new productions of his skill' at Luneberg, Philadelphia reminded his potential audiences that

he is not to be placed in the class of charlatans and imitators, or to be compared with them as he dares, without boasting, to say that his skill has been applauded by the Royal Imperial as well as by the Prussian and Swedish Courts with gracious acceptance. He therefore flatters himself that he will be appreciated and applauded here at Luneberg.

One of the fascinating imponderables of conjuring history is whether we should know so much of Jacob Philadelphia if, in 1777, his path had not crossed that of the famous physicist and satirist Professor Georg Christoph Lichtenberg in the university town of Göttingen. Bock's engraving of Philadelphia was executed in the following year. The poet Schiller admitted he knew of Philadelphia only through Lichtenberg's satirical proclamation. It came about this way:

Philadelphia was scheduled to appear in Göttingen early in January 1777. According to one source,[9] subsequently adopted by later writers, [2, 10] Lichtenberg had printed and distributed a satirical broadsheet which so ridiculed the conjurer's performance that he left the town without performing there. Evidence from Lichtenberg's own correspondence, however, clearly indicates that the conjurer did, in fact, appear in the town.[4] Thus, writing to his friend Johann Andreas Schernhagen on 9 January, Lichtenberg said:

Philadelphia is here and has performed these past three or four days before gatherings of some thirty people, at 1 thaler a head. I have excused myself twice when asked to go along to such gatherings but today he is performing at the Kaufhaus and I am here with a ticket already in my pocket. One must meet people on their own ground. Meanwhile he will take off a nice pile of money here.

In another letter, written (in English) on the same day, Lichtenberg also referred to his forthcoming visit to the show:

Philadelphia the supernaturel [sic] philosopher is here now and intends to perform at the Kaufhaus tonight, where I shall see him most certainly.

Lichtenberg did indeed see Philadelphia on 9 January in the main hall of the Kaufhaus, in the company of his friends Dieterich, the bookseller of Göttingen, and Professor A. G. Kastner, the mathematician, and yet the satirical advertisement that banished Philadelphia was dated 7 January. Perhaps Lichtenberg withheld distribution until he had seen the show for himself, so that the embarrassed Philadelphia's departure from Göttingen did not occur until 10 January. Be that as it may, so popular did the satire prove to be that at least three editions were produced within a couple of weeks and Lichtenberg was able to write:

The rumour that I am the author has now subsided and it is attributed to Kastner. It has revealed, however, that satire can act as a complement to the laws. Mr Philadelphia would certainly have made the town 500 thaler poorer without making its people a pfennig wiser . . .

Philadelphia has vanished and no-one knows exactly where he has gone. Some say to Gandersheim.

We now reproduce in its entirety Lichtenberg's advertisement for the conjurer, which undoubtedly owed its origin to the scientist's familiarity with Jonathan Swift's earlier effusion, 'The Wonder of all the Wonders that the World ever Wondered at':

NOTICE

The admirers of supernatural Physics are hereby informed that the far-famed magician, Philadelphus Philadelphia (the same that is mentioned by Cardanus in his book *De Natura Supernaturali*, where he is styled 'The envied of Heaven and Hell'), arrived here a few days ago by the mail, although it would have been just as easy for him to come through the air, seeing that he is the person who, in the year 1482, in the public market at Venice, threw a ball of cord into the clouds, and climbed upon it into the air till he got out of sight.

On the 9th of January of the present year, he will commence at the Merchant's Hall, publico-privately, to exhibit his one-thaler tricks, and continue weekly to improve them, till he comes to his five-hundred-Louis d'or tricks, amongst which last are some which, without boasting, excel the wonderful itself, nay are, as one may say, absolutely impossible.

He has had the honour of performing with the greatest possible approbation before all the potentates, high and low, of the four quarters of the globe; and even in the fifth, a few weeks ago, before Her Majesty Queen Obera at Otaheite.

He is to be seen every day, except Mondays and Thursdays, when he is employed in cleaning the heads of the honorable members of the Congress of his countrymen at Philadelphia; and at all hours, except from eleven to twelve in the forenoon, when he is engaged at Constantinople, and from twelve to one, when he is at dinner.

The following are some of his one-thaler tricks; and they are selected, not as being the best of them, but as they can be described in the fewest words:

1. Without leaving the room, he takes the weathercock off St James' Church and sets it on St John's, and vice versa. After a few minutes he puts them back again in their proper places. N.B.—All this without a magnet, by mere sleight of hand.

2. He takes two ladies and sets them on their heads on a table, with their legs up; he then gives them a blow and they immediately begin to spin like tops with incredible velocity, without breach either of their head-dress by the pressure, or of decorum by the falling of their petticoats, to the very great satisfaction of all present.

3. He takes three ounces of the best arsenic, boils it in a gallon of milk, and gives it to the ladies to drink. As soon as they begin to get sick, he gives them two or three spoonfuls of melted lead, and they go away in high spirits.

4. He takes a hatchet and knocks a gentleman on the head with it, so that he falls dead on the floor. When there, he gives a second blow, whereupon the gentleman immediately gets up as well as ever, and generally asks what music that was.

5. He draws three or four ladies' teeth, makes the company shake them well together in a bag, and then puts them into a little cannon, which he fires at the aforesaid ladies' heads, and they find their teeth white and sound in their places again.

6. A metaphysical trick, otherwise commonly called *Metaphysica*, whereby he shows that a thing can actually be and not be at the same time. It requires great preparation and cost, and is shown so low as one thaler, solely in honour of the University.

7. He takes all the watches, rings and other ornaments of the company, and even money if they wish, and gives every one a receipt for his property. He then puts them all in a trunk, and brings them off to Cassel. In a week after, each

person tears his receipt, and that moment finds whatever he gave in his hands again. He had made a great deal of money on this trick.

N.B. During this week he performs in the top room of the Merchants' Hall; but after that, up in the air over the pump in the market-place; for whoever does not pay, will not see.
Göttingen, 7 January 1777.

A curious feature of Lichtenberg's attack on Philadelphia is the knowledge that the eminent physicist was keenly interested in the theatre and popular entertainment, as his *Diary of a Tour of England 1774* reveals.[11] There we read of his visits to Jackson's Museum of Curiosities in Mr Pinchbeck's Repository, over his shop in Cockspur Street, to George Saville Carey's Lecture on Mimicry, to the Drury Lane Theatre to see Garrick and to Covent Garden Theatre. Perhaps the answer to this apparent contradiction lies in Philadelphia's pretension to the occult in a show that leaned heavily on the application of mathematical and physical principles: possibly this was too much for the scientist to accept.

Lichtenberg's interest in astronomy led, in 1775, to his meeting with Nevil Maskelyne, the Astronomer Royal and ancestor of the magical Maskelynes of the nineteenth and twentieth centuries. Maskelyne took him to a meeting of the Royal Society and to the Greenwich Observatory. Lichtenberg recorded in his diary an amusing exchange which related to Maskelyne's astronomical observations on Schiehallion in the Scottish Highlands:

I suppose, Sir, you went in order to find out some new stars. Did you find any. No Sir said Mr Maskelyne, I could hardly find the old ones.

In passing, it is of interest to conjurers that Lichtenberg's first substantial publication was an essay on probability, *The St Petersburg Problem*, which was published in Göttingen in 1770. It relates to a method of calculating the probable number of times a coin must be tossed before it falls heads rather than tails, and the chances of profit for person A to whom B will pay a ducat if heads falls at the first toss, two ducats if at the second and so on. The essay was intended to serve as a prospectus advertising Lichtenberg's lectures, a practice common for professors at that time but, mercifully, no longer expected!

The precipitate departure from Göttingen did not seriously affect Philadelphia's successes elsewhere. He was in Strasbourg in 1779 from whence he travelled to Basel and Switzerland.

Another intriguing episode in his life occurred in 1783 when he was living in Köthen and endeavoured to interest Frederick the Great in opening trade relations with the USA.[5] Presumably recognizing that a showman, albeit a 'mathematical artist', was unlikely to command the attention of a monarch, his approach was through an intermediary, C. H. Stilcke, the director of a bank in Magdeburg, who forwarded Philadelphia's lengthy memorandum to the minister Schulenberg. On 14 June 1783 Stilcke wrote:

Jacob Philadelphia, a Jew and famous artist who is at the moment in Köthen, submitted the enclosed memorandum to me a few days ago, asking me to submit it to your highness. As I do not know how far your highness is likely to use his plans and ideas will you please let me know whether I order Philadelphia to Berlin or Kahnert to discuss this matter in more detail with your highness.

There are several features of interest in the document, dated 27 May 1783, which throw some light on Philadelphia's background in the USA and also on his self-agrandisement, secretiveness and salesmanship, which make parts of the memorandum worthy of reproduction. The translation follows the rather archaic language used.

From my early youth I have been in America and brought up and educated there, and I have travelled by land and sea in this part of the world. All merchant ports and market places are known to me better than to anybody else, because I made business—legal and illegal—with the English, the natives and the Indians. I went as far as Quebec and 400 miles beyond this. I spent a long time in this part of the world and know very well not only the American language as it is spoken with the Indians but also English and African which is spoken with the negroes. All these languages are more familiar to me than German and there will hardly be anyone in Germany who can claim this.

There will not be shortage in goods sent to America and in goods coming from there, but whether the profits one can gain from making business with America is [*sic*] as high as it could be is the question.

Linen cloth is best sold in Lissabon or Cadice

with 10 to 12 % more profit than in Hamburg, Bremen or Lubeck. The same situation would be applicable to the American places where one must know the markets for special goods and can easily make more profit or lose money. As I know all the places and secrets I offer my services to the Koenigl Preuss Commission. I am prepared to name the ports and towns in which certain goods are most favourable sold and where one can buy at cheapest prices goods it is desired to bring back to Europe.

I also know of certain goods which will make 20 % profit, but I am not prepared to name this at the moment.

I offer to go with the ships three to four times and to arrange the sale and purchase of the goods to start the business. For this I want a pension for my life time. If this and expenses is granted to Berlin in my favour then I am prepared to release the secrets and facts. I am also prepared to inform you about the best time of passage for the ships, as I am experienced in sailing and I went to sea with the most famous English sea-captains Locks and Mechanicus, whose accident would have been avoided by me.

If your Majesty would do this business on his own account he would make a big profit and the profit from the tobacco alone would finance the expense. Within five to six years companions would receive their interests at 6 % and their full capital. It would be of great advantage to establish a company or representation but this is a matter which is far beyond my judgement.

The approach was, not surprisingly in the circumstances, unsuccessful and Schulenberg replied diplomatically to Stilcke on 11 July:

I thank you very much for the memorandum of the jew Jacob Philadelphia concerning American trade and commerce. There are various considerations to be made and we cannot use his ideas at the moment. Would you please inform Philadelphia accordingly.

There is no evidence that the King ever saw Philadelphia's memorandum, indeed it seems extremely unlikely that the minister would have forwarded to the monarch such a curious letter from a conjurer who was now claiming to be an expert trader, navigator and linguist! Perhaps the marvel is that Schulenberg deigned to reply at all.

Apparently when he was not travelling Phila-

Joseph Jacobs (1813–70), English conjurer and ventriloquist, who made a reputation for himself also in America, Australia and New Zealand.

delphia usually stayed at Köthen, where the mother of his two children lived. The son died at an early age but the daughter was still alive in 1846, living in Halle, the aging widow of drummer Creutzmann of the Renouard Regiment. There is no firm record of Philadalphia's death but he sojourned at Schulpforte in 1794–5, was back in Köthen in 1797 and so may well have lived on into the early years of the next century.

Over the English Channel, in Britain, one of the leading Jewish conjurers and ventriloquists during the nineteenth century was Mr Jacobs, who was born at Canterbury in 1813 and died at Sydenham in 1870.[12, 13] Into his fifty-eight years he packed an interesting career of sustained performing and global travelling.

His conjuring career began around 1834 with visits to Dover, Brighton, Bath and other provincial towns with a London début in the spring of 1835 at the assembly room of the Horn's Tavern in Kennington.[14] Thereafter he toured throughout Britain with considerable success.

Initially Jacobs was probably a better ventriloquist than conjurer,[14] but it is evident that in the eighteen-forties, probably influenced by the gorgeous apparatus of Anderson and the elegance of Robert-Houdin, his approach, style and equipment blossomed. Playbills now announced a Temple of Necromancy or an Enchanted Palace, and his descriptive matter bid fair to outdo Anderson himself—no mean feat, as we have occasion to notice (page 111). The 'Wizard of all Wizards' and 'Greatest Mysteriarchist of the Nineteenth Century' are two 1842 examples of his grandiose self-description seen in the illustration of his playbill for the New Strand Theatre.

Already in 1835 Jacobs was performing the Chinese Linking Rings, some two years before Phillipe is supposed to have secured the secret from certain Chinese jugglers.[15] This feat of linking and unlinking a number of examined metal rings into chains and various figures has become one of the classics of magic. A direct comparison of Jacobs' programmes in 1845, prior to the advent of Robert-Houdin in London, with those in 1849-50 afterwards, reveals the extent of the Frenchman's influence on his show and, although there is some justification for the belief that Jacobs lacked originality, there is no doubt he was a good showman who presented his effects in a pleasing and humorous fashion. (And on this topic it is not without significance that, over a hundred years after Jacobs' death, modern audiences may witness the latest magical novelties yet still come back to talk about 'that trick with the metal rings'!) Despite this stricture on his originality, Jacobs was one of the first conjurers to display the feat of changing a bowl of ink into one containing water with goldfish swimming in it; this was around 1845, the year of his first visit to Hull, when one of the local papers commented:

The tricks which were produced—some of them of an entirely new description—were performed in a most masterly manner, and elicited universal approbation. Mr Jacobs also sang an extemporaneous song, the various subjects of which it was composed being given by the audience, and which being of a ludicrous nature, caused the song to be highly amusing. The ventriloquism was also of no mean description. Taking them altogether, the performances were of a first rate order and gave great satisfaction, which was proved by the repeated bursts of applause from an audience both numerous and highly respectable.[16]

Jacobs embarked on a tour of the USA in 1854, followed by visits to Australia and New Zealand in the following two years. He then re-embarked for the USA but returned to Australia in 1857, finally sailing for England in November 1858. However, the conjurer made a third tour of Australia in 1865-6 and it is clear that he created a great impression and gained many friends in the Antipodes during his three visits there.[17]

At Ballarat in 1855 he had a narrow escape from death when fire consumed the United States Hotel where he was staying. Most of his equipment was destroyed in this disaster, which prevented him from appearing again until 25 February 1856 when he was able to re-open in Melbourne with improvised equipment. Fate dealt a further blow during his second visit in 1858, when his apparatus was ruined by water on board ship while returning from Tasmania.

In 1861 Jacobs was, in addition to all his previous grandiose titles, a

Professor of Experimental and Scientific Philosophy whose fame is established throughout Europe, Australia, California, New Zealand, United States of America, Canada, New Brunswick, Nova Scotia &c., who has weathered Cape Horn and the Cape of Good Hope, Crossed the Line several times and who, on board the GREAT EASTERN steam ship on her return Voyage for the Benefit of the Dreadnought Hospital and the Amusement of the Passengers, presented one of his Unrivalled Entertainments in the middle of the NORTH ATLANTIC OCEAN, LATITUDE 50 deg 30 min NORTH, LONGITUDE 38 deg 30 min WEST, an unprecedented and wonderful undertaking in those regions, has the honour to announce his RETURN TO ENGLAND for the purpose of making a FINAL VISIT to all the Cities in which his early attempts were made, and by way of a Farewell to his old and kind Patrons, previously to retiring from his profession.

In the event, and like so many other conjurers before and since who have advertised their 'Final, Farewell Tours', Jacobs did not retire in 1861 and, indeed, undertook a third tour of the Antipodes four years later.

A minor mystery that surrounded Jacobs concerned his first name, for he was billed as Mr Jacobs

The Great Lafayette (Sigmund Neuberger, 1871–1911) and his favourite dog Beauty, on which he lavished extravagant attention.

or occasionally Mr M. Jacobs, but there was never an indication of what the 'M.' represented. However, the puzzle is solved by the following obituary notices in the *Jewish Record*:

JACOBS—On October 11 at the residence of his beloved friend, Mr A. M. Cohen, Mount Villas, Sydenham Hill, Professor Jacobs, aged 58, deeply lamented by his sorrowing friends and family. May his soul rest in peace. Australian and New Zealand papers please copy.[18]

MRS JOSEPH JACOBS and family with Messrs J. s. and H. JACOBS return thanks for visits and cards of condolence during their week of mourning for their late lamented husband, father and brother. 12 Old Bond Street, W.[19]

Thus Jacobs' first name was Joseph, and the initial 'M.' must have been for theatrical purposes only.[20]

A Jacobs playbill for the New Strand Theatre, London, in 1842. The peripheral cuts show Jacobs performing a variety of effects from his extensive repertoire.

Over twenty years after the Wizard's death, a correspondent signing himself 'I.D.' sent an interesting letter to the *Jewish Chronicle* saying of Jacobs:

He was a celebrated conjurer of my early days whom I met when I was a boy at the table of one of my schoolmasters, the Rev. R. Cohen of Sussex House, Dover . . . The Wizard Jacobs performed his amazing feats of legerdemain with the aid of a clumsy attendant in buttons, a sort of Fat Boy out of Pickwick very much enlarged whose unwieldy form seemed always about to burst his ridiculously short jacket and tight breeches . . . he was called Sprightly and the title itself provoked a roar . . . Great was my boyish astonishment to learn when I met the Wizard at dinner that Sprightly was his brother.[21]

In Melbourne, Sprightly was referred to as 'a very amusing but somewhat eccentric attendant', and it is clear that the extinguisher trick with the initial envanishment of Sprightly and an encore in which he vanished, to be replaced by a live goose, was one of the hits of Jacobs' début in that city.[22]

From the Antipodes, let us return to Europe for a vignette of the third of our trio of Jewish conjurers. Although not of English birth, fame, fortune and a spectacular demise all awaited him in the British Isles.

The magical profession has always abounded with eccentrics, as perhaps the reader might suspect. Daily commerce with mystery frequently imbues the practitioner with a variety of idiosyncrasies. One whose eccentricities became legendary even among magicians themselves was Sigmund Neuberger (1871–1911), born in Munich, the son of a Jewish silk merchant and jeweller who took the youth with him to the USA in 1890. There Sigmund entered vaudeville, presenting feats of marksmanship with bows and arrows, and appearing as a quick-change artiste. Eventually some conjuring was incorporated too. He had a talent for impersonation and his characterization of a famous oriental conjurer, Ching Ling Foo, brought him immediate recognition and

The Great Lafayette as 'Dr Kremser—Vivisectionist' in a literally eye-catching, hypnotic lithograph to advertise the Dr Kremser sketches that were a feature of his shows from 1909. Kremser was supposed to be a 'hypnotic surgeon and vivisectionist'. Very few of these posters have survived.

bookings on the renowned Keith circuit. With the flair for showmanship that was always to mantle his activities, Neuberger changed his name to Lafayette by deed poll and acquired US citizenship.

The recently opened London Hippodrome was the scene of his first triumph in Britain, in August 1900. During a three-week season he was driven in a motor car across the circus arena to the stage where, among many startling effects, in his oriental guise he produced from a cloth a bowl of water and a heterogeneous collection of livestock—pigeons, a dog and a turkey, culminating with a piccaninny; this child then vanished from a cardboard tube, to reappear with a twin brother. Lafayette's artistry in quick costume changes was evidenced by his rapid switch from oriental robes to military uniform as he impersonated John Philip Sousa, leading the Hippodrome orchestra in a rousing Sousa march.[23] This formula of magic, music and transformation was the key to his success. Sidney Clarke, writing of Lafayette in 1928, said:

He carried the methods of transfigurations and substitutions to a height of daring and effectiveness that no earlier performer had reached, and no successor has excelled. Travesty, spectacle and large illusionary effects were his specialities, and he took his audiences from surprise to surprise so rapidly that they had no time to think whether what they saw was legerdemain or mere bluff. A crowded stage, many assistants, and magnificent setting and dressing, all impressed the eye, and concealed the fact that as a conjurer Lafayette was by no means in the front rank. As a showman he was easily first. He was blessed with a personality, a love of colour and a sense of mystery, that put him far ahead, as an entertainer, of other more capable conjurers who present a somewhat similar entertainment.[24]

Some three years later Lafayette returned to London, bought a house in Tavistock Square and furnished it extravagantly with antiques and paintings that his extremely high salary (by the standards of the time) of £400 per week commanded.[25] It became his permanent home and was constantly enhanced as his salary increased still further. In 1910, the last full year of his life, he was the highest-paid performer in the profession, receiving £1,000 per week, and was believed to have earned £40,000 during the year.[26] By that time he employed forty-five people, including six full-time carpenters and two electricians.

The house at 55 Tavistock Square allowed full rein for Lafayette's eccentricities. He was a bachelor whose love and tenderness were lavished on his favourite dog, Beauty, given to him by Houdini in 1899. Although Beauty's ancestry was uncertain, Lafayette invented a pedigree[27] and adorned her with a silvered and bejewelled leather collar. The massive front door at Tavistock Square was embellished with the legend 'The Home of the Great Lafayette and Beauty' and, within, a plaque proclaimed 'The more I see of men the more I love my dog'. There was also a notice that informed guests: 'You may drink my wine; you may eat my food; you may command my servants; but you *must* respect my dog.' And woe betide visitors to whom Beauty took a dislike—the animal's welcome entirely conditioned her master's hospitality.

Beauty had her own room and bathroom and, on tour, it was always stipulated in Lafayette's hotel reservations that she must share his suite. Her collar carried silver labels engraved with the names of the exclusive hotels where she had stayed.[27] The radiator of Lafayette's opulent motor car sported her effigy, and his Credit Lyonnais cheques bore her picture, sitting up and begging, beside two bags of gold, appositely captioned: 'My two best friends.'

Lafayette was a small, dapper, clean-shaven almost Napoleonic man who drilled his company with military precision and expected them to salute him when they met in the street. He was solicitous for their welfare but demanded loyalty and respect from them and was never slow to dismiss anyone who failed to match his standards. In a profession noted for its susceptibility to John Barleycorn it is praise-worthy that Lafayette insisted that all his staff be teetotal.

The Edwardian audiences loved The Great Lafayette, and the details of his lavish show were forever etched in their memories.[28] Seated in comfort in one of Sir Edward Moss' theatres, they watched as the curtain went up on 'A Carnival of Conjuring'. In rapid succession Lafayette caught live pigeons from thin air, produced Beauty from a paper-covered gilt frame resting on an easel and fabricated a picture from seemingly haphazardly splashed paint on six separate wooden panels. The curtains then parted on a sculptor's studio with Lafayette working on a

Dr Kremser—Vivisectionist. Pages from the souvenir brochure that Lafayette issued at every theatre he played.

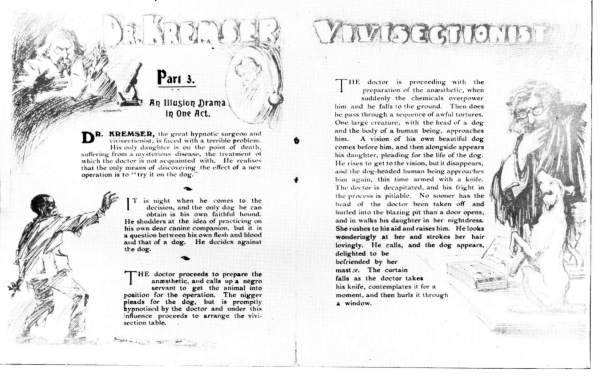

model of Leda and the Swan. Lumps of clay were fashioned into a female form which miraculously came to life, surrounded by fountains illuminated with coloured lights.

Part Three of the show was a one-act drama titled 'Dr Kremser—Vivisectionist', again featuring Beauty. Dr Kremser, the great hypnotic surgeon, is in a terrible dilemma. His only daughter is at death's door suffering from a mysterious disease which the doctor cannot diagnose or treat. He realizes that the only avenue open to him to discover the effect of a novel operation is to 'try it on the dog'. Unfortunately, it is night when he reaches this momentous decision and the only dog available is his own faithful hound. Kremser shudders at the thought but, as it is a matter of his own flesh and blood against that of a dog, he decides against the hound.

The doctor prepares the anaesthetic and calls his negro servant to fetch the animal but, when that worthy remonstrates, Kremser promptly hypnotizes him and, under this influence, the preparations for the operation are completed. However, the doctor is careless in his handling and succumbs to the anaesthetic himself. His frightening, tortured, unconscious ramblings are now enacted on stage. He is approached by a large creature with the head of a dog and a human body, experiences a vision of his own beautiful dog, and then beside it his own daughter pleading for the dog's life. The vision disappears as he tries to reach it and he is now attacked by the dog-headed human armed with a knife. Kremser is decapitated but no sooner is his head hurled into a blazing pit than the door opens and his daughter walks in clad in her nightdress. She rushes to his aid, he simultaneously regains his head and consciousness, and as he bemusedly strokes her hair the dog comes in, delighted to be befriended once more. The curtain descends on Dr Kremser hurling his scalpel out of the window.

Another memorable and less macabre illusion was Lafayette's portrayal of an artist, wearing a long cape and beret, dressing and painting the face of a black assistant who stood in the gilt-framed, open centre section of a three-panel screen. The assistant was decorated with wigs, beards and other properties to make him resemble famous personalities of the day—Lloyd George, the French President, King Edward VII and the Tsar of Russia. As the Tsar stepped out of the frame to approach the footlights, Lafayette walked off stage into the wings. At the second Lafayette disappeared from view, the Tsar removed his beard and wig to reveal none other than Lafayette himself!

A routine that fascinated children was the production of a 'mechanical' teddy-bear. He went through the motions of winding the bear up and it then proceeded to execute a series of slow and laboured somersaults as a prelude to increasingly varied and incredible evolutions. Then it started to read a book and, when Lafayette endeavoured to take the book away, the bear shook its head, stamped the floor and clung desperately to the volume just as would any recalcitrant child.

The Travesty Band enlivened the proceedings, musicians conducted by Lafayette in a series of rapidly changing costumes parodying Sousa, Levi, Strauss, Offenbach and others. The first half closed in spectacular manner with 'Overture 1912'—the famous 1812 Overture used as a descriptive prediction of an invasion in 1912 by the combined nations, and their final defeat. To the full theatre orchestra supplemented by his own musicians and the sounds of offstage guns, the splendidly uniformed Lafayette rode out on a white charger and troops paraded across the stage. It was a great climax of sight and sound.

Lafayette's masterpiece was the pantomimic spectacle of 'The Lion's Bride', occupying some twenty-five minutes of the show. The Arabian Nights plot involved a beautiful Christian princess, the sole survivor of a shipwreck, who falls into the hands of the Pasha and is offered the choice of becoming his bride or being thrown to the sacred Royal Lion. The former fate being, in the imagery of the day, 'worse than death', she chooses the latter and is trussed up ready for feeding time. Meanwhile, the news of her capture has reached her sweetheart, an officer in the Persian Army (naturally portrayed by Lafayette), who mounts his black Arab steed and gallops to her rescue, gaining entrance to the harem by a subterfuge. There he engages in mortal combat with a gigantic negro guard and, victorious, quickly disguises himself as his sweetheart, his features hidden by a yashmak. Other guards enter and bundle him into the lion's cage. The lion roars and leaps out of the cage and, rearing on its hind paws, whips off a false head to reveal Lafayette himself—yet another incredible transformation.

On 1 May 1911 Lafayette commenced a two-week engagement at the Empire Palace Theatre in Nicolson Street, Edinburgh, at the start of a Scottish tour. But tragedy struck on 4 May when Beauty died

The fire-gutted stage of the Edinburgh Empire Palace Theatre on 10 May 1911 following the disastrous fire on the previous evening when Lafayette and eight members of his company lost their lives.

of apoplexy. The illusionist was grief-stricken, and could scarcely get through his shows that evening. Elaborate arrangements were made with Messrs W. T. Dunbar & Sons, well known Edinburgh funeral directors, for Beauty to be embalmed and for the purchase of a plot of ground for the burial.[29] Here some difficulties were encountered but eventually, by agreeing to be buried there himself, he secured a plot for £60 at Piershill Cemetery on Portobello Road. The embalmed animal was placed in a zinc-lined oak casket with silk fittings and a glass lid, and the funeral was arranged for Wednesday 10 May. Each day and each evening after his performances, Lafayette visited the mortuary to see Beauty and quite a sensation was caused in Auld Reekie.

However, this was as nothing compared with the even greater tragedy that was yet to come.

The following Tuesday, 9 May, shortly after 11pm during the second house, Lafayette had just effected his transformation at the conclusion of 'The Lion's Bride' when some of the scenery in the set caught fire. The drop curtain, upstage of the fire curtain, was first lowered, followed by the fire curtain. The latter jammed thirty inches above the stage, being fouled by the drop curtain which had been blown forward by the draught caused by the opening of a door at the rear of the stage. Although the stage was not sealed off from the auditorium, happily the fire did not penetrate across the footlights and the packed audience of three thousand was able to make its way to safety.[30]

Backstage was a different matter, and the fire took a fierce and rapid hold. The Edinburgh Fire Brigade arrived and blackened out the fire by 12.15am, although it continued to smoulder throughout the night. Then came the sad reckoning; nine people, including Lafayette, had lost their lives and a tenth was subsequently to do so. The lion and horse that featured in 'The Lion's Bride' also perished. Among the dead were the seventeen-year-old midget Alice Dale and her understudy, fourteen-year-old Joseph Coats, who animated the mechanical teddy bear.

As in life, so in death. Newspapers on Friday 12 May carried the drama of 'Lafayette's Last Illusion'. Lafayette's body, found on the stage near that of the horse, had been taken through to Glasgow for cremation as there was no crematorium in Edinburgh at that time. The same evening another body had been found in the basement of the theatre beneath the debris, unquestionably that of Lafayette because of two identifiable rings he was wearing. The body already cremated turned out to be that of Richards, a member of his company who bore a marked resemblance to Lafayette and was used as a 'double' in some of the illusions. Lafayette's body was then taken to Glasgow for cremation on the Saturday.

The funeral on Sunday 14 May in Edinburgh was perhaps the most incredible spectacle ever witnessed in the Scottish capital. The day was chosen to permit all his theatrical friends to attend, and the populace turned out in their thousands to line the three-mile route the cortege travelled. The casket containing Lafayette's ashes was placed in a funeral car drawn by four horses; seven open carriages conveyed wreaths and were followed by the illusionist's own motor car conveying Mabel, his Dalmation dog and, on seats outside, his two negro assistants, and then the mourners, some sixty coaches in all.

The casket containing Lafayette's ashes was placed between the paws of the embalmed Beauty and, together, they were interred beneath a wych-elm. Two memorial stones were raised to them, and the curious may today wander into Piershill Cemetery and see these silent witnesses to an event which that

well known Scottish author Alasdair Alpin MacGregor has recalled as one of the most memorable in his youth in Auld Reekie.[29]

The evidence of the inquest suggested that the cause of the fire was probably a short circuit in the cable that fed a lantern on the stage set of 'The Lion's Bride'. On the instructions of Lafayette, in order to preserve his secrets, three of the five exits from the stage were locked and a fourth was barricaded by scenery. For the same reason, apart from Lafayette's company, only the stage manager and theatre fireman were allowed on stage. Immediately after the fire broke out, the barricade of scenery was removed and the fireman opened the door at the rear of the stage, while artistes burst open the door on the opposite prompt side.[31] It was generally believed that Lafayette might have escaped had he not turned back in an effort to save his horse. Three of the company, including Lafayette, were suffocated and partly consumed by the fire while the rest of the victims were suffocated in dressing rooms or on stairs.

The full story did not end until 1913, for Lafayette's brother, Alfred Neuberger, refused to pay the heavy funeral expenses of just over £411 and Messrs Dunbar & Sons had to resort to a High Court action to secure the debt.[32]

These, then, are but three representatives of a legion of Jewish conjurers who have made substantial contributions to the art of conjuring and illusion.[12] The names of others would grace any magical Hall of Fame—for example, Philip Jonas, Philip Breslaw, Carl Hertz, Lewis Davenport, Horace Goldin, Will Goldston, Arnold De Biere, Max Malini and Cecil Lyle—while the greatest of them all, Harry Houdini, deserves and receives consideration on his own as an escapologist (page 193).

9
WIZARDS FROM THE NORTH

Oh, this Wizard, this Wonderful Wizard!
Is native of Scotia's land:
They say he's much gold won—by means of the
the old one,
That he's bound to him heart and hand!

Song, *The Great Wizard of the North*

Scotland's most famous magician was John Henry Anderson (1814–74), whose love of the stage was such that he combined his conjuring with thespian activities and delighted in appearing in the title rôle of *Rob Roy* and as William in *Black-Eyed Susan*. Born in humble circumstances, the son of a tenant farmer at Craigmyle, a few miles from Aberdeen, he was orphaned at an early age and started work assisting the village blacksmith. Release came by joining a troupe of touring players as call boy. Young John subsequently belonged to other companies where he got his first opportunity to tread the boards, although apparently not initially with outstanding success. He later told the story against himself of how, at Hanley, after his first appearance as Romeo, the Irish manager Manley complimented him with 'Ye've brought bad acting, sur, to the greatest height of perfection'![1]

During his time as a strolling player, Anderson saw his first conjurer, Signor Blitz, and was so fascinated he determined immediately to become a magician. To further this ambition he joined the company of a minor showman called Scott, whose grandiose title of 'The Emperor of all the Conjurers' probably accounted for the rest of the fraternity dubbing him 'Baron Munchausen'. John Anderson learned some magic from his employer, including the Gun Trick which he was to feature sensationally during much of his career (page 171), and he also wed Scott's daughter.

He made and acquired apparatus to put together a show, and the tall, handsome fellow made his

John Henry Anderson as a young man. This portrait served as the frontispiece to THE FASHIONABLE SCIENCE OF PARLOUR MAGIC, *a book sold for one shilling to his audiences explaining various tricks and exposing the practices of 'Card Players, Blacklegs and Gamblers'. It also included 'A New Song* THE GREAT WIZARD OF THE NORTH'.

Anderson's bill for the Standard Theatre in Shoreditch (1857).

STANDARD THE. TRE

Opposite the Eastern Counties' Railway, SHOREDITCH

[Proprietor] [J. DOUGLASS.]

THE GREAT WIZARD of the NORTH:

PROFESSOR ANDERSON

THIS EVENING, Monday, June 15th, 1857,
AND EVERY EVENING, in his Entirely
MAGICAL DRAMA, A

Night in Wonder-World

OR, MAGIC, MIRTH, AND MYSTERY!

Produced on a Scale of Grandeur far surpassing anything that has yet been attempted on the Stage

THE MAGNIFICENT PARAPHERNALIA

Of the most Elaborate description, Gorgeous in its Golden Glow and Resplendent in its Jewelled Richness, has recently been Manufactured at a cost exceeding £7000, and was providentially saved from destruction by Fire at the burning of the Luggage Warehouses of the London & North Western Railway. It comprises all that is Oriental in Splendour with all that is chaste in Parisian Elegance

The Theatre will be NIGHTLY VENTILATED by an Improved form of the GREAT HINDOSTANEE PUNKAH Scented with Frangipanni, and diffusing Odoriferous COOLNESS through the House.

First Time during PROFESSOR ANDERSON'S Engagement of the GALLERY OPEN AT THREEPENCE To an Entertainment of the most costly character.

ON MONDAY, JUNE 15th,

AND EVERY EVENING at Half-past Seven,

A NIGHT IN WONDER-WORLD

Or, a DRAMA of the WONDEROUS!

IN THE COURSE OF WHICH THE FOLLOWING

GORGEOUSLY SUPERB APPARATUS WILL BE USED:—

The Casket of the Alchemiste
The Wand of Rosicrucians
The Umbrella of Magic
Glass Goblets of Giraldus
Couch of the Genii
Paradoxical Pan
Cabalistical Candles
Clairvoyant Wand
Coffers au Diable
Anderson's Own Phylophlogiston
The Ampulla Vitrea Inexhaustus
Cagliostra's Carvaffe
Dr. Dee's Mirror

Anderson's Own Metamorphic Tables
The Dioptric Puzzle
Mystic Cards—Devils Punchbow.
Magic-made Canaries
Mysterious Travelling Trunk
Oracle of Peammantiches
Lavatory of Necromancy
Bewitched Flowers
Chair of Comus
Enchanted Target
Anderson's Rifle
The Electric Box
Magneto Electric Vase

The Spirit Rapping Table
The Mechanical Magician
The Magnet of the Pyramids
The Key of Eblis
Circle Endowed with Volition
Effervescent Ink
Venus of the Invisibles
Sketch-book of Bacchanus
Ball of the Invisibles
Mystical Tripod
Vitreo Textile Problem
To a Rostratori Queen
The Globes of the Hindoo

THE GREAT SCENE WILL BE THE

PALACE OF ENCHANTED DIAMONDS,

AND THE PROGRAMME

Act 1	Act 8
THE BIRDS OF FIRE!	THE COUCH OF THE GENII
Act 2	Act 10
MONEY MADE BY WISHING IT	THE WINE VAT OF BACCHUS.
Act 3	Act 11
MAGICAL INTROVISION,	MAGIC WOVE HANDKERCHIEFS
Act 4	Act 12
WILLIAM TELL AT HOME.	The Casket of the Gnomes!
Act 5	Act 13
GREAT GUN TRICK!	CHAIR OF THE WITCHES
The Tocsin of the Invisibles.	Act 14
Act 6	Trunk Mysteriously Corded!
CLEOPATRA'S WEDDING RING.	Act 15
Act 7	TO AUSTRALIA
THE ORACLE of the SIBYLS!	In Ten Minutes!

And in Course of the Evening, (for the First Time in London)

THE HERCULES TRACTION TRICK,

Demonstrating the Power of a Boy of Seven Years of Age, to pull to the Earth the Strongest Man

Between the Parts of the Entertainment,

Mr J. G. FORDE

Will give his Original Monologue, Descriptive of

LOVE AND LAW,

Introducing his Litigious Address, imitative of a

PHILADELPHIA LAWYER,

In which for Facetious power and Volubility of expression, he stands Unrivalled.

☞ NO ADVANCE IN PRICES!

BOX OFFICE OPEN FROM 10 TILL 4. SECURE SEATS BEFOREHAND.

New Private Boxes. Centre Circle. 3s. each Person. Stage Boxes 2s. 6d. each Person. Private Boxes on the Dress Circle. 2s. each Person. Private Boxes on the Upper Circle. 1s. 6d. each Person. The Centre Circle has been fitted up quite private, 1s. 6d. Stalls. 9d. New Orchestra Stalls, 1s.

GALLERY, (First time during Professor Anderson's Expensive Engagements) THREEPENCE

DOORS OPEN at 7. to COMMENCE AT HALF-PAST.

Half Price to Boxes and Stalls at Nine o'Clock.

NO CHILDREN IN ARMS ADMITTED.

début in the new rôle of mystifer at Aberdeen. It was, he claimed in his biography, shortly afterwards, when appearing in Brechin, that he was asked by Lord Panmure to dine with him and entertain his guests at Brechin Castle. Despite gaucheries at the dinner table he carried off his subsequent performance with sufficient *éclat* for his host to give him £10 and to pen the first testimonial he had ever received.[1]

Brechin Castle, 12th March 1831
Sir,—Your performance last night at Brechin Castle much delighted myself and party. You excel any other necromancer that I ever saw either at home or abroad.

I am, Sir, yours etc., PANMURE

In passing we may note that this date is at variance with that quoted on all his advertising matter, where it is given as 24 March 1837. Presumably, when his biography was written much later, he thought it appropriate to have appeared at Brechin as a younger man! Panmure's letter was immediately incorporated into Anderson's billing matter and marked the inception of his extravagant advertising, subsequently to blossom into the most exuberant of any nineteenth-century wizard. A love for incredible names generated a vocabulary of conjuring peculiarly his own, and a lexicologist would have plenty to keep him occupied when reading through a file of Anderson playbills.

The young magician was now billing himself as 'The Great Caledonian Magician', and as such appeared during 1837–8 in Edinburgh, Glasgow, Newcastle-upon-Tyne, Sheffield, Leeds, Manchester and Hull. His bill for the last venue also offered 'A Magical Dye' and promised that 'Any Gentleman with a Head of Grey Hair that he wishes changed to a glossy Black may have it transformed in ONE MINUTE! by applying to Mr A. where specimens may be seen'.[2]

By 1840 Anderson was in London at the New Strand Theatre and had emerged as The Great Wizard of the North, a title he fancifully claimed had been bestowed upon him by his fellow countryman Sir Walter Scott after the famous writer had requested a performance at Abbotsford: 'They call me "The Wizard of the North" but they make a mistake—it is you, not I, who best deserve the title.'[1] As Scott died in 1832 the story is undoubtedly apocryphal. But it made good copy and that was all that mattered. Supported by an impressive list of hundreds of performances throughout Scotland and England, with 'Gorgeous and Costly Apparatus of Solid Silver', defiance was given 'to all Modern Conjurers to Discover or Divine the impenetrable Secrets of the Peculiar one of a Peculiar Profession'. His Cabinet of Cabalistic Phenomena combined Mechanical, Chemical, Electric, Galvanic, Magnetic and Natural Magic and, so he said, the Black Art! He was already performing the Gun Trick and there is no question that he was offering an exceptionally good entertainment.

'Second Sight—who possesses that power?' A rhetorical question posed in 1841 by the Wizard of the North was answered modestly enough by asserting that he himself was the only living being of the present age who was endowed with this miraculous gift, although, as Sir Walter Scott had pointed out in his *Letters on Demonology and Witchcraft*, many persons were supposed to have possessed this wondrous power in the past. To prove his point, the Wizard carried out the following demonstration at the Adelphi Theatre.

A mother-of-pearl case was introduced and six or seven ladies and gentlemen were invited to deposit secretly into it any article that might be in their possession. A gentleman was then requested to write on a slip of blank paper a sentence or sentences in the English language, to fold the paper and place it in the box. The preliminaries completed, any member of the audience could retain the case in his or her possession. Nonetheless, the Wizard was able to read the sentence written on the paper. The feat was then taken from the realm of the apparent psychic to that of conjuring by producing the piece of paper bearing the message from an egg and commanding each article to fly from the box into a locked case held by another member of the audience at the opposite side of the theatre. Anderson would entreat the spectators to put as varied articles as possible into the box and not to restrict themselves to the usual rings, coins and handkerchiefs, so that he would have the fullest opportunity to demonstrate his remarkable powers of Second Sight.

In view of Anderson's previous claim, it must be assumed that his powers of Second Sight were hereditary, for in later years his daughter Louise participated in his presentation of this feat! In fact this subsequent form of demonstration was the style which nowadays is generally referred to as Second Sight, where a blindfolded medium divines objects handed to her partner as he moves about the auditorium.

Anderson's fondness for his daughters was much in evidence when they assisted him with items in his repertoire, and he always managed to convey the impression to an audience that they were being admitted to an intimate family circle. Their modes of address were found rather comical by at least one contemporary[3] who recorded the exchanges between the Wizard and Louise during their performance of Second Sight. After the young lady had been blindfolded, Anderson would go down into the audience:

'Now darling, can you tell me what I am holding in my hand?'

'Yes, dear papa, a watch chain.'

'You are quite right, love; it *is* a watch chain. And now, darling, can you tell me whether it is made of silver or gold?'

'I cannot see very clearly, but I think, dear papa, it must be made of silver.'

'Yes, my dear, you are right' [to one of the audience] 'it is made of silver. Thank you. And now, angel, tell me—is it a gentleman's chain or a lady's?'

'A gentleman's chain, dear papa.'—and so on.

Anderson's flair for turning national and local events to his personal advantage gave rise to what is probably the cleverest of his advertising ideas. On Monday 13 July 1846 he opened at the Music Hall in Jarratt Street, Hull, and his coming had been heralded by large advertisements in the local press. 'First appearance in Hull this eight years of Mr J. H. Anderson the Far-famed Professor!!' Nationally, it was a momentous month, for the great Free Trade crusade had reached its zenith with the repeal of the Corn Laws. Sir Robert Peel, the Prime Minister, had carried the bill after a complete *volte face* from the previous year, but then resigned over the Irish Coercion Bill; and Richard Cobden was a highly active member of the Anti-Corn Law League which had done so much work towards repeal. Somewhat belatedly, the Mayor of Hull called for a Free Trade demonstration on Wednesday 22 July and requested the leading inhabitants to give all persons in their employment a half-holiday in order to celebrate the repeal of the Corn Laws. It was reported that, during the day, 'church bells rang merry peals, and flags bearing suitable inscriptions, were suspended in various parts of the town'.[4]

Anderson, ever alive to the possibilities of a situation, took advantage of this local celebration to

Opportunist advertising by Anderson in 1846 following the Repeal of the Corn Laws. The Mayor of Hull had called for a Free Trade demonstration on 22 July and Anderson, currently appearing at the Music Hall, made capital of the occasion with this delightful bill.

advertise his Temple of Mysteries, and his clever use of the Free Trade theme is seen in the playbill reproduced above which he had specially printed for this unique occasion. Even the prices of admission were to be on the Free Trade principle—*Reduction*. As indeed they were, for sixpence came off the price of all seats and stayed off for the rest of Andersons' visit. His show met with a critic's approbation:

We live in the age of science; this the Wizard of the North has discovered. A more scientific entertainment we never witnessed than the feats of the Wizard, where we find experiments accomplished by Chemistry, mechanism, electricity, hydraulics—which baffle even professors to comprehend. How deeply must the Wizard have studied his profession to have arrived at the eminence he has done: in short the whole is managed upon an incomprehensible principle which seems to set at defiance the laws of nature.[5]

There is more than a suspicion that Anderson stood over the critic while he penned at least part of his report, judging by the phraseology! The Wizard's 'short stay' in Hull was, in fact, of a month's duration, and he took his adieu with a fanfare of advertisements assuring the populace that his departure was caused not by want of patronage but by an engagement in St Petersburg, and that his Mine of Amusement was not exhausted by being worked upon, but, on the contrary, was increasing—still more brilliant and more wonderful.

Anderson's Russian engagement was not a fiction born of his advertising methods. Later in 1846 he was in Russia and performed for Tsar Nicholas, the first British conjurer in that country. The European tour also embraced Sweden, Denmark and Prussia and, on his return to London, he put out a poster that cleverly adapted the painting of *Napoleon's Return from Elba* to show the Wizard of the North graciously accepting the homage of emperors and kings with even the dome of St Paul's and Lord Nelson on his column genuflecting to the 'Napoleon of Necromancy'.

Transport around the world was improving, but there is no gainsaying that many conjurers of the nineteenth century were extremely adventurous and enterprising in their overseas tours. Anderson was no exception: he undertook extended tours in the USA, Canada and Australia. He was in the midst of his second tour of the USA when the Civil War broke out, and had already had a foretaste when his posters advertising the Wizard of the *North* had been torn down by an angry crowd in Virginia!

Queen Victoria's patronage of popular entertainment was extensive. On 27 August 1849 Anderson received a command to entertain at Balmoral Castle on the occasion of her son's birthday. The Wizard acquitted himself well, and celebrated the auspicious event by having commemorative medals struck and by afterwards incorporating mention in his advertising material.

His publications were legion. An audience book, *The Fashionable Science of Parlour Magic*, first published in 1840, went through numerous editions, although it is doubtful if it attained quite so many as

the exuberant Professor would have had its purchasers believe; around 1864 the 250th edition was claimed.[6] Following the wave of interest in spiritualism which stemmed from the strange knockings experienced by the Fox Sisters at Hydesville in upstate New York in 1848, Anderson incorporated *The Magic of Spirit Rapping, Writing Mediums and Table Turning*, as an exposé of the frauds of spirit rappers whom he denounced as 'conjurers in disguise'.

Another, extremely lucrative, venture was his Conundrum Contest, a promotion inviting audiences in each town to submit their best conundrums for the award of a silver trophy or breakfast and tea service. The thousands of riddles and puns entered were printed in booklets, often together with the names of their perpetrators, and sold to eager audiences. They could not even get away from him at table because butter pats distributed to inns and hotels bore the news 'Anderson is here'.

Fire was not only an ingredient of the Professor's conjuring but, unhappily, an element that seemed to pursue him relentlessly throughout his career. On Glasgow Green in 1845, ploughing his profits into the business, he built the City Theatre, a huge structure capable of holding five thousand people, which opened on Fair Saturday, 12 July.[7] The shows mounted by the new proprietor-producer included musical acts and plays in addition to magic. They played to indifferent houses for a while. After only four months, in the early hours of 19 November, a disastrous fire occurred and Anderson's theatre was gutted. He was partially insured but sustained considerable loss and, despite benefit performances on his behalf by friendly theatre proprietors, had to take to the road again to retrieve his fortunes.

The next occurrence was a minor fire at one of the US theatres Anderson played during the early eighteen-fifties. But the greatest tragedy of all took place at the Covent Garden Theatre in London, which he had leased for the winter of 1855-6. His favourite dashing rôle of Rob Roy in Christmas week gave way to a pantomime, for which he had advertised that the scenery had been painted by the celebrated Mr Beverley, thereby raising the ire of Henry Morley when that worthy discovered only

Professor Anderson and his daughter Louise as the Second-Sighted Sybil and Retro-reminiscent Mnemosyne, as they appeared in their advertisements for 'The World of Magic and Second Sight' in 1867.

The Electric and Great Cyclogeotic Retro-Reminiscent Clairvoyant Telegraph Company.

INCORPORATED BY ROYAL CHARTER, 1411.—(NOT LIMITED).

MESSAGES

Are transmitted daily by Visitors from all the Principal Towns in GREAT
BRITAIN and IRELAND, which are replied to with

MARVELLOUS RAPIDITY

by Miss ANDERSON, the SECOND-SIGHTED SYBIL, whose Retro-Reminiscent and Clairvoyant Telegraphic Systems are now in full operation and in

DIRECT COMMUNICATION

With English and Foreign Visitors, *via* the Great Magnetic Line so successfully
laid by the Eminent PROFESSOR ANDERSON, not only over the

CONTINENT OF EUROPE

But encircling THE ENTIRE GLOBE ITSELF, now fully established, in
complete working order; and universally recognised as

The Great World of Magic, Electro Cyclogeotic and Psychomantic Line.

Stations in Hull at which messages are received and forwarded and tickets secured; the charges being the same at any of the Company's stations. Further particulars may be obtained at the Company's Chief Office:—

CENTRAL AND GENERAL OFFICE,

THEATRE ROYAL, HULL.

N.B.—You are requested to give no fee or gratuity to the Messenger, but please Yourself as to extra charges beyond those entered in this sheet.

Charges to Pay.

Admission	..	,,	,,
Cab Hire	.:	,,	,,
Refreshment	..	,,	,,
Total	..	,,	,,

The following message forwarded from _____ Station, { Insert Station at which Message was despatched by the Company

FROM _____ 186

Name and Address. } _____

TO _____

Name and Address. } _____

D.Q.

Professor and Miss Anderson present their compliments, and beg to state that the entertainment "The World of Magic" (which has been given by command of Her Most Gracious Majesty the Queen, at Balmoral and Windsor Castles, also before every Monarch in Europe, and during the last 30 years before nearly a million and a half persons in all quarters of the Globe) will be given every evening at the Theatre Royal, for a short period, at Eight; and every Saturday, at Two p.m., a Day Performance for the accommodation of juveniles and parties living at a distance. This will be positively the last professional engagement that Professor Anderson can give in Hull prior to his final retirement from the stage. Your patronage is most respectfully solicited.

NOTICE.—The chief office, THEATRE ROYAL, HULL, is open every Evening at 7 o'clock, and on Saturday Afternoon at 2 o'clock; when the most astonishing Scientific and Electric experiments are to be witnessed.

CHARGES FOR ADMISSION.

DISTANCE.	ONE PERSON TO STALLS. Dress, numbered, & strictly reserved. Express, Carriage, or Foot.	ONE PERSON TO BOXES. Unnumbered. Carriage or on Foot.	ONE PERSON TO UPPER BOXES. Carriage or on Foot.	ONE PERSON TO PIT. Carriage or on Foot.	ONE PERSON TO GALLERY. Carriage, Cab, or on Foot.
From the Psychomantic Laboratory. Under half-a-mile .... (Considerably)	2s. 6d.	2s. 0d.	1s. 6d.	1s. 6d.	0s. 6d.

No enquiry respecting this Message can be attended to even upon the } production of this paper.

•.• Do not trouble yourself to enter time of delivery or to sign Messenger's ticket.

Wm. M'CALL, Type, 7, Hunter Street, Liverpool.)

.... Clerk.

(By Order.)

S. Artaud, Acting Manager.

one of the scenes was attributable to this scenic artist.[8] Thoroughly soured, Morley considered the pantomime the dullest to be seen in London for a good many seasons and was scathing in its denunciation. From this source we learn of another Anderson publicity stunt, an advertisement requiring 'two hundred young women, none under the height of six feet two, for the pantomime at Covent Garden'! A skit on this topic was evidently introduced into the plot. Probably due to unfavourable notices the pantomime, although running into March, did less well than anticipated and Anderson announced a Grand Carnival Benefit and Dramatic Gala on Monday and Tuesday, 3 and 4 March. We recount elsewhere (page 177) the details of this marathon show.

The climax of the extravaganza was a Bal Masqué held on stage on the second evening, starting after the conclusion of the theatrical performance and lasting until dawn. Precisely what happened is unclear, although it is evident the function degenerated into an unseemly affair and many decent people left, yet at 5am a couple of hundred revellers were still present. Anderson then terminated the proceedings by instructing the band to play *God Save the Queen*, and it was at this juncture that two theatre firemen observed a fire in the carpenter's shop high above the stage. A stampede for the exits followed the shout of 'Fire!'. The flames spread quickly and soon the theatre was an inferno. At 5.30 the roof fell in. Happily no lives were lost.

Then came the reckoning. Anderson, again under-insured, was the subject of accusations, especially when his involvement in two previous theatre fires became public knowledge. On top of that, his bank failed, leaving him heavily in debt. He was not alone: Mr Frederick Gye, the proprietor of the theatre (who was in Paris at the time), lost some £30,000.[9] However, with characteristic buoyancy, the Wizard conjured up some borrowed funds, refurbished his show and resumed his travels, in March 1858 sailing for Australia.

The Covent Garden tragedy marked the onset of failing fortune for Anderson. Although he did well in Australia, expenses were high and profits limited,

Another of Anderson's clever advertising ideas was the issue of forms for the Electric and Great Cyclogeotic Retro-Reminiscent Clairvoyant Telegraph Company in the towns he played. This one was circulated for his appearances at the Theatre Royal, Hull, in July 1867.

and most of the latter had, in any case, to be dispatched to his creditors in Britain. *Via* Hawaii he travelled to the USA, arriving in December 1859. Varied success attended his efforts, but the outbreak of the Civil War sounded the death knell and by the end of 1862 he was heavily in debt. His wife's jewels were sold to provide funds for Anderson and his assistants to return to Britain to try to recoup their losses.[10] Mrs Anderson and three of his children stayed in the USA. Sadly, he was never to see his wife again.

The Wizard resumed his career in Liverpool on 11 January 1863. Five years had elapsed since he was last in Britain. Since then he had covered 235,000 miles and £157,000 had passed through his hands.[1] But his Covent Garden as well as his New World debts were insurmountable, and he was declared bankrupt in 1866. Gone was the gorgeous apparatus but not the indomitable spirit. Anderson embarked again on his Farewell Tour of Britain and there was still the sparkle of publicity.

In July 1867 the Wizard was back in Hull at the Theatre Royal sharing top billing with one of his daughters in 'The World of Magic and Second Sight'. He was stated to be assisted by his four daughters—Louise, Lizzie, Flora and Ada—but these included adopted daughters. Louise Anderson's contribution to the entertainment was substantial, and she was variously described as the Second-Sighted Sybil, the Retro-Reminiscent Orthographist or the Retro-Reminiscent Mnemosyne. Contemporary reports explain these startling appellations.[11]

Miss Anderson performs surprising feats of being able to recount the contents, however numerous, of articles be they never so curious or unique, which may be placed in a vase, to repeat instantly and with a rapidity most extraordinary, the letters forming English words of whatever length or of however uncommon occurrence, either in the proper order or backwards, the latter equally as quick as the former, or she can tell the cards drawn from a pack promiscuously by the audience.

Mnemosyne, the Goddess of Memory, must surely have approved the appropriation of her name in such a cause. But Louise Anderson's attributes extended beyond her theatrical performances, for she was also the authoress of a little volume of poems.

Anderson's love for and use of pretentious sounding names and extravagant adjectives is nowhere better exemplified than in the novel form of advertising matter he distributed during his three-week engagement in Hull. The 'Electric and Great Cyclogeotic Retroreminiscent Clairvoyant Telegraph Company' form was embellished by two medallions, carrying profiles of the Wizard and Louise, which respectively claimed the two companies were 'incorporated' in 1824 and 1860 and carried details of the show and prices in a most eye-catching manner. There was a Grand Fashionable Night under the patronage of the Right Honourable Lord Londesborough, Commodore, and Members of the Royal Yorkshire Yacht Club; but the Wizard's performances clearly did not elicit universal approval for an illuminating rejoinder to two critics appeared in the local press.[12]

PROFESSOR ANDERSON presents his very respectful compliments to Messrs GOY and BOOTH, and has pleasure in intimating to them that a Private Box will be placed at their service this [Saturday] Afternoon when Professor Anderson will endeavour to demonstrate to those gentlemen that the flame of intolerance and superstition which by their breath

they would rekindle is flickering. He further hopes to prove that the march of intellect will totally extinguish it. To those whom Burns calls the 'unco guid', who would debar innocent and poor little children from the enjoyment of harmless and intellectual amusements, Prof. Anderson simply says, 'Come and judge for yourselves'—find out what harm or danger to the morals of these children exists in an entertainment which has received the repeated patronage of the Queen and her children, which has been given before nearly 50,000 children of all denominations, enjoying the benefits of every

A lithograph used by Wellington Young to commemorate his Royal Command performance for Queen Victoria at Arundel Castle on 3 December 1846. He is performing the Inexhaustible Bottle trick against a background of equipment that bids fair to outdo the entire stock of a magic dealer and manufacturer. Young's title, the Great Northern Magician, follows closely that of John Henry Anderson, the Great Wizard of the North.

variety of charitable institutions, and to over Four Millions of people in every part of the globe. If these evidences and that of their own senses fail to convince Messrs Goy and Booth, Professor Anderson had no alternative but to regard them with sincere pity and regret as examples of a prolonged intolerance which he had hoped was unknown in favoured England.

To give emphasis to the point, on the final day of his stay in Hull, Anderson presented 'A Grand Day Performance' to which the children of various local charities were invited free of charge. It was an impressive list. The wily Wizard knew full well the publicity value of his magnanimity and the subsequent letters of thanks to the press on behalf of the recipients gave the *coup de grâce* to his erstwhile critics, Messrs Goy and Booth.

Working for charitable causes is common in the world of show business today, yet well over a hundred years ago Professor Anderson, by his Benefit Performances, donated almost five thousand pounds to public institutions and charities and was made a life governor of eight British hospitals.

The tours continued throughout Britain but Anderson's health began to fail; the weary Wizard died at the Fleece Hotel, Darlington, on 3 February 1874. Scotland's most illustrious magician was borne back to his native heath and buried in St Nicholas' Churchyard at Aberdeen.

One other Scottish magician must claim our attention, the kenspeckle figure of Samuel Murphy Bodie (1869–1939), better known as 'Doctor' Walford Bodie, the Laird of Macduff. With pointed waxed moustache and piercing eyes, Bodie, great showman and ventriloquist, presented what used to be called a 'bloodless surgery' act. As a ventriloquist he was superb in a sketch called 'Fun on an Ocean Liner' which involved some half dozen figures, embracing young and old, with even a negro for greater contrast. The Doctor, styling himself as 'The British Edison', also had an electrical act featuring Madame Electra, and employing equipment that he claimed had cost over £2,000. In those days of gaslight and hansom cabs the principle of the combination of high voltage with low amperage was as unfamiliar to his audiences as was the terrain of the High Andes. Bodie exploited his knowledge to the full, apparently defying death in an electric chair while thousands of volts coursed through his body. Huge sparks and crackling electrical discharges made a great impression, especially when presided over by such a tremendous showman.

That Walford Bodie did not become one of the 'greats' of magic is almost certainly due to his clashes with the medical profession in the course of his hypnotic and bloodless surgery demonstrations. In the early nineteen-hundreds the Doctor was peddling nostrums just as Katterfelto had done in the eighteenth century. The Bodie Electric Drug Company had premises at 163 Blackfriars Road in London and was retailing Electric Life Pills and Electric Liniment. These medicaments were for 'rejuvenating the system' and killing pain 'in man or beast' respectively, and were claimed to work miracles and act like lightning! On stage Bodie would invite up the 'halt and the lame' and go into his hypnotic act, practising 'Bodieism' amd imbuing them with the 'Bodic Force', so that they were apparently then able to march off hale and hearty. While this type of hypnotic act was by no means unique, and the title of 'Doctor' assumed by professional mystifiers a tolerated feature, Bodie transgressed the accepted canons by adding the letters MD after his name. The wanton misappropriation of the higher degree of Doctor of Medicine was too much for the medical profession and it mattered little that Bodie protested the letters stood simply for 'Merry Devil'. He was the subject not only of litigation but also of ragging by medical students in the cities he played.

The most famous of these clashes with students occurred at the Glasgow Coliseum on 12 November 1909, and ever since has been enshrined in local folklore as 'The Bodie Riot'. It achieved wider fame because James Bridie (O. H. Mavor, 1888–1951), the Scottish playwright, was one of the students involved and published his version of the great event in his autobiography.[13] While the accuracy of Bridie's detail has been challenged,[14] the overall story is essentially correct. Earlier in the week Bodie had been hissed and booed by some students in the gallery. 'The magician came down to the footlights and delivered himself very aptly on the subject of the medical profession in general and medical students in particular. He wound up by quoting the poet Burns to the effect that, "They gang in stirks and come oot asses".'[13] This barb led to a mass attack on the Thursday evening when the students pelted Bodie and La Belle Electra with ochre, peasemeal, eggs and decayed herrings before storming the stage. The curtain and fire curtain were rung down

'*Doctor*' *Walford Bodie (1869–1939), the great Scottish showman and ventriloquist, whose 'bloodless surgery' and use of the letters M.D. (Merry Devil!) after his name antagonized the medical profession. This coloured lithograph advertised his electrical act.*

but the academic mob was undeterred, even by the police reinforcements that had now joined the fray. Eventually a halt was called and the students, elated by their success, then endeavoured to treat the premises of a notorious Glasgow quack, Professor Eastburn, in the same manner.

In due course the ringleaders were arraigned before the Bailie at Glasgow Southern Police Court, but they got off very lightly, which is reputed to have elicited the comment from the prosecutor, Superintendent Lindsay: 'Until today I always thought the police were the finest liars in Glasgow.'[14] But Bodie, undeterred, continued on his Merry Devil career, doing well out of the controversy that surrounded his act, until the competing claims of sound films caused declining interest.

Bodie wrote *The Bodie Book*,[15] wherein he dealt with hypnotism, electricity, mental suggestion, clairvoyance and telepathy, *Strange Stories*,[16] some alleged autobiographical tales, and a novel, *Harley the Hypnotist*.[17] During the First World War Bodie and his company were rescued from the torpedoed *Arabia* and lost all their properties but he was commanding a high salary at that time and so was able to refurbish his act.[18] In 1915 he was greatly upset by the death of his son, Albert Edward Bodie, who had already made a name for himself as a clever conjurer. Bodie owned a large mansion at Macduff which he placed at the Government's disposal for use as an emergency hospital during the hostilities.

In the early thirties he purchased what was claimed to be the largest houseboat on the Thames, aptly named *Electra*, but with failing health and declining opportunities the Doctor was now playing only the third-rate music halls, public halls and fairgrounds, a shadow of the former dynamic showman who had topped the bill. He died at Blackpool on 19 October 1939 at the end of a season at the Pleasure Beach, an old weary trouper. Yet those who saw him remember his golden days—the upright figure, in kilt as the Highland Laird or naval uniform for his ocean liner sketch—and revere a great Scottish showman.

Rameses was the stage name of Albert Marchinski (1876-1930), a Yiddish actor from the East End of London, who presented a spectacular costume act of Egyptian magic during the heydays of music-hall. He toured the U.S.A. successfully during 1910-13 and later was involved in an unfortunate theatrical enterprise at Southend-on-Sea, where he died in straitened circumstances.

10
SCIENCE ET LA PRESTIDIGITATION

Il est plus facile de tromper le monde que
de le détromper.

H. Decremps (1785)
quoting Lord Chesterfield

If a time machine could take the adventurous reader back to the eighteen-sixties, and he were so disposed to cross the Channel and wander to Saint Gervais near Blois, in France, he would soon find himself at the gates of 'The Priory', a substantial dwelling set back some quarter of a mile at the end of a drive. The white-painted visitor's entrance, to the left of the iron carriage gates that bar the drive, carries a brass plate bearing the name ROBERT-HOUDIN, beneath which is a gilt knocker with the legend, 'Knock'.[1] Obeying the instructions, the visitor would be unaware that his action had actuated a bell at the Priory which continued to ring until a servant pressed a stud in the hall. This latter action would cause to be revealed to the visitor's startled gaze the sudden replacement of the name ROBERT-HOUDIN by the words WALK IN and the simultaneous sound of the bolt being withdrawn. Somewhat taken aback by the automatic mechanism, he hesitantly enters, the door closes behind him on its own spring, and he begins his walk to the house.

Already, by a combination of electrical ingenuity and psychology, the members of the household have a fairly shrewd knowledge of their visitor. The door, in opening and closing, has set in motion at two different points in its arc, a bell, which thus gives four rings in all—two in opening and two in closing. The

timing and rhythm of this sequence of four tinkles afford the necessary clues to the practised ears at the Priory. One person alone will effect a short, regular foursome of sounds, the sequence being much longer for the hesitant newcomer, confronted by this surprising system for the first time, while a party entering will necessitate a lapse between the initial twosome and the final pair of tinkles as the door closes, their separation being an indication of the number of people entering.

Further refinements extend to the stables where, thrice daily, according to the time of a master clock, electrical connections ensure that fodder is delivered from a square funnel-shaped box to the horse. The master clock serves also two external clock faces, on the gable ends of the Priory and the gardener's cottage respectively, while clockwork provides a striking mechanism for a bell, the motor being wound up by the continual movement of a swing-door in the kitchen. The electrical clock furnishes alarms for early-rising of staff at individual times, by causing a bell to ring loudly and which cannot be cancelled without getting out of bed to press a remote stud. But the master of the house can control time to suit his own convenience, since he is able to retard or advance the clock by a special mechanism and so secure an early meal when he is hungry while also ensuring he is never late to table! There are electrical fire alarms actuated by temperature and a complete burglar alarm system that produces incessant ringing if doors or windows are opened. Over one hundred years ago these were indeed marvels of science in a

L'ESCAMOTEUR *by John James Chalon (1778–1854), one of twenty-four subjects displaying the costume of Paris, was a lithograph published by Rodwell and Martin of London in 1820.*

A portrait of Robert-Houdin in his workshop with some of his inventions.

domestic setting.

Surprised though he might be, the visitor of the eighteen-sixties would, however, have needed no introduction to the name of Robert-Houdin, the foremost conjurer of France, a performer who, after establishing his fame in Paris, first appeared in London at the St James's Theatre on 2 May 1848. Shortly afterwards he conjured before Queen Victoria at a fête in Fulham on 19 July and subsequently had two command performances. When his London season ended on 14 August he went on a tour of the provinces, returning to the St James's Theatre in December. Completing his engagement in April 1849, he then embarked on a second provincial tour which lasted until October. Hailed as 'the sole monarch of the world of wonders', he received from *The Illustrated London News*[2] the comment: 'all other conjurers and wizards, from whatever point of the compass they arrive,[3] sink into insignificant imitators before him'.

Robert-Houdin was born Jean Eugene Robert, the son of an horologer, at Blois in 1805.[4] He inherited his father's skills as a watchmaker and mechanician

and, although intended to become a solicitor, it was finally recognized that this profession was not his bent. Accordingly, he was apprenticed to a cousin as his father had now retired from business. In the course of these formative years Jean Eugene had occasion to visit a bookseller's shop to purchase Berthoud's treatise on horology but, in error, he received the two volume *Dictionnaire Encyclopédique des Amusemens des Sciences, Mathématiques et Physiques* (1792), which contained many conjuring tricks. Fascinated by the new world suddenly opened up, he subsequently recorded in his autobiography that this discovery afforded him the greatest joy he had ever experienced.[5]

Young Robert decided that manual dexterity would be aided by a course of lessons in juggling, which he secured from a Blois corn-cutter who specialized in both activities. After mastering the technique he was soon able to juggle four balls, and then turned his attention to sleight-of-hand, practising assiduously.

Jean Eugene met his future wife, Josephe Cecile Eglantine, the daughter of a Parisian horologist, Jacques Houdin, at a party in Blois, and soon after moved to the capital to become a member of Houdin's staff. They were married in 1830 and the young man, adding his wife's name to his own, henceforth was known as Robert-Houdin. Backed by his father-in-law, he set up his own business, yet all the while was nursing a secret ambition to be a famous magician, and observing attentively the performances of all the conjurers who played in the French capital.

Robert-Houdin's combined skills as a mechanician and magician were exercised with the construction of a Mysterious Clock which, with a completely transparent dial and mounted on an equally transparent column, kept perfect time in the absence of any obvious mechanism, and by a series of mechanical pieces including singing birds. He patented in 1837 a highly successful alarm clock which woke the sleeper and simultaneously presented him with a lighted taper. The would-be magician witnessed automata exhibited by the conjurer Philippe (Jacques André Noel Talon, 1802–78), including one in which a small figure entered a confectioner's shop and emerged with foodstuffs; Philippe had, in fact, been a confectioner himself in Aberdeen! Robert-Houdin subsequently copied this idea for his Pastry-cook of the Palais-Royal, although the motive power was different—his small son was hidden

The Pastry-Cook of the Palais-Royal, Robert-Houdin's 'automaton' which retreated into the shop and returned with confectionery as requested by the audience.

within. But his *chef d'oeuvre* was undoubtedly 'The Writer', a small automaton figure of a man that could write answers to questions or draw sketches of a cupid, dog or heads of reigning monarchs as requested. It was exhibited at the Palace of Industry of the Paris Exhibition of 1844 where Louis Philippe greatly admired its performance and the constructor was awarded a silver medal.

The following year Robert-Houdin's great ambition was consummated with the opening of his own theatre at the Palais Royal where, on the upper floor at 164 Galerie de Valois, an assembly room was converted to provide an elegant drawing room in the

Philippe (Jacques André Noel Talon, 1802–78), a Frenchman who, after a period as a pastry-cook in Aberdeen, became a successful conjurer. He specialized in the Chinese Linking Rings and the production of fish bowls from beneath a shawl. Philippe's curious costume, a hybrid of uncertain origin, was certainly a useful garment for a conjurer!

style of Louis XV. On 3 July 1845 came the first performance of Des Soirées Fantastiques de Robert-Houdin, a programme which was claimed to comprise tricks of his own invention—yet was certainly not the case. But Robert-Houdin was wearied by all the preparations during the period preceding the opening and this première almost ended in disaster. During the second half of the entertainment, nervous exhaustion caused him to flounder and conclude the show with unseemly haste. He was despondent and plagued by doubts of his ability to continue but, spurred by the thoughtless remark of a friend, he shed his discouragement and the following night gave a much better performance. From that moment he progressed steadily, but the turning point which made him the talk of Paris was the introduction into his programme of La Second Vue (Second Sight, page 110) on 12 February 1846. His young son Emile, aged twelve, was the medium and, with his eyes bandaged, the lad described objects submitted by members of the audience. Although the feat was not original to Robert-Houdin, he did introduce a new approach, and audiences flocked to see the presentation, many returning several times hoping to solve the mystery.

The next development was Robert-Houdin's improvement of an Indian suspension illusion, often wrongly referred to as a levitation, in which he capitalized on the recent introduction of ether for anaesthesia, as we recount elsewhere (page 81). Another popular effect was the Enchanted Portfolio, a typical artist's portfolio which was clearly too thin to hold anything but drawings yet, when placed upon small trestles, yielded up an incredible assortment of solid items. Engravings, hats, birds, saucepans and a cage of canaries were climaxed by the appearance of the tousled head of his youngest son; the magician lifted him out to rapturous applause.

It was the Revolution in February 1848, with the closure of the Parisian theatres, that led to Robert-Houdin's first visit to England, new successes and financial rewards. Especially popular was the Inexhaustible Bottle, from which any drink called for by the audience was poured for their delectation. The tour, which embraced also Scotland and Ireland, lasted until October 1849, when the conjurer returned to France, there to resume his performances and shortly to purchase the Priory at Blois.

The tour of Britain had taken its toll, and Robert-Houdin determined to find a successor. He took as a pupil a young man called Hamilton (Pierre Étienne

Chocat), who fulfilled the master's hopes; in January 1852 he simultaneously married Robert-Houdin's sister-in-law, became director of the Théâtre Robert-Houdin, and was designated successor to the founder. In 1853 Robert-Houdin returned to England once again, to be accorded his third appearance before Queen Victoria. Afterwards came his farewell tour of Belgium and Germany and then the return home.

Back at the Priory he devoted himself to researches on electrical devices, recalling the comment made by the judges at the Exhibition in 1844: 'It is a great pity, Monsieur Robert-Houdin, that you did not apply the talent you have evinced in fancy objects to serious labours.'[5] At the Universal Exhibition of 1855 he exhibited several new applications of electricity to clockwork mechanism and was the recipient of a gold medal. These exhibits included a battery-operated electrical mantlepiece clock which served as a master to the other slave dials in the house, similar to the one he had installed at the Priory.

Robert-Houdin was to be recalled to the stage from retirement in a most unusual rôle—no less than that of political emissary. The cause was a threatened uprising in Algeria under the influence of the Marabouts, a religious sect of alleged miracle-workers who were whipping up the principal tribes into a state of ferment and encouraging them to sever their links with France. Colonel de Neveu, head of the political office at Algiers, conceived the idea of the great magician performing for the chieftains of the tribes of the colony to impress them that the Frenchman's powers were far superior to those of the Marabouts, and thereby countering the influence of these fanatics.

Madame Robert-Houdin accompanied her husband on this trip and, because of a revolt in Kabylia when they arrived in North Africa, the fetes arranged for the Arab chiefs were postponed for a month. In the interim, the magician performed at the Bab-Azoun Theatre in Algiers, which he found a valuable experience after two years' retirement from the stage. Eventually the picturesque fetes began on 27 October 1856, and the following day Robert-Houdin gave his memorable performance.

The magician records in his *Memoirs* how the various tribal representatives, their chiefs, civilian and military authorities were all accommodated in the small theatre together with interpreters, and his belief that it was probably the most brilliant assembly to which he had played. Certainly it was the most important in its consequences. His opening effects were designed to relax the audience—the production of cannon balls followed by flowers from a hat, and various objects from a cornucopia. Silver coins were made to fly invisibly across the theatre to arrive visibly in a crystal casket suspended in full view, and sweetmeats and coffee appeared in an empty punch-bowl.

Then came the famous Light and Heavy Chest, first introduced in 1845, the performance of which presents an interesting study in applied psychology. The effect is that a small, light, wooden box with a brass handle becomes so heavy it cannot be lifted. On the stage at the Théâtre Robert-Houdin in Paris it was presented simply in that fashion, the magician by mystic passes over the box apparently causing it to become immensely heavy. For the Arabs, however, the presentation was entirely different. Asserting that his demonstration had already given proof of his supernatural powers, Robert-Houdin claimed that he would deprive the most powerful man of his strength. A brawny Arab, having accepted the challenge, was asked: 'Are you very strong?' On replying in the affirmative, he was asked to pick up the box, which he did with disdainful ease. 'Now I shall rob you of all your strength and you shall become as weak as a little child', and, making mesmeric passes at the Arab, the magician cried: 'Behold! you are weaker than a woman; now try to lift the box.'

And tug, pull and strain as he would, muscles rippling under his dusky skin, the challenger could not raise the small box even a millimetre. Panting for breath he surveyed the box and then decided on a final effort. But as he grasped the brass handle of the box sudden convulsions shook his body, his legs

L'ESCAMOTEUR, SUR LE BOULEVARD, PRÈS LE CHATEAU D'EAU. *Near Porte St Martin and Porte St Denis in Paris, this was a regular pitch for the performer, with nurses and army recruits as his preponderant audience. The artist Brocas features a juvenile pickpocket on the extreme right. Another version of this print was published in 1822 by William Sams of London as* THE JUGGLER OF THE CHATEAU D'EAU.

Robin (Henri Joseph Donckele, 1811–74), a graceful French conjurer who was also popular in Britain. Here he is seen performing the Second Sight with his female assistant at the Salle de Robin in Piccadilly during his first London appearance in 1851.

collapsed beneath him and he yelled in agony until the merciful French magician, with another mesmeric pass, released him from his plight.

The application of science to magic was beautifully illustrated by this trick, for the wooden box had an iron plate let into its base and beneath the stage was a huge electro-magnet that could be switched on at the crucial moment. And even a muscular Arab was no match for the shock from an induction coil which surged through the brass handle in the climax of this feat!

Next came the Gun Trick, with a Marabout threatening to kill Robert-Houdin. The pistol was loaded with a marked leaden ball and the Arab fired it at an apple held on the point of a knife before the magician's heart. The bullet was caught in the apple.

The final feat, and one which made the greatest impact of all, was the disappearance of a young Moor. He was invited to stand on the top of a four-legged table and covered with a large cloth cone, open at the top. A plank was then pushed onto the table top beneath the cone and Robert-Houdin and his assistant carried their heavy burden to the foot-lights where they upset it. The Moor had vanished—only the empty cone remained!

This illusion affected the Arabs considerably, and many struggled to get out of the theatre before they too suffered the same fate as their co-religionist. At this stage the interpreters were asked to convey to the Arabs that the mysteries they had just witnessed were not effected by sorcery but by the natural science of prestidigitation.

A few days later, Robert-Houdin was invited to the Governor's palace where, with all due solemnity, the Arab chiefs, wearing red robes that signified their loyalty to France, presented the magician with a scroll paying homage to him, a manuscript still preserved by his descendants. His political mission was thus triumphantly completed and he returned to France, there to resume his experiments and literary activities, which included his autobiography[6] and three valuable technical treatises on conjuring.[7, 8, 9]

Robert-Houdin, widely acclaimed as the Father of Modern Conjuring and a pioneer of the application of electrical principles to magic and domestic purposes, died of pneumonia on 13 June 1871 at his home in Saint Gervais. His memory is revered wherever magicians meet; Ehrich Weiss adapted his name to become Houdini; and, on the centenary of the anniversary of his death, the French Government issued a commemorative postage stamp depicting his portrait, the Mysterious Clock and the Suspension illusion.[10] No conjurer can ask for more than that.

A contemporary and rival of Robert-Houdin, who shared both his magical and scientific interests, was Henri Robin, whom we also encounter at the Egyptian Hall in London during 1861 (page 152). Robin, whose career as a conjurer outspanned that of Robert-Houdin, opened his own theatre in Paris in 1862 at 49 Boulevard du Temple, near the Place de Chateau d'Eau, and operated for seven years.[11] The Théâtre Robin quickly became a popular rendezvous for Parisians and, with its combined presentation of science and magic, is perhaps best compared with the Royal Polytechnic in London. The walls were hung with porcelain medallions of scientific and magical luminaries such as Archimedes, Galileo, Franklin, Volta, Newton, Cagliostro, Robertson and Vaucanson, and the large stage presented a dazzling array of scientific apparatus and magical equipment. Its proprietor acquired celebrity status, his charming personality and brilliant presentation exciting widespread attention.

We can gauge Robin's popularity and standing by the fact that, when Heinrich D. Rhumkorff (1803–77), the German-born electrical manufacturer resident in Paris, received the Emperor's prize of 50,000 francs for his invention of the induction coil, *L'Illustration, Journal Universel* had this to say:

People are asking themselves 'What is this Rhumkorff coil which has won 50,000 francs?' For those who wish to answer that question there is in all Paris only one establishment able to enlighten them. And it is neither the College de France, nor the Sorbonne, nor the Academy of Sciences, nor the Conservatoire of Arts and Crafts; this unique establishment is the Théâtre Robin.

At a time when electricity was a great novelty, Robin clearly and rapidly explained its properties and employed some of them in his demonstrations. But he opened his show, as he had done over twenty years before, with an impressive feat first introduced by Ludwig Döbler in 1840—the simultaneous lighting of two hundred candles with a single pistol shot. The candle wicks were soaked in turpentine and each was fed by a fine stream of hydrogen gas between two wires, across which, at the critical moment, an electrical spark could be passed, igniting the hydrogen and thereby the candles.

A casket was taken, filled with gold and placed on a stand. An eager member of the audience was invited to help himself and take the casket and its contents. But alas, even Hercules himself could not overcome the powerful electromagnet that held it inviolate. Another application of the same principle was 'The Medium of Inkerman', a drum alleged to have been carried from the battle-fields of the Crimea and which, isolated on a tripod stand, tapped out answers to the questions the spectators posed.

Then the Rhumkorff induction coil was demonstrated. Spectacular sparks arced forty-five centimetres through the air, like lightning in the clouds; and now the sparks impressively traversed a block of glass. Next a series of glass tubes, blown into curious shapes and containing rare gases at low pressures, were subjected to an electrical discharge and glowed in various colours characteristic of each gas. And here a Christmas tree, whose branches slowly covered with hoar frost; just as the audience marvelled at this rapid approach of winter, suddenly the tree was covered with lights, flowers, fruits and toys. Christmas had arrived! Here, then, in the heart of Paris, science and magic truly flourished hand in hand.

The Théâtre Robin at the Boulevard du Temple where Henri Robin presented magic and scientific marvels to fascinated Parisians during the period 1862–9. The Rhumkorff coil and electrical discharge tubes are clearly in evidence.

Monsieur Felix Testot, a French conjurer and juggler, who performed throughout the British Isles from 1824 to 1845. This bill is for Dublin in 1825. Testot's descendants live in Britain and some have been associated with one of the few remaining Flea Circuses in the country.

Now then Ladies and Gemmen, here ye has Signora Diable Humbuggina, the most vonderfullest conjuress that ever vas seed at home or abroad. The most parfect Amphibrous, Nondescript Hannimal that vas ever seed before or behind. She has exhibited her Genus to all the crowned Potentates, and all the principlest Men in all Europe including the Day of Algiers von o'the best Judges in this here Universe. This here living vonder o'the world can conjure dunghill grubs into Knights of all sorts, ride a Donkey, a Lely, and her high horse at von and the same time. Sleep 46 days & nights under the same Tent vith a man, and never be wicious. She can play vise all the grace there ever vas. Columbine, Automaton, Pilgrim, or Dragon, and swallow all sorts of Spiruty liquors by the Gallon and never be the Vorserer — So now is the time before this most surprisingest exhibition closes. Blow the trumpet Denny — Valk up Ladies and Gemmen — Vy dont you blow Broom?

Here's your Works
All from Nature,
no connexion with the Jugglers.

Signora Diable Humbuggina now exhibiting with most astonishing Effect.

Solicit you in General

Ale and strong liquors Good Strong Caroline Brandy

Juggling taught in all its branches.

Books of the travels of this wonderfull Phenomenon to be had within.

CAROLINE FAIR, or MAT PUDDING and his MOUNTEBANK.

Why dang it I tell y' that ere business be all Impositioning like — Do na g'in, I mysel war taken in tother day; but blow my wig if I ha any more to do wi that shew like — do na g'in, It be all my eye and Betty-Martin or my neame beant

John Bull —

11

THEY ALSO CONJURED

When I am a man and can do as I wish,
With no one to ask if I may,
Although I'll play cricket a little, and fish
I'll conjure the most of each day.

E. V. Lucas, *A Little of Everything* (1912)

Conjuring has held a fascination for celebrities in many walks of life and some have become proficient practitioners of the art. Charles Dickens delighted in performing for his family and friends. Mrs Jane Carlyle, writing to her cousin, told of a show she had witnessed at Mrs Macready's home—'that excellent Dickens playing the Conjurer for one whole hour—the best conjurer I ever saw (and I have paid money to see several)'. The earliest record we have of Dickens as a performer appears in a letter he wrote on 3 December 1842 to Professor Felton in America:

The actuary of the national debt couldn't calculate the number of children who are coming here on Twelfth Night, in honor of Charlie's birthday, for which occasion I have provided a magic lantern and divers other tremendous engines of that nature. But best of all is that Forster and I have purchased between us the entire stock-in-trade of a conjuror, the practice and display whereof is entrusted to me. And O, my eyes, Felton, if you could see me conjuring the company's watches into impossible tea caddies and causing pieces of money to fly, and burning pocket handkerchiefs without

hurting 'em, and practising in my own room, without anybody to admire, you would never forget it as long as you live.[1]

It has been plausibly argued that Dickens's interest in conjuring was aroused four years earlier, when *Nicholas Nickleby* was first produced at the Hull Theatre Royal on 26 December 1838, for sharing the programme with the Dickens drama was Ramo Samee, the Celebrated East Indian juggler.[1] Memories of this well known performer surfaced when Dickens wrote an article titled 'An Unsettled Neighbourhood' in 1854, and remarked that Young Slaughter, who managed the business of greengrocer etc., 'was always lurking in the coal department, practising Ramo Samee with three potatoes'.[2]

The skills of Dickens as a conjurer were naturally appreciated by his friends, and he was greatly in demand for their parties and their children's birthday celebrations. When he was staying with his family in the Isle of Wight during the summer of 1849 an amusing magical extravaganza was mounted, which again fell back on and parodied Ramo Samee and colleagues such as Khia Khan Khruse in its billing.

CAROLINE FAIR, OR MAT PUDDING AND HIS MOUNTE-BANK, *a scurrilous attack on Queen Caroline published by G. Humphrey in 1821. Alderman Matthew Wood (1768–1843), friend and counsellor of the Queen, is depicted as a zany on the platform alongside Caroline who is masquerading as Signora Diable Humbuggina, a most wonderful conjuress.*

(overleaf)
Playbill for the first production of NICHOLAS NICKLEBY *at the Theatre Royal, Hull, in December 1838. The celebrated East Indian juggler Ramo Samee was on the programme, and it is believed that Charles Dickens' interest in magic was first aroused by seeing Ramo Samee's performance.*

THEATRE-ROYAL, HULL.

This present FRIDAY, December 28, 1838,

Will be produced, for the THIRD TIME, with Extensive Scenery, and Decorations, an entirely Original Ironical, Local Burletta of Men and Manners, in Two Acts, founded on the celebrated, widely-diffused, extensively-circulated, and universally-admired Papers by "**BOZ**," called

NICHOLAS NICKLEBY;

Or, Doings at Do-the-Boys Hall!

☞ *"It will be our aim, in the Life and Adventures of NICHOLAS NICKLEBY, to amuse by producing a rapid succession of characters and incidents, and describing them as cheerfully and pleasantly as in us lies; advancing thus much, he confidently hopes to enlist both their heartiest merriment and their kindliest sympathies."*—Publisher's Prospectus.

Mr Ralph Nickleby......Mr JOHNSON   Newman Noggs......Mr CRESWICK   Squeers......Mr H. MELLON
Nicholas Nickleby..........................Mr H. HOLL
Mantalini....(a Man Milliner)....Mr M. BARNETT   Smike.....Mrs. CRESWICK
Tix....Mr HOWELL   Scaly....Mr. CROUCH · Servant..Mr. SEYMOUR   Lord Verisopht..Mr. BUTLER
Col. Chowser.........Mr. HUNT   Sir Mulberry Hawk...........Mr ROGERS
John Browdie..(a Yorkshireman..Mr HERBERT   Mrs Nickleby...Miss MELVILLE   Kate....Mrs GURNER
Madame Mantalini......Mrs. BROOKS   Miss Knagg......Mrs. CROUCH   Miss Squeers......Mrs. HUNT
Miss Price........Mrs. H. MELLON   Mrs. Squeers......Miss ANDREWS   Miss Jones...... Miss HOWELL

ACT I.

SARCEN'S HEAD, SNOW HILL, ON A SNOWY MORNING.
THE JOURNEY.

Breakfast for Five—Delightful Prospect—Long Ride and Short Commons—The Yorkshire Pedagogue—The Introduction—Leave-taking—Good 'bye Mother!—Jump up—All right—The Highflyer starts for Yorkshire with "The Hero!"—"Over the Hills and far away."

Madame Mantalini's—The Fancy Dressmaker

First starting in the Wor'd—Dreadful Occupation—High Wages and Short Hours—Kate Nickleby's Introduction to the Man-Milliner—A Duck of a Man.

DO-THE-BOYS HALL, YORKSHIRE.
A WINTRY PROSPECT.

Victim of Avarice!—The Arrival—Nicholas' First Acquaintance with the Mistress of the House—Charming peculiarity of Mrs. Squeers—and brilliant Prospect at D— The Boys Hall—The Letter!—The Runaway.

WORK-ROOM AT MADAME MANTALINI'S.

Bonnet Building—Establishment for Young Ladies—The First Morning—Miss Naggs' Philanthrophy—A Nice Person—Sportive Endearments,—and Family Courtship of Mons. and Madame Mantalini—"Sure such a pair!"

SUNDAY PARLOUR, DO-THE-BOYS HALL!

The Disclosure!—Tender Propensities of Miss Squeers—"Oh! 'tis Love. 'tis love that rules the Camp"—Tea, Cards, and Turn Out—Two Pair of Lovers—Yorkshire Courtship—Jealousy, Race, and Sudden Break up—Ladies in Fits—Nicholas with his arms full—What the Devil shall I do with them.

School Room in the Classical and Commercial Academy
OF DO-THE-BOYS HALL.

N. B. Youth taken in and done for—Interesting Course of Education—Brimstone and Treacle—TABLEAUX—Now for Fuss—throw Physic to the Dogs—Practical Mode of Instructing the Squeerenian System, and Natural Logic—New Light—Injustice Detected !—Barbarous Usage of the Helpless Orphan, and Manly interference of Nicholas—Quarrel, Blow and Fight—Do-the-Boys Hall in an Uproar A Breaking up and Classical Row.

ACT II.—BARN AND ROAD-SIDE!

The Orphan Bey and his only Protector—The Journey to London—Unexpected Friend—A Full Purse and a Feeling Heart.

THE SHOW ROOM AT A FASHIONABLE MILLINER'S

A Touch at the Times—Improvidence, Extravagance—A legal Tender—Writ and Execution—Mantalini's Small Throat and Sharp Razor—A Dem'd Smash.

NEWMAN NOGGS' GARRET.

Scanty Cupboard, and Warm Welcome—Noggs at Home—A Lady's Letter—Indignation and Determination.

GOLDEN SQUARE.—Ralph NICKLEBY'S Counting House.

Upright Guardian—Pocket Book—Grateful Tenant and Benevolent Master—a Discovery—A Prison—What's good for the Man, good for the Master.

DRAWING ROOM AT RALPH NICKLEBY'S.
TABLEAU.

The Money-Lender's Soiree—Rooks and Pigeons—Kind Uncle—Unprotected Niece—Uninvited Guests—Villany and Avarice—and Happy Turn on the Fortunes of NICHOLAS NICKLEBY!!!

THE CELEBRATED EAST INDIAN
RAMO SAMEE,

Who performed before the Glass Curtain of the Victoria Theatre upwards of 100 Nights.

Will appear in the Full Costume of his Country, and go through his Beautiful

EVOLUTIONS WITH SEVERAL GOLDEN BALLS,

Throwing them in different Directions in the most splendid manner.

No person can have an idea of the dexterity of RAMO SAMEE's performance of the above without witnessing it.

Ramo Samee will shoot 12 Eastern Pigeons with his Magic Gun.

RAMO SAMEE will perform his astonishing Feat of

BUILDING A GRAND EASTERN CANOPY!

Which he manages by the movement of Twelve Porcupine Quills, from the Mouth to the Upper Lip, till the Canopy is beautifully erected, after which he will take out the Grand Supporter without the assistance of his hand, leaving the Porcupine Quills and the Canopy perfect, supported upon the Upper Lip.—THE

SPINNING OF THE HINDOO TOP,

Which he catches upon his hand, then placing the Top on the Brass Rod, three feet in length, the point of which is fully as sharp as a Needle; he will then balance it upon his chin, making his obedience to the Audience at the same time, after which he will go through several NEW TRICKS, peculiar to the Natives of his Country, and exhibited in England by himself. THE EXTRAORDINARY FEAT OF

Throwing a real 24 Pounder Cannon Ball,

In the course of which performance, he will throw the Ball between his Feet over his Head, catching it upon the bend of his Arm, he will throw the Ball from the Arm over the Head, and catch it upon the back of the Neck, and from the Neck to the Arm again; he will then throw the Ball round his Head without the assistance of his hands;

With many other Feats, too numerous to mention.

After which, a New Farce, Never Acted Here, written by Mr. Morris Barnett, of

DUCKS & DRAKES.

Marmalade.....................Mr. JOHNSON	Valet..........................Mr. GEORGE
Simon Brill..................Mr. CROUCH	Fisherman.....................Mr. SEYMOUR
Jeffrey Flounder.............Mr. HERBERT	
Grabbem.....................Mr. HOWELL	Polly Brill.................Mrs. CRESWICK
Compound....................Mr. ROGERS	Maid.........................Miss ANDREWS

To conclude with, a NEW FARCE, third time here, called The

BLUE JACKETS;
Or, Her Majesty's Service.

Admiral Trunnion, (a Port Admiral, rich and testy)............Mr. JOHNSON
Charles Herbert, (honourable and romantic) ....Mr. ROGERS
Ben Binnacle, (a superanuated seaman).........................Mr. HERBERT
Mr. Chaser, (an Invalided Master at Arms, Commanding the Bomb Shell).........Mr. CROUCH
Fanny Trunnion, (Daughter to the Admiral, alias Lieut. Firefly, of the Sky Rocket
Fire Ship, and Commander of the Blue Jackets)..Mrs. CRESWICK
Betsy Bodkin, (her Maid, alias Pitch and Tar, a Blue Jacket)......................Mrs. MELLON
Blue Jackets,....Mrs. CROUCH, Mrs. HUNT, Mrs. POWIS, Miss ANDREWS,
Miss MELVILLE and Miss HOWELL, who will go through

THE BROAD SWORD EXERCISE,
AND
DANCE A HORNPIPE OF EIGHT.

On MONDAY Evening December 31st. **FIRST APPEARANCE OF**

MR. SOAN,

Who made so decided a hit at the Theatre-Royal, Drury-Lane.

JANE SHORE.
MORE BLUNDERS THAN ONE.

Larry O'Hoolagan - - - - - - - Mr. SOAN.

RAMO SAMEE.
JIM CROW; or Life in New York.

Jim Crow - - - - - - - - Mr. SOAN

With the celebrated Song of "JUMP JIM CROW."

MORRIS BARNETT, Acting Manager.

PRICES.—Boxes, 3s. Second Price, 1s. 6d.—Pit, 2s. Second Price, 1s.—First Gallery, 1s. 6d
Second Price, 1s.—Upper Gallery, 1s. Second Price, 6d.
Children under Twelve Years of Age, HALF-PRICE at the Commencement.
Second Price to Commence at a Quarter before Nine.
Tickets and Places to be had of Mr. Holmes, at the Box-Office.
Doors to open at Half-past Six o'Clock, and the Performance to commence precisely at Seven.

ROBERT BROWN, PRINTER, PACKET-OFFICE, LOWGATE, HULL.

Khia Khan Khruse,

CHIEF OF THE INDIAN JUGGLERS,

Respectfully returns his most grateful thanks to the Ladies and Gentlemen of YORK for their kind support on a former occasion, and begs to inform them he will repeat his Performance, with a few additions, this present EVENING, when he will go through his much-admired, wonderful, and most interesting

JUGGLING,

AND

Feats of Agility,

In addition to which he will go through many new Feats, Magical Illusions and Experiments, which were never before witnessed in this place.

The admiration expressed by the first Surgeons and Anatomists, sufficiently point out the decided superiority of this truly wonderful Being, who will go through his

PROTEAN TRANSFORMATIONS;

Exhibiting some of the most surprising Evolutions, Serpentine Postures, &c. ever beheld,

WITH SWORDS, CHAIRS, PINS, &c,

With Seven Glasses of Wine upon his Forehead, and a Tumbler of Water upon his Chin,

HE WILL GO THROUGH A SMALL HOOP

Many different ways without disconcerting the position of the Glasses.

He will LIFT a QUART BOTTLE FULL of WATER by a STRAW! And carry it round among the Company to show there is no preparation or Trick in doing it.

CHINESE PERFORMANCES,

The Performer eats a quantity of cut Paper, blazing on Fire; he then draw from his mouth, at least one hundred Yards of white Ribbon, and afterwards as many of Red.

He will Swallow a Small Bell,

Which will be heard to Ring in various parts of his Body.——With

TEN SOLID BRASS RINGS,

In none of which any break can be discovered, he will perform very curious tricks; namely, separating and exhibiting them, handing them about separately for inspection among the visitors, and then at one touch, linking them together in various forms, sometimes like a Chain, a pair of Spectacles, a Globe, &c.; then with talismanic influence, shaking them asunder on the Floor.   The most extraordinary of all other deceptions is the

Swallowing Fifty Sewing Needles,

Which after remaining some time in the Throat, will be pulled out completely threaded. This Trick may be closely examined by all the Spectators, and is particularly recommended to the Knights of the Thimble, as being a novel and most extraordinary way of threading Needles.

Legerdemain

Explored in a variety of Juggling.

With Cards, Handkerchiefs, Rings, Cups, Money, &c.

Qualities of LIQUOR CHANGED,

Water, which may be first examined and tasted by the Company, shall be changed into Brandy, Rum, Hollands, or any liquor the company may please to command.

HE WILL PROVE HIS SUPERIORITY

By Blindfold Performance.

He will make the Cards march from the Pack one by one on the Floor ; change the colour of Sand, &c.; a Half-Crown pass from one Cup to another, at ten yards distance. He will make a certain Card leap from the Pack out of a curious Pedestal, with a variety of astonishing Tricks, too numerous to mention.

A certain Card, chosen from the Pack by any Person, and again replaced, shall then, as if by instinct, Leap from the Pack, and be shown at the top of a curious Pedestal.

HE WILL ALSO

Fry Bacon & Eggs upon a Sheet of common Writing Paper.

HE WILL PRODUCE A

Live Goldfinch,

That will perform several wonderful tricks, such as lying down, sitting down, and tumbling at the word of command   K. K. KHRUSE,

Will Catch in his Hand a marked Bullet from a Pistol,

Which any one may fire at him.——(Should this Trick be objected to, it will be omitted)

A New Grotesque

INDIAN DANCE,

In which he will divide himself into three parts, and personate three distinct characters at once.

TO CONCLUDE.

Stone of 8 Cwt.

BROKEN ON HIS BREAST!!!

Without any deception whatever, which he defies any one to discover.

Playbill for Khia Khan Khruse, Chief of the Indian Jugglers, whose juggling and conjuring performances probably influenced Charles Dickens in his choice of Rhia Rhama Roos as a nom de théâtre *for his drawing-room entertainment in 1849. This programme was at York, about 1816, fairly soon after the juggler had arrived in Britain.*

The Unparalleled Necromancer

RHIA RHAMA ROOS

Educated Cabalistically in the Orange Groves of Salamanca and the Ocean Caves of Alum Bay.

There followed amusing descriptions of six 'wonders' that were to be performed—the Leaping Card, The Pyramid, The Conflagration, the Loaf of Bread, The Travelling Doll and The Pudding. One example must suffice.

THE CONFLAGRATION WONDER

A Card being drawn from the Pack by any lady, not under a direct and positive promise of marriage, will be immediately named by the Necromancer, destroyed by fire, and reproduced from its own ashes.

∴ *An annuity of one thousand pounds has been offered to the Necromancer by the Directors of the Sun Fire Office for the secret of this wonder—and refused ! ! !*

His daughter Mamie enthusiastically recalled her father's performances[3] and her own interest was such that, at the time Colonel Stodare was presenting his sensational new Sphinx illusion at the Egyptian Hall (page 153), she exchanged letters with Dickens on the possible explanation of the mystery.[4]

Another man of letters who embraced the magic art was the poet Dr Oliver Goldsmith (1728–74). The evidence of his skill with coins is furnished by the dramatist and theatrical manager George Colman, the younger, who recounted the following episode which occurred in 1767:

I was only five years old when Goldsmith took me on his knee, while he was drinking coffee, one evening, with my father, and began to play with me; which amiable act I return'd with the ingratitude of a peevish brat, by giving him a very smart slap in the face; it must have been a tingler; for it left the marks of my little spiteful paw upon his cheek. This infantile outrage was follow'd by summary justice; I was lock'd up by my indignant father, in an adjoining room, to undergo solitary

Herr Adalbert Frikell (d. 1889), the son of a distinguished magical father, Wiljalba Frikell (1816–1903). Adalbert gave a Command performance at Sandringham on 8 January 1877 and appeared for three months in 1880 at the Egyptian Hall with Maskelyne & Cooke. A clumsy imposter borrowed his name during the period of his greatest success.

VICTORIA ROOMS, HARROGATE

4 NIGHTS ONLY !!!
Monday, Tuesday, Wednesday & Thursday, Aug. 5, 6, 7 & 8
Each Evening at Eight o'Clock.

Fashionable Morning Performance Tuesday & Thursday at 3
Doors open half-an-hour previous to commencement.

Reserved Seats 3s.   Unreserved Seats 2s.   Back Seats 1s.   Gallery 6d.
SCHOOLS & CHILDREN HALF-PRICE EXCEPT GALLERY
Tickets and places may be secured at Mr ACKRILL'S, Herald Office, and at the Hall.

HERR ADALBERT

FRIKELL

THE FAMOUS CONJUROR AND HUMORIST,
The First of Living Legerdemain Performers (Son of Wiljalba Frikell),
will give his Celebrated and Wonderful Entertainment of

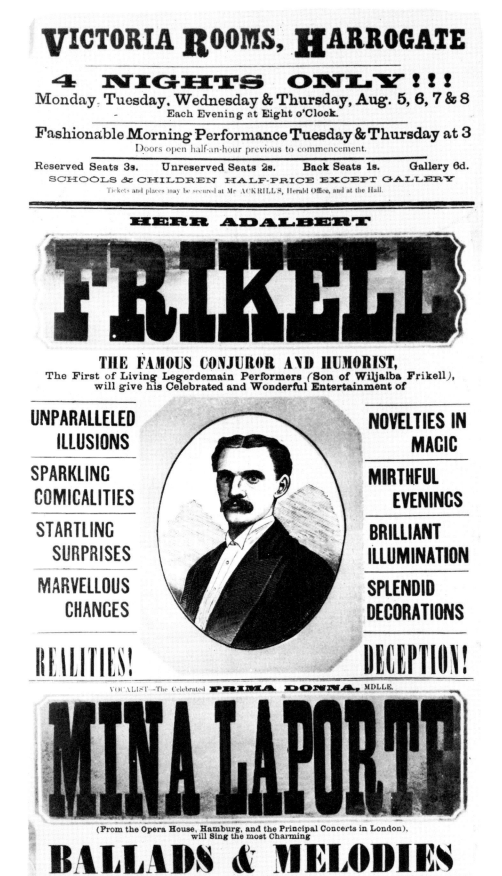

UNPARALLELED ILLUSIONS	**NOVELTIES IN MAGIC**
SPARKLING COMICALITIES	**MIRTHFUL EVENINGS**
STARTLING SURPRISES	**BRILLIANT ILLUMINATION**
MARVELLOUS CHANGES	**SPLENDID DECORATIONS**

REALITIES!   DECEPTION!

VOCALIST —The Celebrated **PRIMA DONNA,** MDLLE.

MINA LAPORTE

(From the Opera House, Hamburg, and the Principal Concerts in London),
will Sing the most Charming

BALLADS & MELODIES

imprisonment, in the dark. Here I began to howl and scream, most abominably; which was no bad step towards liberation, since those who were not inclined to pity me might be likely to set me free, for the purpose of abating a nuisance.

At length a generous friend appear'd to extricate me from jeopardy; and that generous friend was no other than the man I had so wantonly molested, by assault and battery; it was the tender-hearted Doctor himself, with a lighted candle in his hand, and a smile upon his countenance, which was still partially red, from the effects of my petulance. I sulk'd and sobb'd, and he fondled and sooth'd; till I began to brighten. Goldsmith, who, in regard to children, was like the Village Preacher he has so beautifully described, for

'Their welfare pleased him, and their
cares distress'd'

seized the propitious moment of returning good-humour; so he put down the candle, and began to conjure. He placed three hats, which happen'd to be in the room, upon the carpet, and a shilling under each: the shillings, he told me, were England, France, and Spain. 'Hey, presto, cockolorum!' cried the Doctor, and, Lo! on uncovering the shillings which had been dispersed, each beneath a separate hat, they were all found congregated under one. I was no Politician at five years old, and, therefore, might not have wonder'd at the sudden revolution which brought England, France and Spain, all under one Crown; but, as I was also no Conjuror, it amazed me beyond measure. Astonishment might have amounted to awe for one who appear'd to me gifted with the power of performing miracles if the good-nature of the man had not obviated my dread of the magician; but, from that time, whenever the Doctor came to visit my father

'I pluck'd his gown, to share the good
man's smile;'

a game at romps constantly ensued, and we were always cordial friends, and merry play-fellows.[5]

Sir William S. Gilbert, the lyricist of the Savoy Operas, was a very competent conjurer and his pre-occupation with magic philtres, love potions and the like was much in evidence in some of the opera plots. His biographers remarked: 'Gilbert was at one time an admirable conjurer, and bought many books on the art of conjuring, which he apparently read to

good purpose . . . It may be worth noting the rather remarkable common tastes of Gilbert and Dickens, whom he loved so well. Both were excellent conjurers, and both were childlike in their love of acting and dressing up.'[6] It has been claimed also that Gilbert met Houdini when the escape king first came to Britain and that 'Gilbert then excelled in pure dexterous rope manoeuvres and escapes'.[7] One can only observe that, if such an encounter did occur, it seems unusual and most uncharacteristic that the American did not capitalize on his meeting with such a famous person. Or did perhaps Gilbert, with his renowned and pungent wit, pass some comment that the young Houdini failed to appreciate?

It is illuminating that, following Gilbert's visit to Brighton in 1878, the following staccato entry appeared in his diary for 18 February:

Went to Frikell [conjurer] in evening—atrocious entertainment—left when half over—atmosphere putrid.[8]

The recipient of Gilbert's barb was apparently Adalbert Frikell who, barely a year earlier on 8 January 1877, had given a command performance at Sandringham. However, there was at least one imitator who 'borrowed' Frikell's name—and, since the latter, the son of a distinguished conjurer Wiljalba Frikell (1816–1903), was acknowledged to be an excellent performer, it seems possible that the critical diarist saw an inferior plagiarist. Gilbert's second opera, *The Sorcerer*, had made its début at the Opera-Comique only three months before his visit to Brighton, and perhaps 'Frikell' did not measure up to George Grossmith as John Wellington Wells, 'the dealer in magic and spells'. Certain it is that Frikell would not be purveying Oxy-Hydrogen Love-at-first-sight Philtre in four-and-a-half and nine gallon casks!

There is a depth of fellow-feeling for the conjurer, however, when Gilbert, in *Princess Ida*, has Cyril inquire:

*Are you indeed that Lady Psyche, who
At children's parties drove the conjurer wild,
Explaining all his tricks before he did them?*

as many a children's entertainer can testify!

One novelist who became a member of the Magician's Club of London certainly did meet Houdini. Sax Rohmer (Arthur Henry Ward, 1883–1959) had a great interest in the occult and it was his work *The Romance of Sorcery* (1914) that brought them together. Houdini wrote to Rohmer to say how much he had enjoyed the book and that he hoped they would meet. However, the First World War intervened and it was not until late 1919, when the novelist made his first trip to the USA, that he and Houdini finally met. There was mutual attraction and it was Houdini who aroused Rohmer's interest in conjuring and illusion, and so widened the fascination he had previously reserved for the occult. Their friendship was firmly cemented when Houdini helped Rohmer out of an impossible situation that had been created by an error of writing in a serial story for *Collier's Weekly;* the magician suggested a way out of the impasse and got Rohmer 'off the hook'.[9, 10]

After Houdini's death, when Sir Arthur Conan Doyle attacked the illusionist in print for his persecution of spiritualists and simultaneously attributed his remarkable escapes to psychic powers,[11] Rohmer sprang to Houdini's defence and, in consequence, his previously cordial relationship with Doyle became rather strained. The memory of Houdini clearly remained a vivid one for Rohmer and thus, some eleven years after the escapologist's death, he wrote a series of short stories about a master illusionist called Bazarada, as a tribute to Harry.[12]

Charles Lutwidge Dodgson (1832–98), the Oxford don who attained greater fame as Lewis Carroll, the creator of *Alice in Wonderland*, than as a lecturer in mathematics, was also a clever conjurer. As a boy, living at Croft Rectory on Tees-side, he would dress up in a long white robe and a brown wig to amaze his audiences. Puppetry likewise claimed his attention and, with the help of the family and the village carpenter, he constructed a marionette theatre for the presentation of plays which he himself wrote.[13]

Mr W. H. Cremer's Saloon of Magic was situated variously at 27 New Bond Street and 210 Regent Street, London, where both amateur and professional conjurers could purchase equipment and requisites. Lewis Carroll was frequently a customer on his visits to London.

Carroll's fascination with conjuring is clearly discernible in the fantasy of *Alice in Wonderland*, which employs a series of conjuring motifs such as a White Rabbit and a watch in the course of its intriguing narrative. John Fisher, in a masterly analysis of the influence of magic on the tale,[14] has spotlighted 6 April 1863 as the key to much of this fantasy. Carroll was then spending a few days at Cheltenham, and the entry for his diary records a rainy day which ended with a party going in the evening to see 'Herr Döbler, a conjurer'.[15] This individual was almost certainly George Buck (1836–1904) of Bristol, an excellent sleight-of-hand performer. Buck had appropriated the name of an internationally famous Viennese conjurer, Ludwig Leopold Döbler, a superb artiste, who had played with enormous success in Britain in 1842, retired from the stage in 1848 and died in 1864. While the local papers did not announce Döbler's presence in Cheltenham on that particular night, they did advertise Professor Pepper's appearance at the Assembly Rooms[14] with his famous Ghost illusion (page 88) and, since Buck subsequently billed himself as a pupil of Professor Pepper, it is not inconceivable that he was associated with Pepper's show.

The thesis developed by Fisher is that Carroll's introduction to the Pepper's Ghost illusion gave new horizons to his vivid imagination and surely catalysed *Through the Looking Glass*, with the mirror as the central theme of the book. Certainly it generated two additional chapters in *Alice in Wonderland* which were added after Carroll had been to Cheltenham.[16] These were 'A Mad Tea Party' and 'Pig and Pepper', and the latter, as well as including a highly significant name in its title, embraced the Cheshire Cat which 'vanished quite slowly, beginning with the end of the tail, and ending with the grin'—a lovely description of the Ghost effect!

Carroll's diary indicates also that he visited the Egyptian Hall on Saturday 24 June 1876 to see Maskelyne and Cooke who were then exhibiting Psycho (page 162). His familiarity with the motive power of the Chess Playing Automaton of de Kempelen (1734–1804) led him erroneously to assume that a dwarf was concealed within. The spiritualist seance Carroll found astonishing, and he records that Lord Westmorland was the volunteer to be shut up in the cabinet.[17]

Isambard Kingdom Brunel (1806–59), the famous engineer of the Great Western Railway and architect of the ill fated *Great Britain* paddle steamship, was an amateur conjurer, at least until the time when a most unfortunate contretemps with a coin trick almost cut short his career.[18],[19] He was at the very height of his fame when, on 3 April 1843, he was amusing his children with the feat of passing a half-sovereign from his ear to his mouth, and the duplicate coin concealed in his mouth slid down his throat. There the coin remained for six weeks despite increasing efforts to dislodge it and the attendance of Sir Benjamin Brodie, the eminent surgeon and physician to Queen Victoria.

The news of the accident spread through London like wildfire, causing much dismay. Brunel meanwhile developed a cough, which Brodie believed was due to the coin having passed into the trachea. In consultation with the surgeon, Brunel designed a special pair of forceps, two feet in length, which afterwards became known in the profession as 'Brodie's forceps.' A tracheotomy was performed but the surgeon's attempts to remove the coin proved unsuccessful.

The resourceful engineer then hit on the idea of using centrifugal force to dislodge the coin. Brunel rapidly sketched out an apparatus consisting of a board pivoted between two uprights, to which he could be strapped, and then rapidly revolved head over heels.

The equipment was quickly made, but the first attempt to dislodge the coin brought on such a paroxysm of coughing that it was feared he would expire; however, this subsided and, on 13 May, Brunel directed that the frame should again be tried. This time it was successful: the coin shifted and fell from his mouth. To his friend Captain Claxton of Bristol he wrote that evening: 'At four $\frac{1}{2}$, I was safely and comfortably delivered of my little coin; with hardly an effort it dropped out, as many another has, and I hope will, drop out of my fingers.'

This incident had aroused such national concern that when, that same afternoon, Macaulay called at Brunel's home in Duke Street, Westminster, and

Conjuring table and apparatus of the Victorian era as depicted by Henry Novra whose Magical Repository was established at 95 Regent Street, London, in 1844. When Charles Dickens and Forster bought the entire stock-in-trade of a conjurer in 1842 no doubt that worthy would repair smartly to a similar repository, possibly that of W. H. M. Crambrook who issued the first known magical catalogue.

learned the happy news, he raced off to the Athenaeum and ran through the august Club yelling: 'It's out! It's out!'—without incurring any displeasure, for everyone knew, without question, to what he referred.

Richard Barham has immortalized this unfortunate episode in *The Ingoldsby Legends* where, in 'The House-Warming' we read:

All conjuring's bad! They may get in a scrape
Before they're aware, and whatever its shape,
They may find it no easy affair to escape.
It's not everybody that comes off so well
From leger de main tricks as Mr Brunel.

There is no record of whether Brunel ever repeated this particular trick or, indeed, of him giving any subsequent conjuring performance!

Ionia, the Goddess of Mystery, was the younger daughter of Charles De Vere, the Parisian magic dealer, and his wife Okita. Ionia's spectacular illusion act opened in 1911 at the Hippodrome, Birmingham, and subsequently toured Britain and the continent of Europe. She was in Moscow in 1917 at the time of the Revolution, when her show was pillaged, and she spent three months in the cellar of her hotel.

12
EGYPT AND THE SPHINX

Mark ye this, ye breakers of images, that in
one regard, the stone idol bears awful semblance
of Deity—unchangefulness in the midst of change—
the same seeming will and intent for ever and
ever inexorable! You dare not mock at the
Sphynx.

A. W. Kinglake, *Eothen* (1844)

During the last three decades of the nineteenth century one place in England above all others was uniquely associated with magic, a place redolent of mystery, a place that simultaneously enchanted and indelibly impressed all those fortunate enough to enter its portals. Conspicuous by its alien appearance, it stood proudly on the south side of Piccadilly— The Egyptian Hall, England's Home of Mystery— with its exotic entrance prosaically flanked by a provision merchant and a homœopathic chemist. There, from 1873 until its demolition in 1905, Maskelyne and Cooke purveyed magic and illusions on the grand scale; indeed their very names *were* magic to generations of Victorians.[1] Yet they were not the first to exhibit wonders on these premises for the Egyptian Hall had had a long and honourable history of entertainment, perhaps remarkably in view of the fact it was erected by William Bullock in 1812 with the laudable object of educating the masses whilst incidentally lining his own pockets. It was built to house the museum that he had previously exhibited at 22 Piccadilly.[2]

Bullock was a Liverpool silversmith and jeweller who, through his contacts with seafaring men, was able to sustain an interest in natural history by purchasing from them various curios and specimens, including some reputed to have been brought back from Captain James Cook's voyages. Between 1795 and 1809 he exhibited his collection on Merseyside and then, after augmenting it with purchases from the Leverian Museum, decided to move it to the

Metropolis. The premises at 22 Piccadilly, already familiar to us from the exhibitions and entertainments of Katterfelto and Astley, now housed Bullock's Liverpool Museum which quickly became the focus of fashionable London and, in consequence, a great attraction for everyone. So popular did it become that Bullock commissioned the noted architect Peter Frederick Robinson to design a museum for him to occupy a site at 170–2 Piccadilly. Robinson, whose later work included the Swiss Cottage at St John's Wood, designed a building in the Egyptian style embodying a facade ornamented with two huge Coade stone statues of Isis and Osiris, a cornice surmounted by two outward-facing sphinxes and a tablet bearing a scarab. Another tablet proclaimed LONDON MUSEUM, yet Bullock referred to the building as the Egyptian Temple and, almost inevitably, the public called it the Egyptian Hall. There were shops on the ground floor which were occupied initially by a bookseller and by Richard Reece, a physician and herbalist who called his premises the Medical Hall.

The building opened in the spring of 1812. The new edifice was not aesthetically pleasing to everyone. Leigh Hunt observed that its absurdity rendered it a good advertisement and said: 'It gives a blow to the mind, like a heavy practical joke.'[3] But the joke was certainly not on Bullock, who brought his flair for showmanship into play to aid the scientific arrangement of the exhibits and to produce, for the first time in England, museum specimens arranged in their natural or habitat groups. He claimed to possess

about fifteen thousand exhibits that had cost him £30,000.

In 1815–16 Bullock added a Roman Gallery for the display of classical art he had acquired from Italy, and also mounted a highly profitable exhibition of Napoleon's field carriage, which had been captured after the Battle of Waterloo. He secured this vehicle from the Prince Regent for £2,500; what General Blücher, who had brought it to England to present to the Prince, thought of the deal is not on record.[4] The crowds swarmed to the Egyptian Hall to view the carriage, some ten thousand a day, and the result of an overwhelming case of 'Napoleonitis' that infected the British nation was a return of £35,000 for Bullock. It proved too financially successful, however, for the future of the Museum, which subsequently could not match such spectacular returns; and in 1819 he auctioned the contents, after first endeavouring to sell them to the University of Edinburgh and to the British Museum. The sale lasted twenty-six days, at the end of which Bullock had realized only £9,974 13s.[5] The way was now open for the Egyptian Hall to become a suite of exhibition and sale rooms and, for the next fifty years or so, to attract as diverse a procession of showmen, artists, lecturers, freaks and entertainers as ever graced the London scene.

The first conjurer to appear at the Egyptian Hall did not, however, do so in that guise, for a more illustrious mantle had fallen upon his broad shoulders since the days when he had been a familiar and imposing figure at the fairs, taverns and theatres throughout the British Isles. Giovanni Battista Belzoni arrived at the Egyptian Hall in 1821, appropriately enough as an Egyptian explorer and traveller, exhibiting examples of Egyptian art and a facsimile model of two chambers of the tomb of Seti I, which he had opened and explored in 1817. His career is a romantic and fascinating one by any standards.[6, 7, 8] He was born at Padua in Italy in 1778, the son of a barber, and left home at the age of sixteen to work in Rome, possibly initially at his father's trade. For a period he entered a monastery, where he was able to make good some of the deficiencies in his education and to learn the principles of hydraulics. The idea of a monastic life seems not to have appealed for long to this handsome young man of remarkable stature and physique—he was about six feet six inches tall, and broad in proportion. So, seeking adventure, he travelled around Europe with his brother Francesco, finally arriving in England in 1803. Giovanni soon found an English wife, Sarah, who henceforth devotedly shared his adventures.

At Sadler's Wells Theatre on Easter Monday, 11 April 1803, Signor Belzoni made his first appearance in England as the Giant Cormorant in a serio-comic pantomime called *Fee! Faw! Fum! or Jack the Giant Killer*. He was in good company: Charles Dibdin Junior had written and produced the piece, which included the renowned Grimaldi and Jack Bologna, the famous harlequin, in its cast. Belzoni's rôle was essentially that of the speciality act, a feature of pantomime retained to the present day. Billed as 'The Patagonian Samson', he presented a strongman act which was climaxed by a most impressive feat unique to himself. Having donned an iron frame fitted with ledges and weighing over a hundredweight, he then took up and arranged eleven men on this structure and, thus encumbered, he moved around the stage in an easy, graceful manner, waving a flag in each hand.

Considerable uncertainty surrounds Belzoni's rôle in the introduction of aquatic effects at Sadler's Wells in June 1803. Whether his previous knowledge of hydraulics was adequate to sustain an innovatory lead, or whether he learned much from seeing others construct the Exhibition of Hydraulics that Dibdin presented as *Fire and Water*, and for which Bologna devised a spectacular display of fountains and coloured fire, must remain conjecture.

However, the tank that was installed beneath the stage became the scene of an unexpected addition to the programme. One evening, as Belzoni was carrying his human pyramid around the stage, the boards gave way under the enormous weight and cast the strong man, his passengers, harness and all into the deep waters. A commendable rescue operation was executed by the stage hands, and a dripping, wet giant took his bow with solemn if somewhat dampened dignity.

After several months at Sadler's Wells, playing some small parts in addition to his feats of strength, Belzoni embarked upon the life of an itinerant showman for the next ten years, appearing in most

Giovanni Battista Belzoni (1778–1823), strong man, conjurer and Egyptologist. In the guise of the Patagonian Samson he appeared at Sadler's Wells Theatre in 1803, shortly after his arrival in Britain.

parts of the British Isles. Quite early in his career he was visited by Thomas Smith, a former keeper of Prints and Drawings at the British Museum, who committed to his volume *A Book for a Rainy Day*[9] a colourful description of his encounter with Young Hercules in the booth of Gyngell, the conjurer, at Bartholomew Fair.

The gorgeous splendour of his Oriental dress was rendered more conspicuous by an immense plume of white feathers which were, like the noddings of an undertaker's horse, increased in their wavy and graceful motion by the movements of the wearer's head. As this extraordinary man was to perform some wonderful feats of strength, we joined the motley throng of spectators at the charge of only threepence each.

After he had gone through his various exhibitions of holding great weights at arm's length etc. the all-bespangled master of the show stepped forward and stated to the audience that if any four or five of the present company would give, by way of encouraging the 'Young Hercules', alias the 'Patagonian Samson', sixpence apiece, he would carry them all together round the booth in the form of a pyramid.

With this proposition my companion and myself closed and after two other persons had advanced the fine fellow then threw off his velvet cap surmounted by its princely crest, stripped himself of his other gewgaws and walked most majestically, in a flesh-coloured elastic dress, to the centre of the amphitheatre, where four chairs were placed round him by which my friend and I ascended, and after throwing our legs across his lusty shoulders, were further requested to embrace each other which we no sooner did, cheek-by-jowl, than a tall skeleton of a man, instead of standing upon a small wooden ledge fastened to Samson's girdle, in an instant leaped on his back with the agility of a boy who pitches himself upon a post too high to clear, and threw a leg over each of our shoulders; as for the other chap (for we could only muster four) the Patagonian took him up in his arms. Then, after Mr Merryman had removed the chairs, as he had not his full complement, Samson performed the task with an ease of step most stately without either the beat of a drum or the waving of a flag.

Belzoni was booked by John Astley, son of the famous Philip, for the Christmas season of 1803–4, opening on Boxing Day, at the Royalty Theatre.

Astley's Amphitheatre was currently being rebuilt, following the disastrous fire that had destroyed it. So Belzoni continued there until 21 January, presenting 'a most curious Exhibition of Hydraulicks', which presumably derived from his Sadler's Wells experience, besides his customary feats of strength. He was thus yet another carrying on the 'waterworks' tradition that had been established by Henry Winstanley's Water Theatre just a century before. Belzoni's expertise in creating hydraulic spectacles was undoubtedly exploited in various theatres in Britain during the following years, augmenting the rather limited scope that the strong-man act provided for securing a living and which necessitated his nomadic existence. There are various references to Belzoni which enable his travels to be sketchily outlined, and his fairly regular appearances at Bartholomew Fair established.

Belzoni in his rôle of conjurer had emerged by 1812 for, on 24 February, he was at the Theatre in Patrick Street, Cork,[10] announcing that it was positively and definitely the last night of his representations 'when he will introduce a FEAT OF LEGERDEMAIN which he flatters himself will astonish the Spectators, as such a feat never was attempted in Great Britain or Ireland. After a number of Entertainments, he will

CUT
A Man's Head Off ! !
And put it on again ! ! !'

As showman's licence, we may excuse him for overlooking the ancient lineage of the decapitation illusion, going back beyond Scot's first explanation of the feat in 1584. The statement on the bill that this last night is 'by the request of his Friends', and for one night only (even though two nights more had been announced), suggests that he had outstayed his welcome in Cork.

The following 26 February, Belzoni was in Oxford, the City of the Dreaming Spires, performing at the Blue Boar Inn, St Aldate's, 'By Permission of the Rev. the Vice-Chancellor and the Worshipful the Mayor'. His fulsome playbill opened in rather obsequious fashion:
Strongly impressed with a due sense of gratitude for the very favourable reception he has experienced from the Noblemen and Gentlemen of the University, humbly returns his most sincere thanks, and respectfully begs leave to acquaint them, that on the above Evening he will repeat his Novel

Performance, when no exertion shall be wanting to render it worthy of their notice.

The Performance will commence with
THE GRAND SULTAN
OF ALL THE CONJURORS
Who, for this Evening, will disclose the manner in which some of the most intricate tricks are performed in the Art of Legerdemain

SIGNOR BELZONI
will perform several Italian, Scotch, English and Irish Airs, on his
MUSICAL GLASSES
Hitherto not performed here

After which he will introduce his celebrated Scene, the Delineations of LE BRUN'S
PASSIONS OF THE SOUL

———————

THE ROMAN HERCULES
Will display several striking Attitudes, from the most admired antique Statues; among others, The Celebrated Fighting Gladiators; With interesting Groupes from the Labours of Hercules—The Instructions of Achilles—and other Classical Subjects; uniting Grace and Expression with Muscular Strength. To conclude with the truly amazing Herculean feat of CARRYING
A GROUPE OF SEVEN MEN
During which he will play Two Flags, with the greatest Facility. As a proof of his muscular strength he will lift up a FIRELOCK, 14 pounds weight, by the muzzle, at Arm's Length, with Two additional Pounds Weight at the But End

The whole to conclude with a Grand and Brilliant Display of OPTICAL ILLUSIONS (never performed here) entitled the
AGGRESCOPIUS
Which Signor Belzoni has brought to the greatest perfection. The objects which are represented in this Optical Illusion will change their postures, and so far will they seem animated to the Spectator, that some of them will actually change their countenances.

Admission was two shillings and six pence; the show started at half-past six and ran, according to the bill, for precisely two and a half hours.

One undergraduate member of Belzoni's Oxford audience wrote, some fifty years later[11] and with the wisdom of hindsight: 'Well do I recollect Belzoni, even at this distance of time—his lofty stature, his youthful, pleasing, and even genteel appearance, which caused much speculation in my mind as well as in that of others, who and what he could be, and how such a person could be a mere *conjuror and showman.*' This patronizing remark places in sharp focus the low esteem in which the contemporary itinerant performer was then held and, it seems fair to say, not only by Oxford undergraduates. The sentiments fully vindicate Belzoni's subsequent reticence about, and efforts to conceal, his showman origins when, barely seven years later, he returned from Egypt a comparatively wealthy and famous man.

This same erstwhile undergraduate, who signed himself 'I.W.', also recalled an amusing incident during Belzoni's performance. Some of the younger members of the University, who, in the time-honoured fashion, had imbibed too freely, presuming upon the showman's apparent youth and modesty, put forward one of their number to create a general diversion and confusion by slyly extinguishing the lights. Belzoni, perceiving what was intended, said very quietly and civilly to the young blood, 'Sir, I will trouble you not to meddle with the candles.' Discretion was undoubtedly the better part of valour when confronted by the Patagonian Samson, and the showman had no further trouble!

Soon after his Oxford appearance, Belzoni and his wife left Britain for Lisbon, where his thespian activities continued, and he travelled between Portugal and Spain until the Peninsular War ended and Napoleon was banished to Elba. This signal event also marked Belzoni's renouncement of the theatre and the start of his new adventures. To Egypt he went in 1815, ostensibly to make his fortune by instructing Muhammed Ali and the populace in the techniques for raising water to irrigate their parched lands. By all accounts the Egyptians were not particularly receptive to his wares and, in difficulties, he then had the bright idea to approach Henry Salt, the British Consul General, who, before taking up his post that year, had been urged by Sir Joseph Banks, President of the Royal Society and a Trustee of the British Museum, to collect Egyptian antiquities for that institution. Belzoni was signed on and used his skills and influence with the natives to bring the famous head of Rameses II, Young Memnon, from Thebes to ship-

PALAIS ROYAL,
Argyll Street, Oxford Circus, W.
WONDERFUL
TALKING

MACHINE

The Exhibition is not limited to simple talking, but is enhanced by an explanatory description of the method of producing the various sounds, words, and sentences, visitors also being allowed to inspect every part of the Machine. It is not only interesting to the Scientific as illustrating the theory of acoustics, but to the public in general, and especially to the young,—to whom it offers an inexhaustible fund of wonder and amusement.

EXHIBITING HOURLY. From 12 noon, till 10 p.m.
Admission, 1s.   Reserved Seats, 2s.   Children, 6d.

Euphonia, or the Wonderful Talking Machine, was exhibited by Professor Faber of Freiburg at the Palais Royal and Egyptian Hall. Despite the approval of the Duke of Wellington, it was not a success.

board for London. Subsequent to this triumph, he spent the next three years exploring and excavating, discovering the buried temple of Abu-Simbel and the valley of the Royal Tombs, opening the grotto-sepulchre of Seti I and the second pyramid of Gizeh.

The showman turned greatest Egyptologist of his day returned to London in 1820 with his treasures and, to herald his forthcoming exhibition at the Egyptian Hall, published his *Narrative of the*

Operations and Recent Discoveries within the Pyramids, Temples, Tombs, and Excavations, in Egypt and Nubia.[12] The following year, on 1 May, the Exhibition opened and was a huge success, the event coinciding with and benefiting from the crowds of influential people who were in London for the coronation of George IV. There were 1,900 visitors on the first day, paying half-a-crown each.

The Great Hall of the Egyptian Hall housed a 1:6 scale model of Seti's tomb; there was a 1:12 wax model of the second pyramid; and, together with a profusion of artifacts, they comprised a brilliant presentation of ancient Egypt for the British public. The exhibition continued for just over a year and then, in June 1822, the contents were sold at auction.

In the autumn of 1823 Belzoni was restless for new adventures and set out on a voyage of exploration to Timbuktu. He was traversing Benin with the King's permission when, stricken with dysentery, he died at Gato on 3 December 1823. So ended the saga of the first conjurer who appeared at the Egyptian Hall, yet not as a mystifier but as a famous Egyptologist. The many mystifiers who followed Belzoni's steps to the Egyptian Hall during the nineteenth century did not need to hide their prestidigitatorial prowess under any such bushel, however illustrious it might be.

Belzoni's name was happily, if rather fictitiously, perpetuated by John Henry Anderson, the Wizard of the North, when his programmes for 1846 announced 'The Grand Egyptian Feat, entitled THE BELZONIAN CREATION. Water, Fruit, Flowers, Birds, Quadrupeds and Fish, in their Chrystal Fountains— all Produced from Nothing!' Anderson's billing matter claimed that this feat was originally discovered by Belzoni who, during his sojourn in Egypt, became acquainted with several of the greatest Egyptian necromancers, but, although on the most friendly terms, they would not divulge to him the secret of the trick. Yet 'by that indefatigable perseverance, which was characteristic of this truly great man, he at last discovered the Secret, and to the no small surprise of the Eastern Magicians, performed it before the Pacha in Alexandria'. How did Anderson come by this great secret? By mere accident. At an Old Book Stand, he purchased an old Scrap Book of Belzoni's in which the whole mystery was revealed! A good story with which to clothe a production trick, and Anderson never let veracity interfere with his aggressive advertising technique. Interestingly, so far as records tell, Anderson himself never appeared at the Egyptian Hall during almost

The Egyptian Hall, Piccadilly, with General Tom Thumb's miniature coach and ponies at the entrance.

forty years as a professional conjurer. However, according to one source,[8] Jack Bologna, the once-famed Harlequin who had trod the Sadlers Wells boards with Belzoni in 1803, in his later years served as a black-faced assistant to Anderson.

In 1832 an exhibition at the Egyptian Hall of the Royal Clarence Vase, 'capable of containing 5,400 bottles of wine'[13] gave way to the Double-Sighted Scotch Youth—a purely coincidental juxtaposition! Young Louis Gordon M'Kean's double vision was attributable not to alcohol but to clairvoyance, and his showbills claimed that, although blindfolded and seated with his back to the audience, he could distinguish colour, read either print or manuscript, tell the hour of the day on a watch or declare any other fact 'as precisely as the clearest sighted person'. Members of the company could produce coins, keys or trinkets of any description and he would instantly tell them how many there were, whether composed of gold, silver, brass or copper and the dates and values of the coins. He was succeeded in 1845 at the Egyptian Hall by another apparently paranormal individual, 'The Mysterious Lady', whose impact was immediate and dramatic. She, too, presented her back to the spectators but never revealed her face. Contemporary reports tell of her naming the spots upon dice, cards held at considerable distance from her, where she could have no possibility of seeing them in the normal way, and of repeating accurately words whispered to the gentleman in the audience who conducted the proceedings. It was impressive then and is still impressive today when carried out swiftly and surely.

Hard on the heels of the Mysterious Lady, in the summer of 1846, came Professor Faber of Freiburg, with his Euphonia, a genuine talking machine that did not rely on the voice of a hidden accomplice. The torso of a figure (referred to in contemporary reports as a Turk, although the illustration in *The Illustrated London News* scarcely bears this out[14]) rested on a table, with draperies to conceal the mechanism by which his voice was produced. The Professor sat at an adjoining keyboard and was able to regulate the supply of air to a bellows, which served as lungs, and to control the action of a rubber tube (trachea), rubber ligaments or ivory reed (larynx) and the movable jaw, to produce a semblance of the human voice. The machine could converse haltingly in English, French, German, Latin and Greek and, after a few introductory sentences, the spectators were invited to request the Turk to speak whatever words or phrases they chose.

The show was not a success, despite the approbation of that inveterate exhibition-goer, the Duke of Wellington, who, having initially suspected that ventriloquism was the *modus operandi*, was instructed in the operation of the machine and with creditable results. Thereupon he certified that it was an extraordinary production of mechanical genius. Faber's exhibition was, in fact, introduced to Britain from the USA by Barnum, although presented at the Egyptian Hall by his agent.[15]

General Tom Thumb (1838–83), the US midget Charles S. Stratton, was six years old when impresario Phineas T. Barnum first brought him to Britain in 1844.[16] They set up an exhibition at the Egyptian Hall and, following an audience with Queen Victoria at Buckingham Palace on 23 March, the great British public flocked to see the manikin who so intrigued Her Majesty. Barnum was thus poised to repeat his earlier New York triumphs with the little fellow. The fascination that the midget obviously held for the Queen possibly derived from the former practice of having Court dwarfs; be that as it may, Tom Thumb was commanded to appear on two further occasions within a month and the seal was set on fashionable London, despite the sardonic commentary by *Punch*:[17]

We had only to reflect upon the countless acts of patronage towards the arts and sciences—had only to remember a few of the numerous personal condescensions of the Queen towards men of letters, artists and philosophers—to be assured that Tom Thumb would be welcomed with that graceful cordiality which has heretofore made Buckingham Palace and Windsor Castle the homes of poetry and science. Continental monarchs stop short in their royal favours at full-grown authors and artists; but the enthusiasm of Her Majesty Queen Victoria, not content with showering all sorts of favours and rewards upon the literary and artistic spirits of her own country and age, lavishes with prodigal hand most delicate honours upon an American Tom Thumb whose outstanding genius it is to measure in his boots five-and-twenty inches!

There were many more attacks in a similar vein by *Punch*, and, as they all linked Tom Thumb with Queen Victoria, their publicity value to Barnum was inestimable for the social cachet attached, and not solely on the principle that it doesn't matter what they say so long as they are writing about you.

Tom Thumb's appearances at the Egyptian Hall ended on 20 July 1844 and were followed by a tour of the provinces and a visit to Paris, which lasted until December 1845, when he returned to London. During Christmas week he made a farewell appearance at the Egyptian Hall and people had to be turned away. A series of provincial appearances had been arranged by Barnum prior to their return to the USA but, scenting still greater rewards, Barnum booked a room at the Egyptian Hall for another series of farewell lectures to commence on Easter Monday 1846. Unwittingly he set the scenario for a macabre event.

Benjamin Robert Haydon, the artist, had also secured a room at the Egyptian Hall from Easter Monday to hold an exhibition of his latest works, *The Banishment of Arisitides* and *The Burning of Rome*. He was hoping to emulate his triumph of 1820 when, in the same locale, and with canvases which included *Christ's Triumphal Entry into Jerusalem*, he made a profit of almost £1,300. While Haydon's practice of showing his work in such surroundings, with neighbours who were in the entertainment industry, did not endear him to his fellow artists, he was heavily in debt and desperately needed money which a venue such as the Egyptian Hall had the potential to attract. Unfortunately for him, he was pitted against Barnum's greatest star attraction. The

Charles S. Stratton (1838–83), alias General Tom Thumb, who took Queen Victoria and many Londoners by storm from his first arrival in Britain in 1844. This bill shows the twenty-two-year-old midget with various representations from his programme.

VILLIKINS

EQUIPAGE

COURT DRESS

AMERICAN TAR

HIGHLANDER

MY MARY ANN

NAPOLEON

GLADIATOR

SAMSON

THE ORIGINAL

GENERAL TOM THUMB

THE SMALLEST MAN ALIVE.

Albert Smith (1816–60), who deserted medicine to become a writer and great showman. His occupancy of the Egyptian Hall dominated the eighteen-fifties and THE ASCENT OF MONT BLANC *became a remarkable success story. This sketch is by Harry Furniss.*

crowds came to the Hall in their thousands, but they did not patronize Haydon. The artist, who, as an admirer of Napoleon, was not enamoured by the midget's impersonations of the great man, now took a positive dislike to him. He inserted an advertisement in the *Times* on 21 April:

Exquisite Feeling of the English People for High Art—GENERAL TOM THUMB last week received 12,000 people, who paid him £600; B. R. HAYDON, who has devoted forty-two years to elevate their taste, was honoured by the visits of 133½, producing £5.13.6.

It did not advance his cause and the exhibition ended with Haydon further in debt. On 22 June the artist shot himself in the head with a pistol: the bullet did not kill him outright, so he seized a razor and finished the suicide by gashing his throat.[16]

A remarkable success story that spanned almost the whole of the eighteen-fifties was the occupancy of the Hall by Albert Smith.[18] Qualified as a physician,

he had given up medicine for a literary career, contributing to *Punch*, writing novels of London life and launching *The Man in the Moon*, a monthly periodical and rival to *Punch* that ran from January 1847 to June 1849, thirty issues in all. He was also a great traveller and had toured not only Europe but also the Levant and the Middle East. Current interest in those latter regions was high following the recent publication of a trio of books—*Eothen* by Alexander W. Kinglake (1844), *The Crescent and the Cross* by Eliot Warburton (1844) and *Notes of a Journey from Cornhill to Grand Cairo* by William Makepeace Thackeray (1846). Smith entered into the lists with *A Month at Constantinople* (1850), which was not very favourably reviewed but provided a springboard for his first essay into showbusiness, *The Overland Mail*—'A Literary, Pictorial and Musical Entertainment', at Willis's Rooms in 1850. It combined a travelogue with dioramic pictures painted by William Beverley (the foremost scenic artist of the day), humorous sketches, impersonations, songs and anecdotes, all relating to the idiosyncrasies of the English travellers and others he had met along the route. Smith delivered his lines rapidly, with an air of spontaneity that suggested the thoughts had just occurred to him, and his style resembled more that of a drawing-room entertainer than a theatrical performer. *The Times* compared him favourably with Charles Mathews.

In 1851 Smith and Beverley went to Chamonix, Beverley to paint the views and Smith to ascend Mont Blanc, which was to be the subject of his next entertainment. Smith and three companions, with a support party of staggering dimensions—sixteen guides and eighteen porters carrying an enormous quantity of food, wine and spirits—set off on their mission and Smith succeeded in his objective. So it came about that, on 15 March 1852, *Mr Albert Smith's Ascent of Mont Blanc* opened at the Egyptian Hall to a very favourable reception, running into August, with a second season starting in November. By this time the Hall had been transformed into a piece of Switzerland with the exterior of a two-storied chalet, carved balcony, and shutters with a lighted, curtained window; the wall of the chalet was raised when the views were shown and lowered in the intervals. There was a souvenir shop to the right of the chalet, and, to the left, a representation of the Aigle Noir Hotel at Grindlewald. A waterfall tumbled over rocks, turning a mill-wheel and cascading into a pool that fronted the stage. The spectacular

effect won plaudits and the show prospered accordingly, running for season after season until its two-thousandth and final performance, on 5 July 1858, by which time it had earned Smith £30,000, despite *The Times*' stricture on 6 October 1856 that 'Mont Blanc has become a positive nuisance'.

A feature of Albert Smith's *Mont Blanc* was a little ventriloquial duet using his hand, which was painted to resemble the face of an old woman, with a handkerchief tied round like a scarf. The fist was doubled and the knuckle of the thumb moved up and down to give the mouth movement. According to Bellew,[19] Smith had a stand of red cloth which made a very good scarlet cloak for the old lady when his painted and hooded hand was rested on the top. The rustic love duet was started by 'John Giles' in a

The Talking Hand, the ventriloquial novelty as depicted by William Hogarth in AN ELECTION ENTERTAINMENT, *published in February 1755. The operator was acknowledged to be a likeness of Sir John Parnell, a Dublin attorney.*

rough, bass voice. Bellew says:

Those who recollect poor Albert Smith's enjoyable personation of the village swain will remember the arch manner in which he was made to sing the last two lines. There was no talking hand for Giles, who was supposed to be out of sight behind the screen.

I

[He] *As I was a working at my plough,*
Fol de riddle lol-lol lol da.
I felt just here [hand on stomach] *I*
doant know how,
I turned my head, just for to see,
When looking r-reeound, WHY(!) *there*
stand the-e-e!
[Quickly] *Loike Wenus a' coming from the sea.*
Fol de riddle lol-lol lol da.

To this the woman makes bashful reply and, in some four verses, love having been professed and accepted, the duet ends with

[She] *With all my heart*
[He] *Next Sunday come—*
[She] *We'll married be—*
[He] *As sure as Fun*
[Both] AND YOU AND I WILL THEN MAKE ONE,
Fol de riddle lol-lol lol da.

The Talking Hand is of ancient origin, although precisely when it was first performed is unknown. The earliest representation of it is to be found in William Hogarth's *An Election Entertainment*, Plate I of four 'Prints of an Election', published in February 1755. In this print we see an individual 'diverting the company by a face drawn with burnt cork upon the back of his hand'. The man making the Talking Hand and singing *An Old Woman Clothed in Grey* was acknowledged by Hogarth to be a portrait of Sir John Parnell, an eminent attorney of Dublin and nephew of the poet Thomas Parnell, who persuaded Hogarth to include him in this print on the grounds that, being so well known in Ireland, his face would help the sale of the engraving.[20] Perhaps there was more than a touch of the blarney in his request!

The first full evening show of magic at the Egyptian Hall was presented in 1861 by Robin (Henri Joseph Donckele), a French performer who was born at Hazebrouck in 1811. In his own country, as we have seen (page 127), Robin was the greatest rival of the most famous of French conjurers, Robert-Houdin, with whom he engaged in acrimonious claims to the invention of the inexhaustible bottle trick or 'Any Drink Called For', a feat which had its origin in the 'curious barrel' described by Van Etten in *Mathe-maticall Recreations* over two hundred years earlier. It was not Robin's first appearance in England, for he had played an extended engagement from 1850 to 1853 which included a performance at

Windsor Castle on 25 April 1851. The 'Salle de Robin' proved extremely popular, and his programme in 1861 included an effect called 'The Enchanted Christmas Tree' embracing a distribution of souvenirs amongst the audience.

Robin, as already described (page 127), applied science to his magic, and this cultured man, of distinguished appearance and sharp wit, made a considerable impression upon his London audiences, despite his limited command of the English language. Like Robert-Houdin, Anderson and other mystifiers of the period, he presented a very convincing demonstration of second sight with his female assistant.

In 1865 the Sphinx itself came to the Egyptian Hall. It was brought there by Colonel Alfred Stodare, who despite his 'title' was not the latest of the Egyptologist exhibitors to rent a room in the Hall. Nor was the Sphinx that great creature from near the pyramids 'more wondrous and more awful than all else in the land of Egypt', as Kinglake described it, but a novel scientific illusion and one which Londoners certainly acclaimed as the most wondrous they had yet seen in their capital.

Mr Alfred Inglis, *alias* 'Colonel' Stodare, was born in Liverpool in 1831, although Frost[21] records him as 'a well educated Frenchman'. The seal of success on his appearances at the Egyptian Hall was set by the introduction of two illusions, both new to his audiences there—the Sphinx and the Indian Basket Trick, as well as another eastern effect, the Indian Mango Trick, or the Instantaneous Growth of Plants.

In the Basket Trick, with appropriate dramatics, a blindfolded young lady was forced to enter a large, rectangular basket raised upon a low table. Stodare took a long sword which he frenziedly and repeatedly thrust into the basket, to the accompaniment of hideous screams from the occupant, gradually dying away as she presumably succumbed to the onslaught. Having duly worked up suspense, the basket was then tipped over to show it empty while the young lady, removing her blindfold, tripped in at the rear of the auditorium, none the worse for her misadventure. This illusion was a familiar one to Eastern travellers, as also was the Mango Trick, in which a seed was taken, pushed into a little mound of soil and covered with a cloth. After a suitable incantation, the cloth was removed to reveal a germinated seed just emerging from the soil. It was covered

ALLEZ VOIR
LE COUPEUR DE TÊTES AU
BRITISH CIRCUS IMPÉRATOR

again and this time, when uncovered, the plant had grown further; the sequence of covering and uncovering was repeated until the seed had apparently grown into a sizeable mango tree.

After two hundred performances at the Egyptian Hall, the Colonel introduced his latest masterpiece on 16 October 1865. He called it the Sphinx. Entering, Stodare carried a small square box which he placed on an undraped three-legged table. He informed the audience that it contained the head of an ancient Sphinx and lowered the front of the box to expose to

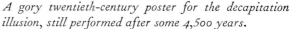

A gory twentieth-century poster for the decapitation illusion, still performed after some 4,500 years.

view what seemed to be precisely that, an Egyptian-style head with closed eyes. The performer retired to a position near the front of the stalls, a move designed to obviate the possibility of ventriloquism playing any part in what was to follow. He then called upon the Sphinx to open its eyes, which it did, to smile and to make a speech. Its compliance was total. 'Not only with perspicuity but with something like eloquence' did it utter some twenty lines of verse, according to an admiring report in *The Times* for 19 October 1865. After closing the box, Stodare then concluded the performance by informing his audience that the charm by which he was enabled to revivify for a time the ashes of an ancient Egyptian, who had lived and died some centuries ago, lasted but fifteen minutes. As that time had now elapsed, the head which a few moments ago had astounded them with its eloquence, had now returned to its original dust. And so it had! Stodare opened the box and in the place of the head was a pile of ashes. The *Times* critic went on to say:

This certainly is one of the most extraordinary illusions ever presented to the public. That the speech is spoken by a human voice there is no doubt, but how is a head to be contrived which, being detached from anything like a body, confined in a case, which it completely fills, and placed on a bare-legged table, will accompany a speech, that apparently proceeds from its lips, with a strictly appropriate movement of the mouth, and a play of the countenance that is the reverse of mechanical?

The answer to that question had, in fact been provided by Thomas W. Tobin and not by Stodare himself. Tobin was the Secretary of the Royal Polytechnic Institution, formerly the Royal Gallery of Arts and Sciences, that had been masterminded in 1838 by Sir George Cayley, the Yorkshire physicist, experimental engineer and aeronautical pioneer, with the object of providing instruction with amusement. The Sphinx was based on the optical device that Tobin had earlier built for Professor John Henry Pepper's lectures at the Polytechnic, and which was patented by them in 1865 as the Cabinet of Proteus. And, let it be whispered softly, it was one of the few illusions that depend exclusively on the use of mirrors.

The Sphinx became the current rage of the metropolis, and the Colonel was summoned to perform for Queen Victoria on the occasion of the Princess Royal's birthday.

Poor Stodare did not enjoy his well merited success for long. The following year—on 22 October—he died of consumption at the early age of thirty-five. For a period his wife endeavoured to continue the show at the Egyptian Hall with the assistance of a minor entertainer of the day, Firbank Burman. Unfortunately Madame Stodare's show did not make the necessary impact for survival, and it faded from the entertainment scene in 1867.

Stodare left three technical manuals for magical posterity, *The Art of Magic* (1865), *A New Handy Book of Magic* (1865) and, posthumously, *Stodare's Fly Notes* (1867). The last volume had previously been published serially for the edification and delectation of the youth of Britain in Routledge's *Every Boy's Annual*.

There followed at the Egyptian Hall in 1867 Signor Rubini, who also performed the Indian Basket illusion but who, according to a contemporary, invested it with little drama. The same observer described Rubini's decapitation illusion, in which a young lady apparently lost her head to the performer's sword, as being conducted as if she were at the hairdresser's, so utterly devoid of emotion and showmanly presentation was it! Rather more startling were performances provided during the same year by The Aissouas—Arab conjurers, snake and scorpion-eaters—who were fresh from their gustatory successes at the Algerian Concerts featured at the Paris Exhibition.

These then were the purveyors of magic and allied arts who helped this entertainment oasis in Piccadilly through its first half century, and up to the point in its history when magic became inseparable from it.

13
Maskelyne & Cooke — Royal Illusionists

And the magician who escapes from the box:
what is he but Adonis and Attis and all the
rest of the corn gods that are buried and rise?

Edmund Wilson (1895–1972),
on 'John Mulholland and the *Art of Illusion*' (1944)

The eighteen-seventies heralded the start of over thirty glorious years of continuous association of the Egyptian Hall with magic. The first of the magicians during this period was Alexander Herrmann, born in Paris in 1844 and younger brother of Carl (Compars) Herrmann who had appeared in London in 1848 with 'La Suspension Ethéréene' (page 82). Alexander learned his magic by travelling with his brother, but then struck out on his own account. For over a thousand consecutive nights he appeared at the Egyptian Hall, from 1870 until 1873, precisely embodying the public's image of a magician, with goatee beard and mephistophelean appearance. He returned to the USA in 1875, took out US citizenship and there remained, apart from occasional tours abroad, becoming a famous magician in the Americas.[1]

Exponents of the arts allied to magic were also in evidence—Woodin of Carpet Bag fame appeared in 1871; 'Lieutenant' Walter Cole with his ventriloquial entertainment 'Merry Folks'; Bullock's Royal Marionettes; and the Christy Minstrel Fantoccini in 1872. In the latter year Professor Pepper and Mr Tobin presented 'The New and Wonderful', a series of popular scientific lectures and demonstrations in the style of the Royal Polytechnic, with musical interludes which included an historical and dramatic sketch titled 'The Temptation of Paganini'.[2]

But 1873 was to prove the key year in the chronicles of the Egyptian Hall, for there descended upon it two relatively unknown young men who were to transform the whole course of magical history. Their names, Maskelyne and Cooke, were

soon to become household words in England, synonymous with magic itself.[3] How their careers in wizardry began is a fascinating story which takes us initially to the fashionable spa of Cheltenham.

John Nevil Maskelyne, the son of a saddler and a descendant of Nevil Maskelyne (1732–1811), the Astronomer Royal, was born in Cheltenham on 22 December 1839. As a boy he had a penchant for things mechanical and, on leaving school, gravitated naturally to an apprenticeship with a watchmaker and jeweller. His leisure pursuits included conjuring, plate-spinning—a skill he had learned from a magician called Blitz Junior—playing the cornet in the local amateur band and singing in the church choir. Maskelyne became interested in the spiritualistic phenomena which were then the vogue in Britain but had his credulity shaken when a friendly medium asked him to repair what he chose to call a 'surgical appliance'. In effecting the repair, Maskelyne discovered that the device, if attached to the operator's leg, would be capable of producing table raps, the method of communication much favoured by the 'spirits'. His vigilance was now aroused and so, when the American spiritualistic mediums the Davenport Brothers arrived in Cheltenham on 7 March 1865, Maskelyne was one of the members of the audience who went up on the stage at the Town Hall to ensure that no trickery was involved and that the manifestations really were, as claimed, attributable to spirit agency.

The Brothers were duly tied up under the direction of their manager, the Reverend Dr J. B. Ferguson, and shut in their cabinet. The cabinet resembled a

large wardrobe with three doors, and a bench was fitted to the back and ends. At the top of the panel of the centre door was a diamond-shaped opening covered by a piece of black cloth. The brothers sat facing one another at either end of the cabinet and an assortment of musical instruments, comprising a guitar, violin and bow, tambourine, brass horn and couple of bells, was placed on the bench between them. As it was an afternoon séance the windows of the Town Hall were curtained to exclude the light that was held to be inimical to spirit activities. What happened next is best told in Maskelyne's own words.[4]

During the séance I was seated on one side of the stage with a row of darkened windows at my back. Once, while the centre door was opening and instruments were flying out of the cabinet, a small piece of drapery fell from the window behind me. A ray of sunshine shot into the cabinet, lighting up Ira Davenport, whose actions thus became visible to me. There sat Ira, with one hand behind him and the other in the act of throwing the instruments out. In a trice both hands were behind him. He gave a smart wriggle of his shoulders, and lo! when his bonds were examined he was found to be thoroughly secured; so firmly bound, in fact, that the ropes were cutting into the flesh of his wrists. But I had discovered the secret. Ira Davenport's movements had taught me the trick, and I knew that with a little practice I could do it. 'Ladies and Gentlemen', I said, addressing the audience 'by a slight accident I have been able to discover this trick'. This statement was at once challenged by the gentleman who engaged the performers. I at once replied that it was a feat of dexterity and could not, therefore be performed without practice, adding that, to prove my statement, I would there and then make a promise to put the trick into practice, and at the earliest possible moment I would undertake to present a replica of the entire performance in the same hall.

Together with his friend, cabinetmaker and fellow band member, George Alfred Cooke, Maskelyne worked hard to duplicate the feats he had seen and, a few months later, on Monday 19 June 1865, the pair made their first appearance as illusionists. The

The cover of a book sold to audiences at Maskelyne & Cooke's entertainment around 1876.

bills announced that at Jessop's Aviary Gardens in Cheltenham

MESSRS MASKELYNE AND COOKE

The only Successful Rivals of the DAVENPORT BROTHERS will give a GRAND EXPOSITION of the ENTIRE PUBLIC SEANCE

They advertised that all the Davenports' tricks would be done in open daylight to show the possibility of accomplishing them without the aid of Spiritualism, together with others, original and more astonishing, including what was subsequently to prove a classic illusion in their hands, escaping from a wooden box. Maskelyne was locked in a deal box, three feet long by two feet wide and eighteen inches in depth with a few small holes drilled in the ends, which was securely corded by members of the audience. The box was then put in a cabinet, bells placed upon it and the doors closed. Almost immediately the bells began to ring and they were shortly thrown out of the cabinet. On opening the doors Maskelyne was found seated on top of the still locked and corded box.

Maskelyne's and Cooke's local acclaim was such that they were emboldened to embark on a professional career and they set out to conquer the provinces. They soon discovered that the life of a professional conjurer could be a hard one. During the winter of 1865–6, when they were struggling to make ends meet and almost about to abandon their new calling, there came an event which was to prove the turning point in their fortunes. A young man called William Morton saw their show in a hall in Bold Street, Liverpool, and had the courage and foresight to finance a tour on 'fifty-fifty' terms. He continued as their named manager for some twenty years, and saw them firmly established in the West End as one of the most widely known attractions of the metropolis. To his initiative may be attributed the foundation of the Maskelyne dynasty as England's conjurers supreme.[5]

Morton was born at Royston in Hertfordshire in 1838 and, by the time he came into contact with Maskelyne and Cooke at the ripe old age of twenty-seven, he had been variously, printers' devil, newspaper reporter, solicitor's clerk, book and music seller and entertainment provider. This last venture, in Southport, ended in disaster and, almost penniless, he had become advance agent for Arthur Lloyd, the comic singer who was later destined to become the idol of the London Pavilion. It was at the end of his tour with Lloyd that he met Maskelyne and Cooke. After a period on the 'fifty-fifty' terms, a contract was drawn up for a fixed salary, with Maskelyne and his wife receiving four pounds ten shillings and Cooke two pounds ten shillings per week.

Under Morton's management they appeared in most of the major cities and towns in Britain and finally in London. After Morton's formal association with the illusionists had ceased, he branched out into other theatrical ventures, building up the Greenwich Theatre, then fallen on bad days, to a reputable house attracting the best managers—such as Ellen Terry and D'Oyly Carte. In 1894 he moved to Hull to become a very successful theatre manager and owner, and also a pioneer of cinema, building the Princes Hall, the first theatre in Hull specifically designed for films. Morton became a well known and highly respected citizen of Hull, and very much a local 'character'. In his ninety-fifth year he started to write his autobiography, titled *I Remember*, which he published in 1934.[6] It included a chapter on his association with Maskelyne and Cooke, and also his

recipe for longevity—total abstinence, with a diet chart for three meals a day (the last one at 5pm being a cup of weak tea and six slices of bread and butter) and the scrupulous avoidance of confectionery and sweets! Morton achieved his ambition to become a centenarian on 24 January 1938, and on 5 July of the same year died peacefully at his home.

Maskelyne and Cooke appeared at the Crystal Palace in 1869 and, after further provincial tours, they were back in London at St James's Hall in April 1873. By that time they had been rewarded by a private showing for the Prince of Wales at Berkeley Castle in 1870 and were now billing themselves as 'The Royal Illusionists and Anti-Spiritualists'. They then moved across Piccadilly to take up a three-month tenancy of

Harry Kellar (1849–1922), the famous American magician, presented his version of WILL, THE WITCH AND THE WATCH *during the period 1905–7 as* THE WITCH, THE SAILOR AND THE ENCHANTED MONKEY. *Like several other of his illusions, it was copied from Maskelyne & Cooke's programme.*

THE WITCH, THE SAILOR AND THE ENCHANTED MONKEY.

the Small Hall at the Egyptian Hall where they opened on 26 May 1873, a tenancy that was to continue, subsequently in the Large Hall upstairs, until the end of 1904, when impending demolition of the building necessitated Maskelyne's removal to St George's Hall.

Let us now recall something of the programme that amazed audiences during those early years at the Egyptian Hall. The Box Trick, first introduced at Cheltenham, had been expanded into a sketch called 'Will, the Witch and the Watch' or 'The Mystic Freaks of Gyges'. The scene was a village green, the period November 1799. In the foreground was a mahogany trunk, with canvas cover and cord, and the Village Lock-up, which was essentially based on Tobin's Cabinet of Proteus (page 154) and had double doors. Two of the audience were invited to examine the apparatus and to remain on the stage throughout the playlet. To describe the scenario we can do no better than use the illusionists' own description:[7]

The story opens with Miles Mooney, a watchman, beguiling the time between which he 'runs 'em in' by thinking of the village beauty, Dolly, who is, unfortunately, hard-hearted and unkind towards him. Dolly enters, and, like the saucy Irishman he is, Miles attempts to kiss her. Dolly screaming, her own true love—Will Constant, a regular British Tar—rushes to the rescue and at once becomes an object of the watchman's professional zeal; but the Sailor not being 'unworthy of the name', knocks Miles down, who thereupon springs his rattle, and his superior, Daddy Gnarl, enters to his assistance. Between them they secure the sailor and place him, a prisoner, within the Lock-up. An old witch now appears . . . who flings coloured flames about with her hands, and behaves peculiarly, but as she undertakes to deliver the sailor from bondage Dolly is not disposed to be exacting about her appearance.

The doors of the Lock-up are then opened, and it is empty! The sailor has disappeared! The witch has evidently been true to her word! Miles, thunderstruck at the sailor's escape, sees a comical gorilla jibbering at him from the Lock-up, and at once wishing himself 'miles away', rushes off. The beast creeps to its hiding place, and Joe Kilbull, a butcher, enters with Miles, the latter in a state of great trepidation, as he imagines the beast he has seen is a visitant from—'below'. Miles gives Joe a highly coloured account of the beast, and the

butcher determines to see for himself, but on opening the Lock-up finds it empty. The gorilla again appears and is pursued; Joe, managing to get in the rear, cuts off the poor beast's tail, which still shows signs of animation and hops about the stage in a most extraordinary manner. For being thus cur-tailed the gorilla revenges himself by dragging Joe into the Lock-up, whence sounds of mortal strife proceed, but when the doors are opened both have disappeared leading one to suppose that the beast has swallowed Joe and afterwards performed a like operation upon himself!

However, all surmises are set at rest by the butcher coming from the midst of the audience with a graphic description of his tussle with the gorilla; and the latter putting in an appearance, from the Lock-up again, is this time knocked down and secured in the Trunk which is locked, corded, and the knots sealed by gentlemen from the audience.

The Trunk is now placed (with its "Darwinian progenitor of the human race" inside) in the Lock-up and the watchman left in charge, but in five seconds, or less, the gorilla's paws are thrust through the apertures in the doors, and Miles hearing a noise within thinks it wiser to have the trunk outside; accordingly, it is lifted out, still locked, and with the knots upon the cords sealed. It is opened, and found—empty!

The old witch here re-appears upon the scene, and completes her promise to Dolly of restoring her lover, who steps out of the Lock-up where he was placed at the opening of the piece. With the union of the lovers the curtain falls upon one of the most mysterious and farcical of extravaganzas.

The reader will have noted that the plot invests the gorilla with a tail, an anatomical inexactitude which may be forgiven in the interests of magic. As the gorilla was first made known to zoology only in 1861, the scientific topicality of the playlet at least will be apparent.

By describing 'Will, the Witch and the Watch' in detail it is possible to get some idea of the bewildering series of appearances, disappearances and transpositions which characterized the sketch and which, with various modifications continued to be presented (later as 'Will, the Witch and the Watchman') for over thirty years.

While new items were introduced from time to time, Maskelyne and Cooke's repertoire remained

VICTORIA ROOMS, CLIFTON.

Tuesday, Nov. 16th, to Saturday, Nov. 20th; each Evening at 8.

Day Performances, Wednesday and Saturday, at 3.

CULLIFORD & SONS, LITH. LONDON.

MASKELYNE & COOKE'S.
MARVELLOUS ENTERTAINMENT, FROM THE EGYPTIAN HALL. LONDON.

fairly constant. Their presentation, however, changed considerably as new magical sketches incorporating the illusions were introduced and existing playlets underwent significant modification and development. Some of their 'evergreen' illusions employed in this way included the levitation of a human being, variously Mrs Maskelyne, Maskelyne or Cooke, rising from the ground to a considerable height in full view and on a fully lit stage, and the decapitation of a besmocked Gloucestershire farmer, whose severed head was then set on a table and continued to converse with his 'surgeon'. The Box Trick, either as a separate item or as part of a sketch, continued to be a featured item, as was Maskelyne's plate-spinning. By dexterous finger work he was able to keep six dessert plates spinning on a table top— 'waltzing, galloping and dancing quadrilles'— and to spin one plate down an inclined plate only four inches wide, then up a spiral and down again onto the table. Duplication of the spiritualistic feats of the Davenport Brothers also played a prominent rôle in their programmes.

One performer appearing under the Maskelyne and Cooke banner who must claim our attention in the chronicles of the Egyptian Hall is the outstanding French conjurer Buatier De Kolta (1848–1903). He came to the Egyptian Hall in 1875 and presented a startling new effect, 'The Flying Cage'. The magician held up a wire cage containing two canaries and, instantaneously, without any cover, both cage and birds vanished completely. He then elaborated on this trick by using a large cage set on a wooden platform and a female assistant dressed as a canary. She entered the cage which De Kolta covered with an opaque cloth. On the count of three he pulled the cloth away and the cage and its human canary had completely disappeared. This illusion was called 'The Captive Flight'.

De Kolta's most famous illusion came to the Egyptian Hall in 1886, initially presented by Charles Bertram assisted by Mlle Patrice, since the inventor was still successfully showing his originations in Paris and could not arrive in London until Christmas. This was 'The Vanishing Lady'. A newspaper was spread on the stage to obviate the possibility of a trapdoor being used and a chair set upon it. The lady took her seat and was covered completely by a cloth.

A lithograph used by Maskelyne & Cooke when they were on tour.

Buatier De Kolta (1848–1903), the outstanding French conjurer and illusionist, whose startling new effects, the Vanishing Birdcage and the Vanishing Lady, astounded Egyptian Hall audiences in 1875 and 1886 respectively.

It having been indicated that she was still there, the cloth was then whipped off and she had disappeared. She was later led onto the stage.

Maskelyne and Cooke's magic was, over the years, leavened by singers, musicians, entertainers at the piano, ventriloquists and quick-change artistes, as well as by the introduction of other magicians, some of whom we shall mention later. It was a hallmark of distinction for a conjurer to appear with Maskelyne and Cooke, and one that was eagerly sought but not readily gratified for, as we have just observed, their programmes did not change a great deal. In consequence Maskelyne occasionally missed a rising star. One of these was none other than Houdini, for, when that young man was down on his luck in the USA and contemplating trying to break into the theatre in Europe, he wrote to Maskelyne at the Egyptian Hall to ask for an engagement. The reply he got, dated 24 March 1898, said simply

Dear Sir,

I have no room for any addition to my company. I seldom change my artists.

Yours very truly,
J. N. Maskelyne.[8]

This letter has considerably piquancy in the light of Houdini's meteoric career in Britain and Europe, for two years later in London he became, overnight, a top-of-the-bill attraction, virtually on Maskelyne's own doorstep.

In 1875 a sensational new item was introduced—an automaton called Psycho who played cards with members of the audience. Psycho was a small figure of a Hindu, some twenty-two inches high, seated cross-legged upon a small box which, in turn, rested upon a clear glass cylinder, thereby disproving any connexion with the stage. Members of the audience were invited to inspect it closely. First, Psycho would perform arithmetic calculations set by the audience, opening a little door beneath his left hand and sliding numerals in front of an aperture to give the correct answer. Then he would play whist with three volunteers from the audience. The cards were dealt and those for Psycho were placed by Maskelyne singly and upright in each of thirteen numbered holders set in an arc before him. When it was Psycho's turn to play he would swing his arm across and, with finger and thumb, pick up the card, lift it to display it to the audience and then bring his arm down, when Maskelyne would remove the card and throw it on the table. The remarkable aspect of Psycho was not merely that he played cards but that he frequently won! Among the celebrated players who contested the automaton was 'Cavendish' who, in *The Field* on 27 January 1875, commented: 'the wonder therefore is, how the figure can play whist at all, and how it can apparently exercise intelligence in choosing the appropriate card.'

How Psycho and the other illusions appeared to a Norfolk clergyman is recorded in that worthy's diary for 23 May 1876:

In the evening to Maskelyne and Cooke's celebrated seance in which there is an automaton figure on a glass tube (to prevent suspicion of collusion) which played whist with three of the visitors and solved the most difficult arithmetical problems.

A programme for the Royal Aquarium, Westminster, in March 1889, printed on crepe paper, and featuring Buatier De Kolta with his illusion 'The Cocoon'.

There were other marvels—too marvellous to be amusing.[9]

Was there for this cleric just a hint of diabolic sorcery in what he saw?

Psycho was the joint inspiration of Maskelyne, whose watchmaking skills and mechanical ingenuity were brought into play, and John Algernon Clarke, a farmer from Long Sutton in Lincolnshire, who had brought to the conjurer his original but impractical idea for a machine that could play cards. They were immensely gratified by the furore that greeted Psycho, comparable in many ways to that associated with De Kempelen's famous chess-playing automaton almost a century earlier.[10] The advertising value of Psycho to Maskelyne must have been enormous, for it was the subject of a succession of articles, poems and cartoons in the national press, and probably stimulated him to further efforts in this direction. Thus, in due course, he introduced three other automata to the Egyptian Hall, although none of them enjoyed the same popularity as Psycho. The first was Zoe, a mechanical lady who drew heads of celebrities with a pencil, and who made her début in May 1877. In the following year came Fanfare and Labial, evoking memories of Maskelyne's bandsman days, for the former was a automaton boy cornet player and the latter played the euphonium. Their inventor completed the trio with a trumpet obligato in a spirited rendering of 'The Death of Nelson'.

After four thousand consecutive performances, Psycho was withdrawn on 10 November 1880 in order that his overworked mechanism might be overhauled. Simultaneously, the reward of £2,000 that had been offered for the correct solution to the mystery was cancelled. The mechanism was never revealed by Maskelyne but the fact that he and Cooke took out a provisional patent in 1875 for an improved means for actuating automatic mechanism by compressed air or gas as a controlling power may offer a clue, or, alternatively, a red herring! Psycho eventually returned to the programme and, in the fullness of time, he was presented to the London Museum, where he may still be seen, inscrutable as ever. He did emerge, however, on a very special occasion and under strict security guard. That was when he graced the Annual Banquet of The Magic Circle at the Café Royal in October 1973, to mark both the centenary of Maskelyne and Cooke's first appearance at the Egyptian Hall and the posthumous award of the Magician of the Year Trophy to his inventor. Grandson Noel Maskelyne received a bronze head of his grandfather—a Maskelyne for a Maskelyne!

The bent for invention extended outside the theatre, and Maskelyne was responsible for a typewriter with differential spacing, a ticket punch and a coin-operated lock, amongst many others. However, as his grandson pointed out, every time he ventured outside the atmosphere of greasepaint and footlights he failed conspicuously, with the notable exception of work for the War Office in connexion with the rapid filling of balloons at the time of the Boer War.[11]

Maskelyne's enthusiasm for conjuring was almost matched by his fervour for challenges and litigation, the former usually leading to the latter and often resulting in heavy expenditure, which he always regarded philosophically as a good investment for the attendant publicity gained. His first London encounter was with a magician styled Dr H. S. Lynn (Hugh Washington Simmons), who was appearing at one of the other rooms in the Egyptian Hall when Maskelyne and Cooke arrived there in May 1873. Lynn was an accomplished performer with a racy line of patter who had started his magical career in Australia and worked in the Orient and the USA where, in Boston, he apparently studied medicine. He presented a version of Maskelyne's Box Trick which he endeavoured to pass off as his own invention in his book *The Adventures of a Strange Man* (1873). Subsequently he produced an extension of the decapitation illusion which included the amputation of limbs. This latter illusion was called 'Palingenesia' and advertised as 'Another Man Cut Up Tonight!'. It proved a great attraction and became essentially Lynn's 'signature tune'.

Maskelyne attacked Lynn's Box Trick in a pamphlet he published in 1873 titled *The History of a Mystery!*, and they continued to feud for some time. This same illusion eventually cost him a considerable sum of money, for Maskelyne had a standing offer of £500 to anyone who could duplicate it. In 1898 two young men, Stollery and Evans, accepted the challenge and Maskelyne's untenable position was quickly revealed; in order to demonstrate that they were not precisely duplicating his method, even though the effect appeared the same, he would have been forced to reveal the secret of his box, and this he understandably was not prepared to do. So, even although it required two juries to secure a decision, and a decision that proved unfavourable to the

illusionist, he promptly appealed, lost his case, took it to the House of Lords and lost again!

Interest in spiritualism was revived in London in the autumn of 1875 when an American medium, 'Dr' Henry Slade, was prosecuted by Professor E. Ray Lankester. Maskelyne, who had recently written *Modern Spiritualism* exposing some of the methods used by bogus mediums, was called by the Crown as an expert witness. Slade was a so-called 'slate medium'; that is, he caused messages to appear on slates and claimed they were produced by spirits. In the witness box Maskelyne demonstrated exactly how such messages could be obtained without spirit intervention and Slade was sentenced to three months' jail—although he escaped on a technicality and fled the country.

A new development of the levitation illusion stemmed from the most famous and controversial of the phenomena of the medium Daniel Dunglas Home (1833–1886)[12] who, it was alleged, floated out of one upper-storey window and in at another at Ashley House, Westminster, in 1868. While a critical analysis of the evidence has completely undermined

John Nevil Maskelyne with his automata. From left to right they are Psycho, Fanfare, Labial and Zoe. A drawing made in 1878 for the ILLUSTRATED LONDON NEWS.

the credibility of the witnesses,[13] it provided an excellent plot for Maskelyne who, standing erect at the front of the stage, floated up to the top of the dome of the Hall in full view and, with two lanterns trained upon him, turned to a horizontal position and then floated gracefully back.

The spiritualists also furnished Maskelyne's last costly litigation, although this was in 1906 after the move to St George's Hall. Archdeacon Colley, the Rector of Stockton in Warwickshire, put up £1,000 and publicly challenged Maskelyne to reproduce phenomena which he claimed to have witnessed more than thirty years previously by a certain 'Dr' Monck. These included the extrusion from the medium's side of a cloud of vapour from which a spirit form materialized. Maskelyne duly presented an illusion which he called 'The Side Issue', closely based on this description, and claimed the money, intending to present it to charity. Colley declined to pay and so Maskelyne sued. The court case was an amusing one but the illusionist lost because Colley claimed that the spirit form he had witnessed returned to the medium's side whereas Maskelyne's spirit walked off stage, and therefore the phenomenon had not been duplicated. Although Maskelyne explained that he could have made the spirit disappear in that way but had refrained because it would have spoiled the trick as an illusion, creating an anti-climax, it was of no avail. He went back to St George's Hall determined to re-stage the illusion. Before he could do so he received a letter from Colley's solicitor withdrawing the challenge, so Maskelyne was once again out of pocket although attracting crowded audiences as a result of all the attendant publicity.

John Nevil Maskelyne's two sons, Nevil and Edwin Archibald, both became part of the Maskelyne company of illusionists, as in turn did three of Nevil's sons, Clive, Noel and Jasper, and England's Home of Mystery continued to draw audiences until, in 1933, St George's Hall was sold to the British Broadcasting Corporation. John Nevil had died in 1917, Archibald in 1920, Nevil in 1924 and Clive in 1928, leaving Noel and Jasper to continue the family tradition. Differences between Jasper, Noel and the fourth brother James led to closure in 1933, when Jasper went on the road with a smaller show. In 1936 Jasper wrote *White Magic*,[11] the story of the Maskelyne family and, following his war service as a Major in the Royal Engineers Camouflage Experimental Section, wrote *Magic—Top Secret*, which told of his war-time experiences.[14] For a period in the post-war years he took out a magic show again and brought pleasure to thousands but, with the pecline of live theatre and music hall in the nineteen-fifties, he emigrated to Kenya where he died in 1973. With the death of Noel Maskelyne in 1976 the long line of Magical Maskelynes came to an end, a dynasty that has no parallel in the annals of British conjuring and one which, in presenting a theatre of magic continuously in London for sixty years, cannot be matched anywhere in the world.

Maskelyne's Egyptian Hall stage launched several young performers who were destined to become famous magicians, one of whom, David Devant (1868–1941), was eventually in 1905 taken into partnership with Maskelyne himself. Devant was born David Wighton, the son of an artist, James Wighton, and had taken up conjuring about the age of twelve. He moved through a succession of varied

JUST AS WE EXPECTED. MR. MASKELYNE HAS DEALINGS WITH HIS SATANIC MAJESTY.

A cartoon of John Nevil Maskelyne (1839–1917) which appeared in ENTR'ACTE *in 1887.*

jobs until in 1885, when he was seventeen, he adopted the name of Devant and gave his first public performance in a schoolroom in Kentish Town Road. There he had the salutary experience of discovering that a member of his audience was none other than the redoubtable Professor Hoffmann, author of the classic textbook *Modern Magic* (1876), which had revolutionized the literature of conjuring.[15]

After this event he began to meet other magicians and became an habitué of the Egyptian Hall, where he studied the styles and techniques of the magical masters who trod those hallowed boards. Thus fortified, he began to perform around London and the provinces and at the start of the eighteen-nineties broke into the music hall field. He had already added hand shadows to his repertoire (page 189) and had devised a new illusion, 'Vice Versa', in which a man changed into a woman in a thin, isolated cabinet, despite members of the audience holding the ends of tape tied around his waist.

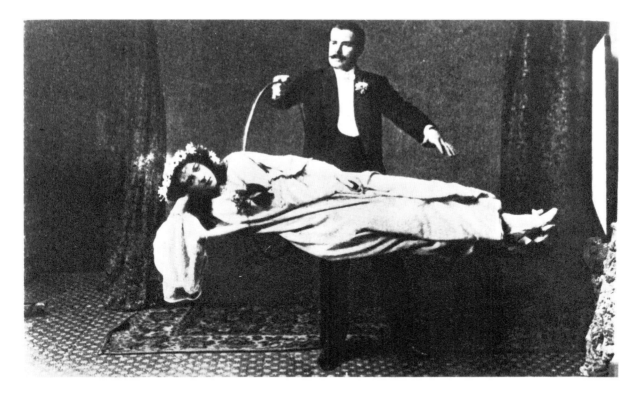

David Devant performing 'The Sylph', another version of the levitation illusion.

Devant's chance came in 1893 when Charles Morritt, a clever conjurer, inventor and former owner of the City of Varieties Theatre at Leeds,[16] who had been with Maskelyne for four years, left the Egyptian Hall to establish a show of his own at the Prince's Hall, Piccadilly. Devant auditioned specially for Maskelyne at the Trocadero Music Hall and was engaged. As his illusion was not suitable for Maskelyne's stage he was asked to think out an alternative one. Thus was created 'The Artist's Dream', in which a picture of a young woman came to life.

Devant's great success as a conjurer was undoubtedly due to his personal charm and his refreshingly new approach to the art. For example, early in his career he discarded the magic wand, which hitherto had been *de rigueur* for all aspiring conjurers, and also the use of any apparatus which gave the impression of having been made especially for magical purposes; he reasoned that suspicion would thereby be allayed.

An intriguing aspect of Devant's presentation was his 'drawing-room' style, even though he was

The levitation illusion presented by the Belgian illusionist Servais Le Roy (1865–1953), with his wife Talma floating in the air.

performing on stage. Such was his charisma that young and old alike were immediately transported into his whimsical fairyland of magical delights. Conjurers still alive today who were fortunate enough to have seen him in his prime will tell you that they, too, fell wholly under his spell. Sophisticated critics though they may be, invariably they refer to Devant as 'The Master'. Recognition of his pre-eminence came in 1912, when he was chosen for the first-ever Royal Command Performance for King George V at the Palace Theatre in London—the only conjurer on the programme and in the company of such artistes as Harry Lauder, Anna Pavlova, Cinquevalli, Harry Tate, Vesta Tilly, Fanny Fields and George Robey.

On that auspicious occasion he was assisted by his young daughter Vida and by the nine-year-old Jasper Maskelyne, John Nevil's grandson, in the trick known as 'A Boy, a Girl and Some Eggs'. The children were shown an empty hat from which Devant commenced to extract eggs, passing them to the children to hold. As the seemingly never-ending supply of eggs continued to be drawn from the hat the dilemma of the youngsters with hands and arms full of eggs, endeavouring to avoid dropping and smashing them on stage (thoughtfully covered with a sheet to catch the mess), created perfect situation-comedy in addition to the mystery. Later, both Devant[17] and Jasper Maskelyne[11] were to record that the child assistants on this particular showing were far more interested in the occupants of the Royal Box than in the magic!

The lustre of England's Home of Mystery was enhanced by a number of outstanding illusions which flowed from Devant's fertile and inventive mind. In 'The Birth of Flora', rose-petals were dropped into a bowl of fire which was transformed into a huge basket of roses from which appeared a lady, Flora the Goddess of Flowers. Another beautiful but more amazing illusion was 'The Mascot Moth'. The moth was played by a lady whose costume had wings, which she folded about her as Devant approached with a candle. In full view, in the centre of a lighted stage, she simply vanished from his arms as he tried to embrace her. Yet another, noisier, illusion was 'Biff', which involved a motor cycle and its rider. After several laps of the stage the cycle entered a wooden crate which was hoisted in the air. A pistol was fired—or, latterly, a ray was directed—at the crate, which disintegrated leaving not a trace of motor cycle or rider.

In surveying the long list of Devant's creations one facet stands out—he did not use the theme of mutilation at all. The element of horror was banished from his performances, and the image of the kindly uncle sharing his magical treat was never dispelled. Perhaps that was part of his greatness.

Devant took the Maskelyne and Cooke show on tour in the late eighteen-nineties and early nineteen-hundreds. Then, in 1905, following Cooke's death and the move to St George's Hall, he became Maskelyne's partner and for the next ten years Maskelyne and Devant's Mysteries were the Mecca for all magic-lovers visiting London. The partnership was dissolved in 1915 when Devant went his own way once again, touring the major variety theatres.

But, at the zenith of his career, tragedy was lurking in the wings. During the First World War he was stricken with a disease that led to an increasing palsy and paralysis, and which finally necessitated his retirement from the stage in 1920. This consummate artist ended his days in the Royal Home for Incurables at Putney, where he died in 1941 mourned by magicians throughout the world.[18]

14
THE GREAT GUN TRICK

There's a curse on the bullet-catching trick.

Will Dexter, *The Riddle of Chung
Ling Soo* (1955)

There can be few, if any, conjuring feats that have captured the popular imagination so much as 'Catching a Bullet'. It has been featured regularly for some two hundred years, with Philip Astley (1742–1814),[1] the famous equestrian and founder of the modern circus, claiming to be the originator in his book *Natural Magic: or, Physical Amusements Revealed* published in 1785. This volume contained twenty-four tricks and was a plagiarism of Thomas Denton's *The Conjurer Unmasked* (1784), itself a translation of Henri Decremps' *La Magie Blanche Dévoilée* published in Paris in the same year.[2] One trick was substituted by Astley, namely the Gun Trick, which he claimed to have invented in 1762. It is headed 'A Pistol loaded with Powder and Ball, and discharged at any Person who dexterously receives the Ball on the Point of a Knife or Sword'. Despite Astley's claim, the first record of this feat appeared as early as 1631 in a treatise titled *Threats of God's Judgements* by one Rev. Thomas Beard.

It is not long since there was in Lorraine a certain man called Coulew, that was over much given to this cursed art, amongst whose tricks this was one to be wondered at: that he would suffer harquebusses or pistols to be shot at him and catch the bullets in his hand without receiving any hurt; but upon a certain time one of his servants being angry at him, hit him such a knock with a pistol (notwithstanding all his great cunning), that he killed him therewith.

Coulew was thus the first of a long line of conjurers to be killed by firearms, albeit not by a bullet in his case; many of his successors, however, fell victim to the business end of the guns. No wonder then that

the suspense, danger and occasionally fatal outcome served to keep the 'Bullet Catch' in the public eye.

In the eighteenth century Katterfelto also performed this trick, and it has even been suggested that he might have been the first to present it in Britain, in 1781.[3] In Katterfelto's version any spectator could load the gun with powder and ball and then fire it at a glass bottle; the ball would drop in the bottle or before it, without breaking the glass.

John Brenon, from Dublin's fair city, was a conjurer and expert on the slack wire, and his wife was a conjurer, too—in fact, one of the earliest female performers on record and the first to perform in the USA. Brenon was obviously a most skilful exponent of the Gun Trick for, while balanced on his slack wire, he would allow a gentleman from the audience to fire a loaded pistol at him and would catch the bullet in a silk handkerchief.[4] He was performing this version of the feat in New York in 1787 while his wife, not to be outdone, enlivened her dexterity of hand by permitting any gentleman to cut off the head of a fowl 'which would be restored to life in a surprising manner'.[5]

A playbill printed in Armagh in 1787 advertising the 'so much famed English Hussar', who presented dexterity of hand in its various branches, reveals that he concluded his performance with the Art of Gunnery, another name for the Gun Trick. 'The Hussar gives liberty to any Gentleman to load a Gun or Pistol with Powder and Ball and lets him fire at him, and receives the Ball on the Point of a Sword or Knife;—this he does without any Coat of Armour in defence of his Body.' The similarity of the wording of this description to the text of Philip Astley's *Natural Magic*, published only two years previously, makes it possible that the English Hussar was either Astley himself or one of his company, for they were exceptionally popular in Ireland, having first appeared at the New Circular Riding School on the Inn's Quay at Dublin on 17 December 1773 where they proved a sensational success.[6] Astley's Learned Horse Billy even featured as a special act with a dwarf called the Corsican Fairy. The Astleys returned year after year to Ireland and in 1789 Philip erected the Royal Amphitheatre in Peter Street, Dublin, under a Royal Letter Patent of 23 April 1788 which permitted him to present his circus for seven years between 29 October and the following 29 January but expressly forbade the presentation of regular plays. It was a familiar situation, because Astley had been arraigned and even imprisoned for contravening the laws that regulated theatrical performances.

Sometimes rumour outstripped fact with the Gun Trick. Such was the case with an Indian juggler called Kia Khan Khruse who landed in Britain in 1815 as part of the troupe of 'The Four Surprising Indian Jugglers just arrived in this country from Seringapatam' under the leadership of Ramo Samee, a performer who was to become a household name during the next thirty or so years. Kia Khan Khruse was rumoured to have been a victim of the bullet catching trick. Thus Dexter[7] has given a highly dramatic account of how he was killed outright at the Pall Mall Music Hall in Dublin in 1818 at the hands of a marksman who used his own pistol instead of the juggler's weapon. However, an advertisement for the troupe dated 26 August 1818 seems to refute this untimely end:

Mr Ramo Samee, principal performer, wishes to intimate to the public that there is no truth in the statement as to one of the jugglers dying in consequence of Swallowing the Sword, or being shot with a pistol in Ireland.

Khruse must have parted company from Ramo Samee's troupe in 1818 for the playbill illustrated shows him appearing under his own aegis at the Old Ship Rooms in Brighton on 25 May 1818. Billed as the Chief of the Indian Jugglers, from Lisbon, instructed in the Caves of Salamanca, his performance was divided into two parts which featured contortionism and balancing feats followed by legerdemain. He worked his magic with swords, rings, balls, knives, handkerchiefs, ladders and money, and also displayed his 'superiority' by performing blindfold.

Playbill for Kia Khan Khruse at Brighton (1818), in which he refutes the rumour that he was killed while performing the Gun Trick.

Such delectable items as frying a number of eggs on a sheet of writing paper, turning a ball into a toad, barley changed into wheat and three shillings into a horse's foot were part of his repertoire. It was also stated that 'He will fire a pistol, charged with 12 pins, at a pack of cards thrown up, and lodge the pins in the identical card which had been drawn and returned to the pack by one of the company'. The principal feat in relation to our present interest was, however, contained in the statement:

And again (though it has been said he was killed in performing this astonishing Trick), he will catch in his hand a marked Bullet, added to the powder-loading of a Pistol, which any one present may fire at him for that purpose.

Kia Khan Khruse, within the next couple of years or so, had become sufficiently famous in his own right to be featured under the letter 'K' in an alphabetic *Arabian Nights* with the formidable title of *Aldiborontophoskyphorniostikos* published for children by Dean & Company around 1820.[8]

K, Kia Khan Khruse, the Conjurer, transmogrified them into Pippins, because Snip's wife cried Illikipilliky! lass a-day!

Whether this nonsense appealed to the children is difficult to say!

In the nineteenth century the most successful exponent of the Gun Trick was undoubtedly Professor John Henry Anderson, the Great Wizard of the North. Not only did he feature the effect for much of his career, but, to his credit, he also survived it, to die eventually of natural causes in Darlington in 1874. Now, as we have had occasion to note elsewhere (page 111), Anderson was one of the greatest magical advertisers, and it is not surprising therefore to find him also claiming to be the sole inventor of the Gun Trick and describing it as 'the most wonderful feat ever attempted by living man'. There was even an invitation to 'Bring your own gun'. He used this featured effect to conclude his show, and for a very

Annie Vernone, 'the Only Female Professor of Modern Magic in the World', was seventeen when she appeared in Hull in 1857, and was assisted by her seven-year-old sister Florence. She claimed to be an American and featured the Gun Trick 'never before performed by a lady'.

Grand Opera House.

HARRY L. HAMLIN, Manager.

Announcement Extraordinary!

SUNDAY, SEPT. 5.   BY SPECIAL REQUEST.

ADELAIDE HERRMANN

Will on this night only perform her late husband's

ORIGINAL AND SENSATIONAL BULLET CATCHING ACT.

She stands as a target and catches the bullets fired point blank at her by six local Militia-men under the command of a Sergeant. The regular military rifles and the regular United States Government ammunition will be used in this test. Adelaide Herrmann will not handle or even touch the ammunition, which goes directly from the hands of the parties from the audience, who will mark the bullets, to the soldiers composing the firing party. The rifles will be then loaded by the soldiers, who, at the word of command, will face Adelaide Herrmann and fire at her point blank. Adelaide Herrman will catch the previously marked bullets in her hand and return them to those who marked them, still warm from the barrels of the rifles.

Adelaide Herrmann (1853–1932) at the Chicago Grand Opera House in 1897 caught in her hand six bullets fired by militiamen.

good reason which was unambiguously stated in his advertising matter. Thus Anderson's playbill for the New Strand Theatre, London, in 1840 proclaimed the Gun Trick and went on to say:

of which unique and brilliant feat he is the *absolute Inventor*, and it is so perfect a delusion, as almost to justify the supposition of INVULNERABILITY. In this splendid invention, he distinctly assures the Public, that the extraordinary Mystery of the trick is not effected by the aid of any accomplice, or by other conceivable devices, as the Public frequently, and in some instances correctly imagine, but that any Gentleman may really Load the Gun in the usual manner, inserting himself A MARKED REAL LEADEN BALL!! The Gun being then Fired off at the Wizard, he will instantly produce and exhibit the same bullet in his HAND. The above, although a most Extraordinary Deception, one that creates greater speculation than the others, is not a pleasant Experiment, particularly to Ladies; consequently it will not be performed till all the other Delusions are finished.

So, out of consideration for the fairer sex, Anderson enabled them to see the rest of his programme and then to withdraw discreetly, thereby avoiding witnessing the 'unpleasant' Gun Trick experiment. One wonders just how many availed themselves of the Wizard's thoughtfulness—Victorian ladies were often made of sterner stuff than later generations credit.

One such little lady was Annie Vernone who, in 1857 at the tender age of seventeen years, was billed as 'The Only Female Professor of Modern Magic in the World'. Assisted by her sister Florence Vernone, who was just seven, she was one of the treats for Hull Fair week at the Theatre Royal. Not only was Annie impervious to the unpleasantness of the Gun Trick but also to the bullets themselves, for the playbills announced she would introduce this celebrated trick, 'Never before performed by a Lady', and allow anyone to try to shoot her, catching the bullet in her hand and thereby proving her invulnerability! Annie Vernone appears to have been the first of the very few female exponents of the bullet catch during the two hundred years of its flamboyant performance.

A later, more famous, magicienne who occasionally performed this illusion was Adelaide Herrmann, widow of the renowned Alexander Herrmann, who was an extremely popular and successful magician in the USA during the last three decades of the nineteenth century. After Herrmann's death in December 1896, Adelaide carried on her husband's show, initially with the assistance of Leon Herrmann, Alexander's twenty-nine-year-old nephew. This arrangement endured for three seasons until their clashing personalities led to the dissolution of the partnership, when Leon took out his own show.

Adelaide continued on her own, indomitably and successfully; indeed she was seventy-five before she finally retired from the stage; she died in 1932 at the age of seventy-nine.

Alexander Herrmann performed the bullet catch solely on special occasions and usually for charity functions. Throughout his career he exposed himself to the marksmen—he used five or more—on only seven occasions. It has been recorded that Adelaide could not bear the sight of Alexander facing the firing squad and invariably locked herself in her dressing-room when he presented the feat.[9] However, within nine months of her husband's death from a heart attack, Adelaide was offering herself as the target. By special request, on Sunday 5 September 1897, at the Chicago Grand Opera House, it was announced that she would perform her late husband's sensational effect, with the assistance of six local militiamen under the command of a Sergeant. This she accomplished successfully, catching six previously marked bullets in her hand and returning them to those who had marked them while they were still warm from the barrels of the rifles.

The Gun Trick has always been a dangerous one to perform because the gun is out of the conjurer's control at the critical time of firing. Anderson was well aware of the dangers since, as a young man, as we have seen, he had been apprenticed to a magician named Scott who, it will be no surprise to learn, also claimed to have been the inventor of the Gun Trick. Scott's face was terribly scarred from a button which a spectator had secretly dropped into the barrel of the gun during the performance of this feat. The youthful Anderson learned the trick from Scott and also pulled off a trick of his own, for he married Scott's daughter and then struck out to make his own career as a conjurer with his new wife.

Anderson had a close call with the Gun Trick on at least one occasion. Arthur À Beckett[10] has recorded an incident which involved a friend who was, as he put it, 'an admirable amateur conjurer'. Opinions may differ as to the admirability of his friend in view of subsequent events when that worthy offered himself as an assistant to the Wizard of the North. He took the gun and ammunition and duly loaded it. At this stage it was the custom of the Wizard to give the bullet a final tap with his wand to ensure that it was rammed down properly, an operation which was vital to the subsequent success of the feat.

This the amateur knew and politely declined the Professor's assistance.

Anderson did not insist but coolly walked to the side of the stage and then called out: 'Now, sir, take a good aim at me and fire!'

The amateur conjurer hesitated, as he was well aware that the gun he held was really loaded.

'Fire, sir, fire!' cried Anderson.

The amateur lowered the weapon and, saying he could not let it off, returned it to the Wizard who immediately, under the pretext of checking whether it had been properly loaded, effected the necessary operation. He then handed the gun to someone else. But, before the gun was fired, he addressed the audience: 'Ladies and Gentlemen, the person who has just resumed his seat knew my trick, and foiled it. If he had fired, this, probably, would have been my last appearance before you. But he hadn't sufficient nerve to shoot me!'

As the realization that Anderson had risked his life, rather than confess himself beaten, swept across the house, the applause swelled into deafening tumult. And À Beckett wryly remarked that his friend told him he felt rather small and regretted his penchant for practical joking. As well he might!

The impact that Anderson made with the Gun Trick is evident when one realizes he served as the inspiration for a one-act play which was published in 1856. As a thespian himself, he doubtless derived much satisfaction from this event even though he was pilloried by it.

The Great Gun Trick—A Magical Squib in One Act, was written by Christian Le Ros, the pseudonym of William J. Sorrell, a member of the Dramatic Author's Society and author of *The Amateur's Handbook and Guide to Home or Drawing Room Theatricals*. The publisher was Thomas Hailes Lacy, a well known theatrical bookseller of Wellington Street, Strand, London, and the play a twenty-page paperback which sold for the princely sum of sixpence. The author in his introduction said:

The idea of this little piece was suggested by an ingenious advertisement issued by the Wizard of the North during his performances at the Lyceum

Adelaide Herrmann, widow of the Great Herrmann, carried on her husband's show for thirty years after his death in 1896. 'The Flight of the Favourite' was the transposition of a girl from one raised cabinet to another.

Theatre, in the autumn of 1855; and it is almost needless to say, that whatever point there may be in THE GREAT GUN TRICK, is due to the celebrity of Mr Anderson—while whatever success it may have achieved, is entirely owing to the great talent of our most accomplished comedian, Mr Charles Mathews.

Clearly the play was considered worthy of the technique of Charles James Mathews, Junior, who held the supreme place in the sphere of light comedy at that time, and of being staged at a principal London theatre, the Theatre Royal, Drury Lane. Additionally, its topicality must have ensured its success. Thus there was a nice allusion to Albert Smith's *Ascent of Mont Blanc* at the Egyptian Hall in Piccadilly, currently all the rage of London, with: 'At last I heard of a man in Piccadilly who was making lots of money by a mountain—I dare say you've heard of him—we all know lots of Smiths—there's one here, not a bad fellow neither, but that's between ourselves.'

The plot concerns one Augustus Trinklet, the Great Wizard of the SSW by E, Legitimate King of Conjurers—Emperor of all the Wizards from whatever point of the compass they may come, fantastic, romantic and necromantic. He soliloquizes how his life was saved at St Valerie-sur-Somme by a young woman who rejoiced in the name of Sophonisba. Having saved him from the river she then disappeared from his life and he has been searching for her in vain ever since. His only clue is her pale green silk bonnet, which she had left behind on the riverbank.

The show starts and, after a marked half-crown is discovered in a ball of wool, Trinklet calls for an assistant from the audience. This turns out to be Snap, a bailiff, who is intent on serving a writ on Trinklet. Snap is vanished by means of an extinguisher, and a further assistant now comes up.

Strange quirk of fate! This is Brown to whom Trinklet owes £100. Brown's coat is torn in two and restored. His small dog is now wrapped in paper, vanishes, and reappears in a basket, and then Brown is asked to participate in The Great Gun Trick. Only in this case Trinklet announces: 'I am enabled to adopt an entirely new method of performing this celebrated trick; to prevent the possibility of collusion, *I* fire the gun and a *stranger* catches the bullet.' Brown is far from enamoured of this idea and, in the ensuing events, inadvertently lends

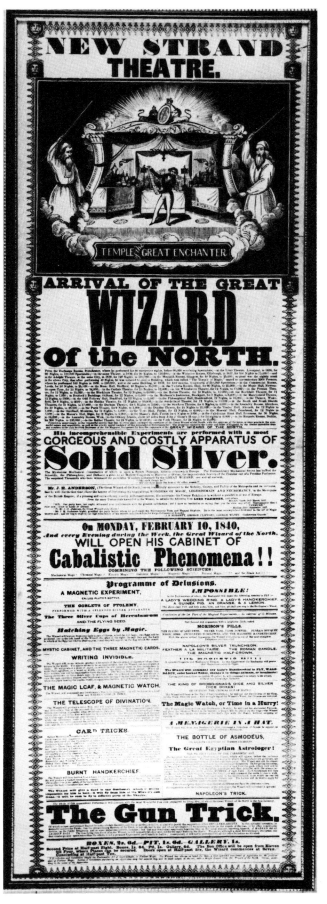

Trinklet a £100 note instead of a fiver. The £100 note is then transposed with the bailiff's writ, on the principle that exchange is no robbery.

Now a lady's bonnet is required; one is borrowed from a private box on the stage, a pale green silk bonnet—*the* bonnet! Sophonisba is found. She rushes on stage. 'Good gracious,' Brown exclaims, 'that's my daughter! What are you doing in London, miss? I left you at your Aunt's in Berkshire. I'll teach you to run after conjurers.'

After further vicissitudes all ends happily, needless to say, with Brown giving his blessing to the marriage and allowing Trinklet to keep the £100 note.

The stage instructions inform us that the scene is a stage prepared for a Wizard's Performance and the play calls for a cast of eight. The time is 1855 and we are told: 'The stage is fitted up for the performance of a Conjuror. Table C. and R. and L. Apparatus, &c; Large Extinguisher near R.H. table. Automaton figure in glass case, L.H.; the arrangements not altogether completed.'

When the curtain rises two of the cast, Buttons and Dibbles, are discovered, the latter seated. A little of their dialogue is not without interest:

BUT. Now turn round and let's look at you. A little more paint on the left cheek—your wig a little more over your eyes; fight your way to a good place in the pit—look as wonder-struck as you can—and 't would puzzle a conjuror to find out you had ever been in a play house before.
DIB. Am I to have the padlock through my cheek tonight?
BUT. No.
DIB. Or drink three quarts of beer and have it drawn out of my fingers ends into a funnel?
BUT. No; indeed!—these tricks are only fit for a country audience; *here* we must have something newer and more genteel. You're to lend a silver watch and strongly object to it being smashed with a hammer—to have six eggs taken out of your hair, and bellow lustily at ten sovereigns in a leather bag being turned into peppermint lozenges.

Mathews had one piece of by-play in *The Gun Trick* which apparently always caused much merri-

Anderson had emerged as the Great Wizard of the North by the time he arrived at the New Strand Theatre in London in 1840. He made great play on his use of solid silver apparatus and he included the Gun Trick in his performances.

ment.[10] At the commencement of the farce he would produce an umbrella and, attaching it to a wire that came from the flies, call attention to it. He would declaim: 'Ladies and Gentlemen, will you please observe this umbrella. It is of ordinary but strong silk and the handle is readily identifiable. Here, examine it for yourselves.' Whereupon he would pass it around.

When he regained possession he would say: 'Now I shall attach it to this wire, and I must request you to watch it. I particularly wish you to see that it is touched by no one.'

Then the play would run its course without any further allusion to the suspended brolly, and it was still there when the curtain fell. At this juncture a confederate in the audience would call out 'The umbrella!' and the cry would be taken up. Charles Mathews re-entered, seemingly rather surprised by the noise. Then he appeared to remember the umbrella and hastened to remove it. The cries were followed by dead silence as the audience waited expectantly for some miracle to be performed with it. Mathews merely smiled and, tucking the brolly under his arm, remarked: 'Ladies and gentlemen, I am infinitely obliged to you. The fact is I am always losing my umbrella—especially behind the scenes of this theatre. So I thought that if I could induce all of you to keep your eyes upon it, it would be quite safe. Thank you very much indeed.'

And with a bow he would retire amidst general hilarity.

If Henry Morley, the prolific nineteenth-century author, is to be believed, Anderson did not take too kindly to the initial appearance of *The Great Gun Trick*.[11] In his *Journal of a London Playgoer* for 19 January 1856, Morley refers to the piece as a pleasant quiz upon the conjurings and claptraps of the Wizard of the North and observes that, as the caricature threatened to prove a little more amusing than the conjuring itself, the Covent Garden Wizard was up in arms. Hitherto Anderson had carried on the war by means of posters or cartels, but a direct attack was now threatened in the shape of a farce 'courteously' entitled *Twenty Minutes with an Impudent Puppy*. In the event the counter attack was not successful for Morley's next entry on 16 February recounts that Mr Charles Mathews was still making merry as the Wizard of the South-South-West by East at Drury Lane while, at Covent Garden, the Wizard of the North had given up the attempt to retaliate with a small squib that would not go off

satisfactorily. 'The public threw so much cold water on it, that after a little hissing it went out; and the great Professor resumed the career of actor upon which he had entered'—a reference to Anderson's appearances as Rob Roy and as William in *Black-eyed Susan*.

However, a rapprochement between Anderson and Mathews was obviously soon achieved for, on the Covent Garden playbill for 3 March, advertised as Professor Anderson's Great Carnival Benefit, it was announced that Charles Mathews would himself appear in the celebrated Drury Lane farce of *The Great Gun Trick*.

The Carnival Benefit was a marathon endeavour. It started at 1pm with the Covent Garden pantomime *Ye Belle Alliance;* which was followed at 4pm by a two-act drama, *Time Tries All;* then at 5.30pm came Anderson himself in the Scottish drama *Gilderoy;* succeeded by the opera *La Sonnambula* at 7pm, leading up to Mathews and *The Great Gun Trick* at 9.15. After this farce, at 10.30pm Mr Leigh Murray joined forces with Professor Anderson to 'imitate Mr Charles Mathews, Mr Charles Kean and Professor Anderson in the New Squib entitled *What does he Want?*' In this item Anderson introduced part of his conjuring repertoire and Murray, made up to resemble Charles Mathews, appeared as a rival conjurer and performed some tricks that were claimed to be 'entirely his own' and in respect of the performance of which the audience was 'requested to order from the nearest dairy a large supply of the "milk of human kindness" '.[12] Even then the evening was not yet over for those with sufficient stamina—it concluded with a Grand Ballet. Prices of admission for this twelve-hour extravaganza ranged from five shillings in the Grand Balcony to one shilling in the Gallery, which seems to be an incredible bargain. The second night of the Great Carnival, on Tuesday 4 March, was devoted to the Great Wizard's Grand Bal Masqué, an evening which ended in tragedy in the early hours of the Wednesday, when the Covent Garden Theatre was burned down (page 115).

Anderson made the most of *The Gun Trick* and in his advertising matter capitalized on the ready-made plot that Le Ros had presented him with; he was still using it eleven years after the play was written. Thus in July 1867 Professor and Miss Anderson were presenting their Royal Entertainment 'The World of Magic and Second Sight' at the Theatre Royal in Hull. Throughout the Wizard's three-week stay the amusement columns of the *Eastern Morning News*

£1,000 REWARD!

TO

YOUNG LADIES

AND OTHERS.

On the Evening of Monday, July 8th, there was a Young Lady in the Stalls of the Theatre Royal, who lent to Professor Anderson a Bonnet, trimmed with Pale Green, which the Wizard burnt to ashes, and afterwards restored to her in perfect condition. A gentleman in the Reserved Seats chanced to see her face in an after-part of the Evening, and recognized her as one to whom he was indebted for the safety of his life, while residing at Valerie-sur-Somme, in France, in the year 1866. At that time she did not, he believes, learn his name, nor did he have an opportunity, though he much wished it, of obtaining hers. Fortune now seems to offer him a chance to repay the debt of gratiude he owes her in a manner which may possibly be agreeable to himself and his preserver. Will she communicate with him, or if a false modesty prevents her doing so, will she kindly allow a friend to be the medium of her message? In the event of her altogether declining, the above sum will be paid to anyone who was present at the time who may know her, and will forward her Name and Address to Messrs. Boone and Creswick, Solicitors, Parliament-street. The Lady herself can communicate with the advertiser by addressing "Sir Charles S————— to be left at the General Post Office." Whether she will please to make herself known, or whether a remorseless fate should prevent the advertiser ever discovering her name, he will never during life forget Valerie-sur-Somme nor the evening on which they both saw the Wizard at the Theatre Royal, July 8th.

PRINTED AT HILL'S STEAM WORKS, 35 CHURCH-LANE.

carried extensive advertisements for the show and the news columns considerable reportage.[13] One of these advertisements had the eye-catching heading

£1000 REWARD—TO YOUNG LADIES AND OTHERS

and it was used also as a daybill, as the accompanying illustration shows. Perusal of the text quickly reveals Anderson's indebtedness to Le Ros for a most unusual theme. The pale green silk bonnet and the subtle introduction of a member of the aristocracy as the female-searching individual is, in the modern idiom, 'pure Anderson'!

Whenever magicians foregather and discuss the Gun Trick there is one tragedy above all others that exercises their minds, a tragedy that took from their midst one of the most talented members of their profession.[7] It was the second house on a Saturday night, 23 March 1918, and Chung Ling Soo, the Celestial Chinese Conjurer, was completing his week's appearances at the Wood Green Empire in North London. Included in his spectacular show was the Gun Trick, under the guise of 'Condemned to Death by the Boxers—Defying their Bullets'. A Chinese assistant stepped to the footlights and invited two gentlemen from the audience to assist Chung Ling Soo to demonstrate how he escaped from the Boxer bandits in the Chinese uprising of 1900. On this fateful Saturday two discharged soldiers came up and were invited to inspect the powder and ball for two old-fashioned muzzle-loading rifles. Soo poured a charge of black powder onto a tray and ignited it to prove that it was gunpowder. Meanwhile, a little female Chinese assistant had gone *via* the run-down into the audience and had asked two people to select two round lead bullets from a box. The chosen bullets were then secretly marked by cutting initials or other insignia on them with a knife, so that they could be identified later. They were placed in a cup and borne back to the stage where they were tipped into the hands of the two waiting volunteers. The Chinese magician poured gunpowder into the barrels, followed by wads to keep the charges in place. He removed the ramrods from the rifles and with them rammed the marked bullets home. The volunteers then carefully handed the loaded rifles to two of Soo's assistants, dressed as Chinese warriors, who were to be the marksmen. The volunteers were thanked, shaken by the hand and returned to their seats in the auditorium, their moment of glory over.

Chung Ling Soo now moved slowly to the right

Chung Ling Soo (William Elsworth Robinson, 1861–1918). A photograph mounted on his colourful red, green and gold notepaper.

of the stage, turned and faced the two Chinese warrior marksmen. The little Chinese girl solemnly handed him a china plate which he held up before him, chest height, at arm's length. The marksmen raised their rifles and a hush of expectancy fell over the crowded theatre. Soo braced himself and signalled his chief assistant who gave the command to fire.

Two deafening shots rang out and acrid smoke hung over the rifles. The magnificently gowned magician staggered and fell on the stage. The ripple of applause, beginning to swell, was suddenly arrested as the audience realized that tonight the trick had had an unscheduled climax. The curtain was rung down as, on stage, the bewildered company surrounded the crumpled body of Soo. He was wrapped tenderly in a curtain and, after being attended by three doctors and a nurse, taken by ambulance to Wood Green Cottage Hospital where, at 5am the following day, he died. A bullet had passed completely through his right lung.

While Soo's tragic death made spectacular headlines for the nation's press, it also provided them with the exposure of a carefully kept secret, for the world at large now learned that the inscrutable Chung Ling Soo was none other than William Elsworth Robinson, an American born in New York City on 2 April 1861. While members of the magic fraternity knew all about Soo's impersonation, the public image had been carefully preserved whenever he met the press. In Chinese make-up, he spoke only 'Chinese', which had to be 'interpreted' by his stage manager, Frank Kametaro, for the benefit of the assembled reporters! The legend of these 'Chinese' interviews has blossomed over the years since his death, to the extent that it is often stated that he wore Chinese costume on all occasions. Yet, strange as it may seem, in his earlier days he had not only allowed the secret of his identity to be revealed in the press but also agreed to be labelled as a fraud!

This remarkable disclosure occurred in 1908 when Soo was topping the bill at the Olympia Theatre, Liverpool. Charles Hand, who had been friendly with Soo for about a year, wanted something sensational with which to launch the first number of his new paper *The Liverpool Theatrical News*.[14] Hand suggested to Soo that, having hoodwinked the British public for the past eight years, he would be even

more popular with them if it were revealed that he was not a member of the race that had perpetrated the atrocities of the Boxer Rebellion in 1900 but was really a clever Lancashire man from Bolton. (Here it must be emphasized that the stories surrounding Soo's birthplace are legion and it seems possible he might even have fostered them himself. He has been recorded variously as a Scotsman, Yorkshireman, Lancastrian and even from Birmingham, but his link with Bolton was a real one inasmuch as he had a warehouse for illusions there.) Soo decided to go along with the proposals and indemnities were drawn up by Hand against legal action. The 'Chinese' conjurer signed. The banner headline

CHUNG LING SOO
THE FRAUD

duly appeared in the first issue of the new theatrical paper, giving it a sensational start, and it is evident that William Robinson, *alias* Chung Ling Soo, did not suffer any ill consequences from what might have been a professionally suicidal move.

The inquest on Soo, held at Wood Green Town Hall on 28 March, was adjourned after the Coroner

Obverse and reverse of a beer mat advertising Chung Ling Soo's version of the Gun Trick, 'Condemned to Death by the Boxers'.

See A Dream of Wealth as Presented by Chung Ling Soo. It will not cost you Five Pounds to do so, but whatever price you pay you will say it is well worth it. Five 1914 London SIGNED Chung Ling Soo. Chief Conjurer

had taken formal evidence from members of the company and from one of the doctors, Dr W. R. Porter, who attended him. Mrs Olive Robinson, Soo's widow, who had assisted him on stage as Suee Seen, told of the events leading up to the fatal shooting and of the part she played in ensuring that her husband received the marked bullets to enable him apparently to catch them on the plate. Duplicate bullets were loaded into the guns and a secret mechanism prevented them from being fired. She had no knowledge of the mechanism and neither had any of Soo's assistants. Her husband, she said, always cleaned and loaded the rifles himself and never allowed anyone else to handle them. They had been in use for about twelve years.

When the inquest resumed Mr Robert Churchill, the famous gun expert, was present to describe his findings on the guns which the police had delivered to him without interference after the shooting. It was he who disclosed for the first time the secret of Soo's rifles.[15] Matter-of-factly he reported they were 12-bore single-barrelled muzzle-loading rifles with a small ramrod tube beneath each barrel. In Soo's act the ramrods, used for the loading, were never returned to their tubes, an unusual feature which Churchill had, when witnessing the trick, attributed to the avoidance of undue delay in the build-up to the

Chung Ling Soo used these 'fivers' as a novel form of advertisement, distributing them in the towns where he appeared.

climax of the effect. His examination revealed, however, that herein lay the key to the mystery: the ramrod tube was prepared as a second barrel to the gun. The barrel proper was effectively sealed so that when the percussion cap was fired the flash could not take its normal course and ignite the propellant powder charge which sent the bullet on its way. Instead, the Coroner heard that a separate channel had been bored to give access to the ramrod tube so that the detonating fire was diverted to the blank charge in the lower barrel. Thus the bullet in the barrel proper was normally never discharged and it was the small and harmless charge of powder that Soo had secretly placed in the ramrod tube which made the bang. After each performance Soo would extract the bullet from the barrel and reload the ramrod tube with powder.

The inquest was informed that one rifle was in good condition but the other, which had fired the fatal shot, had developed an imperfection due to Soo's technique for withdrawing the bullet. Normally one unloads a muzzle-loader by withdrawing the bullet with the worm screw that is fitted inside

a brass cap on the end of every ramrod. This, naturally, would have damaged the specially marked bullets that he used, and which his volunteer assistants believed to have been marked by other members of the audience. So after every performance he unscrewed the breech plug in the base of the barrel to remove the bullet and powder. This was the procedure that cumulatively led to disaster. Churchill opined that no muzzle loader could stand up to such treatment for long—normally the breech block would never be removed except by an expert gun-smith, and then only occasionally for the purpose of lapping the inside of the barrel. The result was that the thread had worn to such an extent that the fitting was quite loose.

The final, fatal factor was the mesh of the powder Soo used. It was of very fine grain, almost dust-like. Churchill said for safety he should have used a powder of much coarser texture. With constant loading the fine powder had worked its way along the imperfect thread in the screw of the breech plug until a train of it led to the hole in the nipple that held the percussion cap. And so, on 23 March 1918, the inevitable happened and the exploding cap ignited both the blank charge in the ramrod tube and the fatal charge in the barrel. Police Inspector Cornish confirmed that the rifles had been taken to the gunsmith after the shooting and they could not have been tampered with. The East Middlesex Coroner, Mr A. M. M. Forbes, having assessed all the evidence, brought in a verdict of 'Death from Misadventure'.

We have dealt at some length with the gun expert's evidence for a very good reason. After Chung Ling Soo's death, rumours started to circulate that he had been murdered and even that he had committed suicide. Some writers latched on to these stories since clearly they made good copy. One of them, Will Goldston, was a magician himself, author of many technical books on magic and a manufacturer and dealer in conjuring apparatus. In 1929 he published a book titled *Sensational Tales of Mystery Men* which carried a chapter headed 'Was Chung Ling Soo Murdered?'. Goldston's thesis has been clinically dissected and exposed for what it is worth by Will Dexter,[7] and the farrago of inaccurate statements simply underlines the fact that he was, as his title patently proclaimed, selling Sensational Tales.

The one magician who faced death in hundreds of spectacular ways during his career was the celebrated Harry Houdini—yet he never performed the Gun Trick. Although he had contemplated including it in his programmes and certainly wasn't afraid to perform it, he was earnestly entreated by his old friend Harry Kellar (1849–1922), the Dean of American magicians, not to entertain the idea. Kellar told him: 'No matter what precautions are taken with the bullet-catching trick, it's a damn-fool trick, and the chances for an accident or a "job" are always present.' He wrote insistently and persuasive-ly: 'Now, my dear boy, this is advice from the heart. *Don't try the bullet-catching trick*. There is always the biggest kind of risk that some dog will "job" you. And we can't afford to lose Houdini. Harry, listen to your friend Kellar, who loves you as his own son, DON'T DO IT!' And Harry never did.

Chung Ling Soo used numerous different lithographs which made a glorious splash of colour on the advertise-ment boards. To have reached the highest pinnacle of fame at a time when there were so many expert con-jurers was testimony to his great artistry and by no means merely advertising licence.

15
SOUNDS, SHADOWS AND SHACKLES

The story of Houdini's life proves more
stimulating than we might have expected, and
it makes us think better of humanity than the
lives of many other figures of more
conventional reputation in more
distinguished fields.

Edmund Wilson, *A Great Magician* (1928)

The ability to create illusion is not confined to either the possession of the visual skills of sleight-of-hand or the application of mechanical ingenuity, but extends also to auditory phenomena, as exploited by the ventriloquist, and mimicry—often allied to a rapid change of costume which was the prerequisite of the protean entertainer. These performers were entirely dependent upon their own unaided efforts. The Victorian era witnessed the rise and fall of the single-handed entertainer, although the breed is by no means extinct, and some notable twentieth-century examples could be cited.

Mr W. S. Woodin (1825–88) was one of the first of this talented band who, with the support of a pianist, kept an audience amused and happy for a couple of hours. Some idea of the scope of his performance may be gained from the accompanying playbill for Leith, and we learn a little more from a review of his show at the Music Hall in Jarratt Street, Hull, where he was billed for five nights at the end of April 1868, presenting his Comic Character Entertainment entitled *Baden-Baden* and *Up in the Air*. The *Eastern Morning News* on 29 April noted that Mr Woodin had given the first of his popular entertainments to a select and numerous audience. *Baden-Baden* was descriptive of life on the promenade, at the gaming tables and on the race course. For the last venue Woodin assumed the character of Joe Downey, a Yorkshire jockey, and concluded with 'a good song and the celebrated jockey hornpipe'. The critic noted that the changes in dress were effected with great rapidity and took the audience by surprise.

The second part of the show, *Up in the Air*, involved some mechanical effects. The scene was a house top, reached by all kinds of persons in various ways, embracing events which were 'ludicrous in the extreme', and caused much merriment amongst the audience.

The Reverend Benjamin J. Armstrong, Vicar of Dereham, Norfolk, from 1850 to 1888, was a great theatregoer and his diary[1] for 21 April 1854 records: 'Went with my father to see "Woodin's Carpet Bag and Sketch Book". This Woodin impersonated upwards of fifty characters. His imitations were really admirable and the rapidity with which he changed his dress marvellous.'

A female protean artist of the early twentieth century was Mademoiselle Von Etta (later Vonetta) who was also a splendid illusionist. Her career had started in a romantic manner for, at the age of sixteen, she had eloped and married Vincent Paul, whom she met while appearing at amateur concerts. Initially she worked as a singer, accompanying the lantern slides that her husband projected, and was also an accomplished dancer. Vonetta's own act flourished during the period 1906 to 1914, when she was billed

William Samuel Woodin (1825–88), single-handed entertainer, was a versatile monologuist and quick-change artist. Many of his monologues were written for him by his friend E. L. Blanchard, prolific pantomime writer, who was also a conjurer.

ASSEMBLY ROOM,
LEITH.

FOR ONE NIGHT ONLY !
MONDAY, MAY 4th.

Doors open at Half-past Seven.   *Commence at Eight.*

W. S. WOODIN'S

NEW ENTERTAINMENT

CABINET OF CURIOSITIES.

Tickets to be obtained of Mr. JOHNSTONE, Bernard Street and
Mr. C. DRUMMOND, Kirkgate.

FIRST SEATS · 2s.   SECOND SEATS · 1s.   BACK SEATS · 6d.

CARRIAGES TO BE ORDERED AT TEN.

as 'The only Lady Illusionist, Protean and Quick-Change Artiste, introducing the most Colossal Act ever presented to the Public. The Feminine miracle Worker, performing unaided. A series of Mystifying Illusions. Conjuring, Electrical Dances, Sleight of Hand Act, Dancing, Quick Changes.' She offered £500 to anyone who could prove that she used stage traps, wires or mirrors in her illusions, or that she introduced a double during her rapid costume changes.

Vonetta made her stage entrance in male evening dress and opened by apparently causing smoke to pass from a cigarette to an empty glass. Retiring for a second behind a screen, she reappeared as a Spanish dancing girl and then commenced her marvellous quick-change act, making twenty-four different changes of costume all in the space of a few minutes. She continued with her magic, occupying the stage for over half-an-hour and concluding with a colourful, rousing finale called 'Flags of All Nations'—the production of two enormous trophies of flags, from the second of which appeared three girls.

One of the best known ventriloquists during the first half of the nineteenth century was Mr Love, whose entertainments in his own right, or as part of a general theatrical programme, were extremely popular. William Edward Love was born in London in 1806, the son of a wealthy merchant. He was educated at a preparatory school in Essex and subsequently at Nelson House, Wimbledon, which he left at the age of fifteen. Shortly afterwards he started his career as a ventriloquist.

Love combined rapid costume changes with his ventriloquism. His programme consisted of a series of sketches, each involving several characters, usually written for him 'by Gentlemen of high standing in Circles of Literature', as he so delightfully put it! Titles of these sketches included 'The Peregrinations of a Polyphonist', 'Love in a Labyrinth', 'Love in All Shapes', 'Love's Labour's Lost', and 'Love's Lenten Lucubrations'.

The performances were clearly designed to have educational as well as entertainment appeal, as witness the following long-winded, high-flown statement:

Although Mr LOVE's various Entertainments have been constructed with a view of creating an hour's amusement, and raising a laugh at the expense of some of the more prominent foibles of the age we live in, it is presumed a more important object has been attained. To the historical Student and Antiquarian, his productions cannot fail to prove a source of considerable interest and gratification, as they will satisfactorily elucidate the nature of the means which were resorted to in remote ages, to impose upon the superstitious multitudes, by the Pythians or Priestesses of Apollo at Delphi, the ENGASTRIMANDI of the Greeks mentioned by Oecumenius and St. Chrysostom, and by the Soothsayers, Magicians and Sorcerers (who make so conspicuous a figure in Roman History)

Mademoiselle Vonetta, 'The Only Lady Illusionist, Protean and Quick Change Artiste', who flourished during the period 1906–14. The variety of her costume changes may be appreciated from this striking poster.

assisted by Oracles, Idols, and other instruments of equivocation and deceit. This singular power after having occasioned much controversy between the most eminent Physiologists of Europe, and brought into the field (as is quite usual in similar cases) a host of imitators and pretenders, possessing a vast amount of assurance, but no portion of genuine talent, is at length generally admitted on all sides to be a gift of nature and chance, conjoined with Science, experience of late having shewn the utter impossibility of teaching it, except to those born with the necessary quality Vocal Organ, by the exercise of which, strange voices may be heard to proceed from and given distance in the Air, under the Earth, &c.

It may be worth while to remark that the whole of Mr LOVE's Entertainments are sustained by himself without assistance, or any description of trickery, fraud, confederacy, collusion, or accompaniment, either in sight, or out of sight of the Audience.

Mr Love first came into prominence in the Capital in 1836 when he appeared at the St James's Theatre,[2] concluding a programme which embraced impersonations, songs, dances and monologues, with 'Love's Labour's Lost', an acoustic sketch of eight voices. On Wednesdays and Fridays during Lent he was also to be seen at Almack's Rooms, St James's, with 'Love's Lenten Lucubrations'. In 1838 he produced his 'Ignis Fatui' in Oxford, which apparently was so successful that he hastened to London and engaged Almack's Rooms again for the season. Thereafter he travelled widely and considerably enhanced his reputation in the USA. He labelled himself a 'polyphonist'; i.e., one who speaks with many voices.

Love was a master of the 'distant voice' and his colloquy 'A Reminiscence of By-Gone Times: or Past Ten o'Clock, and a Cloudy Night' gave full scope for this accomplishment. In its course, Love introduced the invisible character Mr Midnight, the Watchman, who was at first heard crying the hour of the night, at an apparent distance of about a quarter of a mile from the Rooms. The imaginary person was then heard in the street, approaching the house, step by step, until he appeared to have arrived under the window; the window was thrown up, and an altercation ensued between Mr Midnight and several of his fraternity outside. The dispute between the parties, after becoming heated, was amicably adjusted, and the sketch at length terminated with a song in which all the persons represented took a part. The characters then wished each other good night, and were finally heard in the act of departing in different directions.

The performer's versatile powers of imitation and vocal expression were impressive and won much admiring comment from the press. *The Illustrated London News* of 25 March 1843, on the occasion of his appearances at the Strand Theatre, said:

He can imitate an 'infant puling in its mother's arms' and an infant laughing on its mother's knee. He can represent an old crone chuckling or an old crone wheezing and uttering malediction both loud and deep. He can depict a merry old man and a cross old man, a blustering boatswain and a solemn Quaker. The tones of the lover and his lass . . . In a word, he can, with the rapidity of thought, bring upon the stage a numerous dramatic corps, so perfect in their respective parts, so diversified in character, and so humorous in their exhibition, that they play those fantastic tricks which make ladies and gentlemen die with laughter . . . if what he represents may be deemed a picture, he is a painter of first-rate genius, and with all that art can do to make him pre-eminent in his profession.

William Edward Love (1806–67), the ventriloquist and polyphonist, whose shows were extremely popular from about 1835 until he suffered paralysis in 1858.

The nature of some of Love's impersonations may be gathered from a report of his appearance in Hull in 1845,[3] when the motley characters included Mr Hicjacket, a garrulous repeater of queer epitaphs; Monsieur Le Baron La France, the facsimile of a confident French Militaire, discoursing with unabashed absurdity upon subjects utterly beyond his knowledge; Mr Graball, the searcher after bargains; Mrs Tomkins, lean, red and sixty; Will Surge, a superannuated Man-of-War's man, a regular Jack Tar, affluent in dry jokes and tough yarns; and last, but not least, Gregory Glitter, a bejewelled and eyeglassed popinjay.

It is an interesting reflection of the times that the Hull critic noted approvingly the enthusiastic audiences which greeted Love appeared 'to be nightly growing in numbers and *respectability*'. In 1851, the year of the Great Exhibition, Love was at the St James's Theatre with his entertainment, which included imitations of the sounds of kitchen utensils as well as other sketches and impersonations— apparently everything *including* the kitchen sink! Four years later, when he was giving a 'London Season' at the Regent Gallery, *The Illustrated London News*[4] saw fit to compare him favourably with an earlier, celebrated exponent of the art of ventriloquism, Alexandre, of whom Sir David Brewster wrote so enthusiastically.[5] 'Brilliantly quick as were Alexandre's changes of personal appearance to suit the exigencies of the subject, Love is quicker. As a ventriloquist Alexandre was singularly excellent; but Love's artistical management of tone is as wonderfully real as it is rapid and complete in transition.' The overall conclusion reached was that Love was superior to Alexandre.

Love's season extended to 300 consecutive nights, culminating with his 2,406th performance in London. Unhappily he was overtaken by paralysis in 1858, when a benefit for him was organized at Sadler's Wells. After suffering nine years of illness, Love died in poor circumstances in 1867. His daughter made her début at the St James's Theatre as a member of the acting company there in the October of that same year,[2] and the theatrical tradition was carried on by his grand-daughter, Mabel Love, the popular principal of many musicals from the eighteen-nineties onwards, and subsequently in legitimate theatre. Postcards of this charming lady sold in their thousands and she was a favourite pin-up in that era which led up to the First World War.

It was in the eighteenth century that theatrical illusion created by shadows of cut-out figures first became a familiar form of entertainment, being imported from Italy—thus Hallam's Great Booth at Bartholomew Fair exhibited 'The Italian Shadows performed by the Best Masters from Italy' as early as 1737—but some forty years elapsed before their popularity was firmly established. Under the title of 'Les Ombres Chinoises', they attracted Londoners in their thousands and the conjurer-equestrian showman Philip Astley quickly added them to his programmes. But shadows produced by moveable cut-out figures are really outside the scope of our survey of conjuring and manual dexterity and we must therefore turn our attention to shadows fabricated by the hands themselves—the art of shadowgraphy.

While the origin of shadowgraphy must ever remain uncertain, it seems likely that the ability to create shadows in the likeness of animals by using one's hands was discovered by prehistoric Man and has been practised in crude form ever since. Precisely when the refinement of the art which led to its use for entertainment purposes first came about is equally unclear, but possibly it was during the eighteenth century. However, it was unquestionably a well recognized form of entertainment by the second half of the nineteenth century, and was incorporated in various volumes of home amusements in addition to being the subject of several publications devoted exclusively to the art. Frizzo, an Italian conjurer, is believed to have been the first to it is to him that the modern shadowgraphist is primarily indebted.[6] Further, Félicien Trewey (1845–1920), who raised the art to such perfection, was first imbued with the idea of becoming a shadowist after witnessing a performance by Frizzo (Enrico Longone) in Belgium.

The depiction of hand shadowgraphy by a visual artist came rather later than that of conjuring and ventriloquism. We have already noted that the Ulm Manuscript of 1404 depicting *Children of the Planets, Luna* incorporates a Cups and Balls performer, while William Hogarth's *An Election Entertainment* of 1755 includes a performance of the Talking Hand. The earliest record of shadowgraphy on the Continent seems to be the painting of Johan Schénau (1737–1806) titled *L'Origine de la Peinture ou Les Portraites à la Mode*, which depicts a scene wherein the man is busily tracing a silhouette of the lady's features, two

Félicien Trewey (1845–1920), superb French conjurer, juggler and shadowgraphist, who was a friend of the Lumière Brothers and first brought their Cinematographe to London in February 1896.

children are similarly engaged with the family cat and a third is making the familiar handshadow of a rabbit.

It may be conjectured that this picture was the inspiration for the first British example, the Scottish artist Sir David Wilkie's celebrated *The Rabbit on the Wall*, which he completed in 1816 and exhibited at the Royal Academy that year.[7] It was a panel, 25in by 21in, painted for John Turner and for which Wilkie received 200 guineas. A candle-lit cottage interior shows the father producing a rabbit shadow on the wall, to the obvious delight of the four children, and especially the youngest on the mother's knee. Wilkie (1785–1841), who was largely responsible for the British taste for art being of a domestic rather than a historical character during his lifetime, painted other topics of peripheral interest to magicians. These included *The Card Players*, painted for the Duke of Gloucester in 1808, *The Jew's Harp* for Francis Annesley in 1809 and *The Empress Josephine and the*

Fortune Teller for John Abel Smith in 1838, the last subject now reposing in the National Gallery of Scotland in Edinburgh.

The handshadow theme as a political cartoon surfaced in 1843 when *Punch*[8] published *Sir Robert Peel and his Presentation Bull* accompanied by supporting text and a poem, with the comment: 'To us it appears like the schoolboy trick of making rabbits on the wall.' One might infer, therefore, that the skilful shadowgraphists who were to lift the art from the realm of childplay to the dignity of a stage entertainment had yet to appear on the horizon.

The first books devoted to shadowgraphy for the instruction of the tyro performer appeared in the late eighteen-fifties. Henry Bursill's *Hand Shadows to be Thrown Upon the Wall* (1859) and its sequel, *Second Series of Hand Shadows* (1860), have recently been reprinted, making these delightful volumes available to a modern readership.[9, 10] But the industrious compiler of *The Corner Cupboard—A Family Repository* (1858), which was stated to 'contain treasures of knowledge upon every conceivable subject, having reference to the health and happiness of the family circle', had, in addition to Parlour Magic, furnished his readers with The Rabbit on the Wall, making the observation: 'This, although it may appear a trifling sport, demands skill in its performance. It may be made very amusing to the little ones and elders of the family circle. Every one must remember Wilkie's admirable picture, representing a family group engaged in the game.' There followed instructions and illustrations for the fox, rabbit and bird shadows.

By the end of the century two of the most prominent professional shadowgraphists, David Devant and Félicien Trewey, were giving lessons, as recounted in the *Strand Magazine*.[11]

Fathers of large families pay Mr Devant eight guineas for a course of ten lessons in the art, that they might amuse their wives and offspring during the long winter evenings. Mamma cuts out and hems the sheet while daddy gesticulates strangely in the endeavour to portray new figures of his own invention. M. Trewey's most interesting pupil was a dentist, who wanted to learn shadowgraphy in order to beguile timid children whilst he removed their offending molars.

Presumably the dentist was a contortionist, too, if he could perform extractions and execute handshadows simultaneously.

Interestingly, both Devant and Trewey were also

Painted by David Wilkie R.A.   London, Published February 3rd 1877, by the London Fine Art Association, by kind permission of Messrs Henry Graves & Co. (Copyright)   Engraved by John Burnet

THE RABBIT ON THE WALL

associated with another form of shadows, those early, flickering, moving images that were to develop into the enormous new industry of the cinema. Trewey was a friend of the Lumière Brothers, and he it was who first brought their films to London to exhibit at the Royal Polytechnic Institution, on 20 February 1896. There followed a series of nightly cinema shows at the Empire Theatre, London, which, starting on 9 March, lasted for eighteen months.

Not to be outdone, the Egyptian Hall announced that on 19 March a series of *Animated Photographs* would be added to their programmes. This competition was entirely due to the initiative of David Devant who, having failed to secure Maskelyne's interest after taking him to see Trewey's exhibition, found that the instrument maker, R. W. Paul, had constructed what he termed an Animatographe, and purchased one.[12] Under contract, Devant then gave exhibitions at the Hall until Maskelyne and his son Nevil were convinced of its success. Despite this arrangement, it was Nevil Maskelyne who introduced the exhibition and who gave an explanation of the development of the new invention to fascinated audiences.[13] These early cinema shows continued to be one of the attractions of Maskelyne and Cooke's programmes for many years, and their former manager, William Morton, was not slow to introduce the novelty to his theatres in Hull. The programme for the Theatre Royal, Hull, in 1900 included, in addition to the main stage attraction,

Maskelyne and Cooke's Animated War and other Pictures, as shown at the Egyptian Hall, London. Every scene representing the War is guaranteed genuine and not theatrically arranged as many now being exhibited in Paris and elsewhere. The series of miscellaneous subjects will be changed every week. Messrs MASKELYNE & COOKE's Animated Photographs can no more be classed with the usual travelling Cinematographe than a flickering rushlight can be compared with a thousand candle power arc lamp.

It was through his cinema venture that David Devant came into contact with Georges Méliès (1861–1938), the French illusionist who had also become excited and involved with the new medium. Méliès was the director of the Théâtre Robert-Houdin in Paris, which he purchased in 1888 from the widow of Émile Robert-Houdin, son of the famous French conjurer. In 1896 Méliès bought one of Paul's machines and started to make films. By 1912 well over a thousand titles had been produced, a number including magical themes, for which he drew on his illusionist experience.[14]

Several other conjurers were closely involved in the early days of cinema,[15] including Carl Hertz (1859–1924), who holds the distinction of being the first to give a film show at sea, in April 1896 on board the steamship *Norman*, and of pioneering films in South Africa and Australia, with Paul's equipment.[16]

But let us return to the shadowgraphists, whose digital skills continued to surprise long after the intrusion of films. Several of the leading exponents around the turn of the century launched into print to describe, in lesser or greater detail, *How to Do It*—the title used by Trewey for his excursion into the literary field. William J. Hilliar (1876–1936), an Englishman who in 1900 started an illustrious American magical periodical *The Sphinx;* Imro Fox (1852–1910), German-born comedy conjurer whose mark was made in the USA; Louis Nikola (1878–1936) who appeared with Maskelyne and Devant; and David Devant himself—all recorded the technique but, as many of their readers quickly found, even the most supple fingers required practice, practice and yet more practice to form a semblance of the many shadows they proffered.

Chassino (Éléonor Chassin, 1869–1955), who was operating in the early nineteen-hundreds, had novelty in as much as he used his feet as well as his hands. A contemporary report [17] explains:

Next followed some shadows made with the naked feet—the great majority if not all the figures, were produced with the legs crossed, i.e. the right foot occupying the position ordinarily held by the left and *vice-versa*. The side of the foot on which is the small toe was facing the screen and the performer was lying on his back on a small low couch.

The legs in the position explained form a flower Vase; then a smaller vase is made by the side of the above, with the two hands. Different pattern vases were constructed using both hands and feet to elaborate the designs. A particularly good effect was produced by the feet and legs forming a Vase

THE RABBIT ON THE WALL *by Sir David Wilkie (1785–1841) was painted in 1816 and is the earliest British example of shadowgraphy.*

while the hands supplied handle ornaments to same in the shape of Foxes heads. This series concluded with the shadow of a full man produced entirely by the two feet.

A famous pair of shadowgraphists were The Joannys, Charles and Maria Drouillat of Barcelona, who specialized in coloured shadows, first produced at Cheltenham in March 1914 using a lantern constructed by Charles. Although coloured shadows became a matter of some dispute in the profession, and even the subject of a patent, the principle was well known to schoolboy scientists and had even been described as long ago as 1838 in *Parlour Magic*,[18] one of those delightful volumes of instructive and recreative entertainment so beloved by our forefathers for furnishing 'ingenious youth with the means of relieving the tediousness of a long winter's, or a wet summer's evening'.

Another of the so-called 'allied arts' is the ability to extricate oneself from a variety of restraints such as ropes, chains, manacles, leg irons and straitjackets, a branch of magic now dignified by the name of 'escapology'. We note elsewhere (page 157) that this particular skill was not at the outset overtly practised, for the Davenport Brothers, who excelled at rope-tie releases, conveyed the impression that they were so securely trussed up that the phenomena which occurred in their presence could not conceivably be due to other than spirit agency. The conjurers of the day (the eighteen-sixties) responded accordingly, and were not slow to demonstrate the very materialistic basis of such feats. But almost thirty years elapsed before the whole emphasis of presentation changed, now to focus attention on the performer's ability to escape from restraints and, importantly, to *challenge* the spectators to prevent him doing so by inviting them to bring or construct whatever devices they chose. The man responsible for this transformation was destined to make his own fame and fortune by the pursuit of escapology—Harry Houdini.

Okito (David Tobias (Theodore) Bamberg, 1875–1963), of a famous Dutch conjuring dynasty, travelled with Howard Thurston's magic show in the USA during 1910–11 doing handshadows. He also made exclusive conjuring apparatus and operated the Bamberg Magic & Novelty Company at 1193 Broadway, New York, during the period 1908–14.

No magician has attracted a greater gaggle of biographers, novelists and film-makers than Houdini, which is simply a reflection of the incredible impact that he made during his lifetime and the enduring and legendary qualities of his feats. Thus, over fifty years after his death, his name is still a famous and familiar one which is perpetually turning up in newspaper articles, either in his own right or, frequently, as a generic term for any aspect of escapes or disappearances, criminal or otherwise. In 1976 he was even used as an advertising theme for British Government Premium Bonds—a trussed up figure suspended by his ankles, dangling above the open jaws of a shark; the caption read: 'The more bonds I have the happier I am. (H. Houdini).' This sort of thing is quite extraordinary, and one can safely say there is no other entertainer—or politician, sportsman or public figure for that matter—who is still such a topical subject half a century after he has departed this sphere.

Houdini was a phenomenon that captured the imagination of the world during the first quarter of the present century, and the sensation he made has carried him through to the present as the most talked-of magician of all time. It is all the more remarkable when one recalls that he died in 1926, at a time when radio was in its infancy and television a thing of the future. Yet, without these aids, he made his mark so indelibly that he is even enshrined in Funk and Wagnall's Dictionary as a verb—'to houdinize'—and there is a Houdini Museum at Niagara.

Although it is my conviction that too much has already been written and re-written about this great artist—often with little that is novel to add—any attempt to discuss the development of magic as a performing art cannot ignore Houdini's vital contributions, and therefore a vignette of his life and work is included here.[19, 20]

Harry Houdini was born Ehrich Weiss, the son of a Rabbi, in Budapest on 24 March 1874. As an infant he was taken by his parents to the USA and brought up in poverty at Appleton, Wisconsin. He ran away from home for a while when he was twelve and, variously, subsequently worked as a shoeshine boy, photographer's help, electric driller and assistant necktie cutter. A good runner, strong swimmer and proficient diver—attributes that were subsequently to stand him in good stead—he joined an athletic club in New York City. In excellent physical condition, he resolved never to drink or smoke.

Ehrich's brother Theodore showed him his first conjuring trick and, by the age of sixteen, he had become obsessed by magic and was giving neighbourhood shows. About this time he read the *Memoirs of Robert-Houdin* and was imbued with the idea of emulating the famous French conjurer. As a friendly pundit told him that, in French, if you added the letter *i* to the end of a word it meant 'like', he decided to add an *i* to Houdin—thus was Houdini born! Harry probably derived *via* Ehrie, a contraction of Ehrich.[19]

With a friend from the necktie factory, Jacob Hyman, Harry worked a double magic act as The Brothers Houdini. The results were disappointing and Jacob left the act, whereupon Harry recruited his younger brother Theo (1876–1945) as a replacement, and they toured Dime Museums of the mid-West.

In 1892 Rabbi Weiss died and Harry thereupon vowed to look after his mother, which he did with tremendous, almost pathological, devotion throughout her life. This caused certain conflicts when he subsequently married, a facet of his personality which has recently attracted psychiatric analysis.[21] Two years after his father's death Harry met Beatrice (Bess) Rahner at Coney Island and, after a whirlwind courtship, married her within a month. She then replaced Theo in the magical act.

At this time Houdini was presenting a standard magic act, closing with a remarkable transposition illusion called 'Metamorphosis' which is still performed at the present day and never fails to astound. Bess's wrists were tied, she was placed in a sack and locked and corded in a wooden trunk. A curtained cabinet was pulled round the trunk and Houdini then, inviting the audience to watch closely, entered the cabinet. Almost immediately the curtains were pulled back to reveal Bess, and the trunk, when opened up, yielded Houdini in the sack with wrists bound.

However, perceiving the value of specialization, Houdini decided to concentrate on tricks and manipulations with playing cards and emerged as the self-crowned 'King of Cards'. Unfortunately it was not a particularly original coronation—there were Card Kings by the dozen—and he quickly recognized that to specialization he must add novelty.

So, in 1895, Harry devised the Handcuff Act, in which he was handcuffed by members of the audience and then effected his escape. This led to more sophisticated releases and the following year

Houdini introduced the straitjacket escape, an idea that surfaced after a visit to an asylum for the insane. The essence of all these escapes was the challenge to his audience to restrain him in such a way that escape was impossible. It was the genesis of the Challenge Handcuff Escape and the concept that transformed a whole field of magic. From this springboard it was natural to extend the scope to escaping from locked prison cells. Harry gradually accumulated a long list of jails that had offered him temporary accommodation and simultaneously afforded considerable publicity when, although stripped naked and medically examined, he managed to escape.

The young newly-weds nonetheless found the going was hard. They performed in Welsh Brothers Circus, with medicine shows, in vaudeville and dime museums and toured the Canadian Maritime Provinces, without the 'break' needed to establish themselves. Looking further afield, Houdini wrote to J. N. Maskelyne at the Egyptian Hall in London (page 162) but without success. Eventually, however, with the optimism and determination that characterized his life, he decided that they would sail for England, without any theatre bookings, and try their luck in London, the recognized centre of theatrical activities. It was a desperate gamble that was to be the prologue to magicdom's most famous 'rags to riches' story.

They sailed for Europe on 30 May 1900 and arrived in a London that was riding on the crest of theatrical and music hall popularity. Numerous theatres existed in the West End and suburbs, and all were playing to tremendous business. The twenty-six-year-old Houdini was fortunate to find a young theatrical agent, Harry Day, who was sufficiently impressed by the American's background and scrapbooks of reviews and testimonials to arrange for him to meet Mr C. Dundas Slater, the manager of the Alhambra. Slater, requiring evidence of his ability to escape from anyone's manacles, effected a visit to Scotland Yard where Houdini astounded Superintendent Melville by the rapidity with which he shed the British handcuffs. And so, within a fortnight of his arrival in Britain, Houdini was contracted to open at the Alhambra in July. From that moment he never looked back and his rise to top billing was meteoric.

Harry Houdini (1874–1926) started his career as a King of Cards specializing in tricks and manipulations with the pasteboards.

Two examples of Houdini's escapes. On the left he is handcuffed in a prison cell and on the right chained to a ladder (1901).

Throughout Europe he travelled, from London to Leipzig and Manchester to Moscow, conquering restraints and audiences alike. European managements competed for his appearances, and five years were to elapse before Houdini returned to play in the USA. By that time he was rivalling Lafayette's high salary. Throughout this period he was accepting new and more fiendish challenges—such as an escape from a mobile jail in Russia, and from the *Daily Illustrated Mirror's* specially constructed handcuffs at the Hippodrome in 1904.

Back in the USA he introduced publicity escape stunts, being thrown shackled from bridges into rivers or being trussed and submerged in packing cases, padlocked into milk churns or leather mail pouches. The more bizarre the restraint the more Houdini and the public liked it.

Houdini attracted a rash of imitators, and dealers in magical equipment were soon offering handcuffs

and escape methods to cater for the increasing demand from professional and amateur alike. While Harry was annoyed and frequently challenged the 'imposters', the plain fact remained that he was pre-eminent in this specialist sphere. But Houdini did recognize the value of legitimate competition and, since the field was ripe for exploitation, sent for his brother Theo and set him up with a duplicate act. Theo started under the name of Harden but soon changed it to Hardeen, and Hardeen he remained for the rest of his career. It was Hardeen who first appreciated the dramatic potential of the straitjacket escape in full view of the audience—prior to this the escape was always effected in a curtained cabinet which some members of the audience wrongly believed held a confederate who released the performer.

The courageous, progressive Houdini became fascinated by aviation in 1909, and bought a Voisin biplane which he took with him on his tour of Australia the following year, accompanied by a French mechanic, A. Brassac. So it was that he became the first person to achieve a sustained flight on that continent, achieving a speed of about fifty miles an hour. Competition in this sphere was fierce too. Ralph C. Banks, proprietor of the Melbourne Motor Garage, was endeavouring to attain this record with a Wright aircraft when Houdini arrived in Australia. The scene of the frenzied activities of these two would-be record breakers was Diggers Rest, about twenty miles from Melbourne. In the end the American triumphed over the native. According to the booklets that Houdini sold to audiences, *The Life, History and Handcuff Secrets of Houdini*, this historic event occurred on 16 March 1910, a date widely adopted by other writers. However, it does not accord with local newspaper reports, which indicate that 18 March was the happy day. Thus on Saturday 19 March *The Argus*[22] carried the report:

HOUDINI FLIES
Trials at Diggers Rest
Three successful flights
Height of 100 feet reached

Harry Houdini's attempts at aviation have been crowned with success. After a month of patient waiting, with only three or four opportunities for the attempt, Houdini made three successful flights at Diggers Rest yesterday morning.

The evidence of Houdini's performance is contained in the following document.

To Whom it May Concern, Diggers Rest, Near
Melbourne, 18/3/1910

We, the undersigned, do hereby testify to the fact
that on the above date, about 8 o'clock a.m., we
witnessed Harry Houdini in a Voisin Biplane (a
French heavier-than-air-machine) make three
successful flights of from one minute to three and
a half minutes. The last flight being of the last
mentioned duration. In his various flights he
reached an altitude of 100 feet, and in his longest
flight traversed a distance of more than two miles.

(Signed) Harold J. Jagelman, Kograh, N.S.W.
        Robert Howie, Diggers Rest
        A. Brassac, Paris
        Walter P. Smith, 4 Blackwood Street,
           North Melbourne
        F. Enfield Smithells, care of Union Bank,
           Melbourne
        Ralph C. Banks, Melbourne Motor
           Garage
        Franz Kukol, Vienna

HOUDINI

Laughs at . . . .   . being incarcerated

Jeers at . . . . chains and bars

Sneers at efforts to   keep him in prison

Chief of the Secret Russian Police LEBEDOEFF has HARRY HOUDINI stripped stark naked and searched then locked up in the Siberian Transport Cell or Caretta, May 10 1903. In Moscow and in 28 minutes HOUDINI had made his escape to the unspeakable astonishment of the Russian Police.

HOUDINI
The
Magician
HOUDINI

HOUDINI
The
Magician
HOUDINI

The Marvel of the Age . .
The Wizard of the Chains
The Demon of the Cells .
The Mystic of the World

NOTHING CAN HOLD HIM! NOTHING!

Handbill for Houdini's appearance at the Holborn Empire, London.

Houdini's record-breaking flight in Australia at Diggers Rest, near Melbourne, on 18 March 1910.

H. J. Vickery, Highgate, England
John H. Jordan, 11 Francis Street, Ascot
Vale

Interestingly, four of the signatories were his friendly rival Banks and his team; Kukol and Vickery were Houdini's trusted stage assistants. Houdini talked excitedly to the press:

Yes, I've done it! When I went up the first time, I thought for a minute that I was in a tree, then I knew I was flying. The funny thing was that as soon as I was aloft, all tension and strain left me. When I was rolling every muscle of me was taut. When she cants over to the turn—you know how she goes when she's rolling—I am always afraid the wing will hit the ground and break. In the air it's different. As soon as I was up all my muscles relaxed, and I sat back, feeling a sense of ease, freedom and exhilaration, that's what it is. Oh! she's great. I know what it is to fly in real earnest. She's like a swan. She's a dandy. I can fly now!

Corroboration of the date as 18 March is given also elsewhere.[23]

Besides his rôle in aviation history, Houdini made significant contributions to the historical side of magic. Early in his career he had become an avid collector of books, playbills and memorabilia associated with the art and when, during the period 1906–8, he published from New York the *Conjurer's Monthly Magazine*, he used much of this material for the basis of historical articles, some of which were subsequently embodied in his classic work *The Unmasking of Robert-Houdin* (1908). Other titles bearing his name ranged from *The Right Way to Do Wrong* (1906), an exposé of the methods of confidence tricksters and swindlers, and *Handcuff Secrets* (1910) to the more unlikely *Houdini's Paper Magic* (1922).

Tragedy entered Houdini's life when, in 1913, his mother died. Grief-stricken, he was released from his contract in Copenhagen and returned to the USA. He had idolized his mother and now, inconsolable, he turned to the possibility of communicating with her *via* spirit mediums. Quick disillusionment followed when, with his unrivalled knowledge of deception and conjuring techniques, he detected many of them employing fraudulent means to supply the information he so keenly sought. Thus he entered the third phase of his life, a crusade against fraudulent spirit mediums who, with the outbreak of the First World War, were reaping a rich harvest from bereaved families.

His preoccupation with spiritualists led to his meeting with that champion of spiritualism, Sir Arthur Conan Doyle, in England in 1920 and subsequently on Doyle's Spiritualist Lecture Tours in the USA. A curious and short-lived friendship ensued between Houdini the sceptic and Doyle the believer.[24] Its short duration was predictable because of their irreconcilable views—Doyle believed that Houdini was a medium who effected his escapes by dematerializing himself.[25] Houdini's denials were ineffective because he was in the classic 'catch' position of not being able to explain to Doyle precisely *how* his effects were achieved without revealing his secrets! Not, one suspects, that it would have made the slightest difference, for Doyle's conviction in spiritualism was total.[26] The breakdown became final when Lady Doyle produced some automatic writing which purported to be a communication from Houdini's mother and which the magician could not accept as genuine because the style and syntax were so alien to those of his mother. Their last letters were exchanged in 1924. Houdini published in the same year *A Magician Among the Spirits* where he laid bare the chicanery he had encountered in his investigations of spiritualism over the years.

Films attracted Houdini's attention around 1918 and, in those days of silent serials, he blossomed as a film actor, bringing audiences to the edges of their seats as each week he was left in an impossible cliffhanging situation, only to extricate himself miraculously in the following week. Naturally Harry was his own stunt man and no stand-in was ever used in these hair-raising episodes. *The Master Mystery* was his first, in 1918, and others included *The Grim Game* and *Terror Island*. Intoxicated by the film world, at the end of 1920 Harry decided to retire from vaudeville and launch the Houdini Picture Corporation, the president of which company wrote and starred in his own films. *The Man from Beyond* was his first effort, an improbable time-lapse tale of him being hewn out of a block of ice (where he had been incarcerated for a hundred years), thawed and pitched into modern life. Another film was *Haldane of the Secret Service*, which had British links since it included a trail of counterfeit banknotes

Poster for a packing case escape challenge to Houdini at Sydney on 12 April 1910.

CHALLENGE
— TO —
HOUDINI

Mr. H. HOUDINI, Tivoli Theatre, City.   Sydney, April 12th, 1910.

Dear Sir,

The undersigned Expert Carpenters and Joiners, **Hereby Challenge You** to allow us to construct a **Large and Secure Packing Case** from **One Inch Timber**, and making use of Two and Half to Three Inch Flat Headed Wire Nails.

We believe we can so nail you in this box, rope it up and then nail the ropes to the box, that it will be **impossible for You to make Your escape.**

If you accept we will send the box along for examination, but demand the right to re-nail each and every board before the test so as to guard against preparation on your part.   Awaiting your reply, we beg to remain, yours truly.

JOHN ANDERSON, "Lynton," Mansion Road, Strathfield.
JAMES WILLIAMSON, Balfour Street. Bellevue Hill.
WILLIAM ELPHINSTONE, 4 Church Street, Camperdown.

On behalf of the firm of E. THORNTON, Contractor and Builder, 42 Castlereagh Street, City.

HOUDINI ACCEPTS THE ABOVE CHALLENGE
— FOR —
FRIDAY NIGHT, APRIL 15

TEST TO TAKE PLACE ON THE STAGE OF

MR. HARRY RICKARDS TIVOLI THEATRE

The Box when finished will be placed in Theatre Vestibule for Public Examination.

HOW HANDCUFF TRICKS ARE DONE
BY IMPOSTERS!

Herr Franz Kukol the **CELEBRATED ILLU-SIONIST OF VIENNA,** and **Mr** Geo. Vickery the **MAGICIAN OF LONDON,** beg to inform the general public that they will appear at the large shop No. 23 and 25 **NICOLSON STREET,** next door to Moss' Empire Music Hall, where they will give performances every half hour, **SHOWING HOW HANDCUFF TRICKS ARE DONE BY ALL IMPOSTERS!**

These gentlemen confess they do not know how HARRY HOUDINI, who is engaged at the GAIETY THEATRE, LEITH, this week, performs his tricks. If they did they would not travel as exposers.

LIKE ALL other BOGUS HANDCUFF IMPOSTERS THEY DO NOT ALLOW ANYONE TO BRING HANDCUFFS.

NO ONE is ALLOWED ON THE STAGE. No one is allowed to examine the trunk they make use of, as **THEY HAVE A TRAP IN THE TOP OF BOX,** similar to other Imitators, and tear open the bottom of the bag they use!

They cannot open any Handcuff unless their own, and they must have a key to fit, just the same as all other Exposers.

THE WHOLE SWINDLE SHOWN FOR A PENNY.

NEXT DOOR TO THE EMPIRE THEATRE, EDIN.
Open from II a.m. to 9 p.m.

JOHN FMRLEY, PRINTER, LEITH.

in Hull and London. This venture ended, alas, in financial disaster and Harry returned to the vaudeville circuits.

The final section of Houdini's full evening show which took to the road in September 1925 was now devoted to an exposure of the methods of fraudulent mediums, and his last appearance before an audience was thus in the rôle of an anti-spiritualist campaigner. The tour took him on 11 October 1926 to Albany where, on the opening night, he broke a bone in his foot performing the Chinese Water Torture Cell escape. In this effect his ankles were locked into stocks which formed the top of a huge tank filled with water. He was lowered head first into the tank and the stocks were then secured with padlocks. Assistants pulled a curtained cabinet round the apparatus and, while the orchestra played 'The Diver', the audience held their breaths to see if they could survive as long as Houdini did. After two or three minutes, when the suspense was overwhelming, the curtains were pulled aside to reveal a gasping, dripping Houdini and the tank still securely sealed. On this particular night the stocks jerked as Houdini was being hoisted up, breaking a bone and preventing him from undertaking the escape.

From Albany the show moved to Schenectady and thence to Montreal, where the fateful event that led to Houdini's death occurred.[19] On Tuesday 19 October he lectured on fraudulent spiritualism at McGill University for Dr William D. Tait of the Psychology Department and afterwards a student, Samuel J. Smiley, showed him a sketch he had made of Houdini during the lecture. Pleased, Harry invited Smiley to make another portrait backstage at the theatre later in the week. He came, on Friday 22 October, with a friend Jack Price and, while Houdini was attending to his mail, started his sketch. Shortly, another student, J. Gordon Whitehead, arrived to return a book he had borrowed from Harry. In the course of conversation, Whitehead inquired whether it was correct that Houdini could sustain punches to his midsection without suffering injury. The magician invited the student to feel his abdominal muscles and, suitably impressed, Whitehead then

An amusing example of the advertising used by Houdini when appearing at Leith, Scotland, at a time when he was plagued by 'exposers'. Kukol and Vickery were Houdini's trusted assistants who were pledged to secrecy concerning his methods. Here, all in the Houdini cause, they were indulging in 'decent' exposure!

A portrait of Bess and Harry Houdini taken in London, which the escapologist has inscribed, referring to his wife as 'the Mrs'.

asked if he might make some trial punches. Houdini immersed in his mail and relaxed on a couch, grunted acquiescence. Immediately Whitehead struck out at him and then followed up with three more heavy blows, much to the consternation of Smiley and Price. Houdini indicated that he was all right but he had not been able to brace himself before Whitehead's first punch was delivered. He thanked Smiley for the sketch and the three students departed.

That afternoon Harry became increasingly aware of abdominal pain which intensified. He struggled through his evening show, concealing his pain from Bess and his entourage and, despite the agony next day, he also completed the Saturday performances. The show had now to move to Detroit to open at the Garrick Theatre on the Sunday night. On the train he could conceal the agonizing pain no longer. A telegram was sent ahead to Detroit to have a doctor available to examine Houdini on his arrival. The train was late into Detroit and so, instead of going to the hotel, where the doctor was waiting with the show's advance man, Houdini and his company went direct to the theatre to set up the show. There he was eventually examined and acute appendicitis diagnosed. Knowing that there was a full house waiting for him, Houdini foolhardily refused to go to hospital. Unfortunately Bess had not heard the diagnosis or she would have intervened at that stage and insisted on hospitalization.

And so the amazing drama was played out. Thirty minutes late, the curtain rose and by some superhuman power Houdini presented the hour-long first act of miscellaneous magic. At the interval he was running a temperature of 104 degrees yet somehow managed to continue and complete the spiritualist exposure act. As the curtain came down he collapsed but still refused to go to hospital and was taken to his hotel. There Bess had hysterics and succeeded in her objective of getting him into the hands of surgeons at Grace Hospital. His ruptured appendix was removed but peritonitis had set in and, in a critical condition, Houdini struggled for his life. On Friday afternoon a second operation was performed but to no avail. The great magician died in Bess's arms at 1.26pm on Sunday 31 October. He had staged his exit on Hallowe'en.

The legends that surround Houdini are legion, and not least are those connected with his death. Robert Lund, the proprietor of the American Museum of Magic at Marshall, Michigan, collected no fewer than seven different versions of how Houdini died. One cannot do better than quote his own inimitable summary.[27]

And there you have the true story of Houdini's death. How he died in the arms of Larry Lewis and Beatrice Houdini in Boston and Chicago while suspended upside down in a glass tank on the stage of the Oriental Theatre while performing on the bottom of the river locked in a casket and suffering from a ruptured appendix and hardening of the arteries, the same afternoon, within twenty-four hours, or five days later. Truth will out.

The assessments of Houdini's character are so diverse as to give a psychologist nightmares. I once asked the late John Mulholland, respected US magician and editor of the conjuring periodical *The Sphinx*, who knew Houdini well, what Harry was really like. John's reply was intriguing. 'Every story you've heard about Harry is true. He could be mean, generous, harsh, gentle, hostile or friendly . . .'

Houdini the personality thus defies categorization, as surely as he defied all his challengers when they brought their handcuffs, leg irons and other restraints. But he will remain for all time 'The Great Houdini—the man who made the impossible possible'.

EPILOGUE

Our revels now are ended. These our actors,
As I foretold you, were all spirits, and
Are melted into air, into thin air.

W. Shakespeare, *The Tempest*

Our idiosyncratic procession of wonder-workers, the jugglers, conjurers, fire-eaters, water-spouters and mind-readers, who have paraded through these pages, comes to a halt with the death of Houdini over half a century ago. It is no bad thing for the historian to stand back for fifty years to endeavour to put his canvas into perspective. Let us simply close with the thought that Houdini died at a time when sound films were about to be launched at a delighted public and when television was still very much an ideal for the future. The succeeding years witnessed the gradual decline of variety and music hall which, with a brief resurgence immediately after the Second World War, virtually disappeared in the nineteen-fifties when television reigned supreme. But variety did not die and, like Phoenix arising from the ashes of the old Palaces of Variety, found a home in the new music halls of clubland. Television still holds sway, and it is a sobering thought that Houdini or Chung Ling Soo could tour the variety theatres of the world and in almost a lifetime be seen by fewer people than the multitude that a brief four-minute exposure on the tiny screen ensures today. That is magic of a different kind! Yet, even in an age of technological marvels, the conjurer and illusionist can still fascinate, bewilder and entertain and, like Houdini, continue to make

THE IMPOSSIBLE POSSIBLE

REFERENCES AND NOTES

The works to which I have had recourse, for
my own information, and to justify my remarks,
are such I have no doubt, as will meet the
the good opinion and approbation of my readers,
suffice to say, that they are scarce, and not
to be found in every library.

Gale's Cabinet of Knowledge (1797)

1 IN THE BEGINNING (pages 11-25)

1 Woodcroft, B. (1851): *The Pneumatics of Hero of Alexandria.* London: Taylor Walton & Maberly. A reissue in 1971 carries a useful introduction by Marie Boas Hall. London: Macdonald Elsevier.

2 Drachmann, A. G. (1972): 'Hero of Alexandria' in *Dictionary of Scientific Biography,* ed. by C. C. Gillispie, *6,* 310–14.

3 Brewster, D. (1832): *Letters on Natural Magic,* 4. London: Murray.

4 *The Apocrypha.* Daniel: Bel and the Dragon *v.* 1–22.

5 Erman, A. (1927): *The Literature of the Ancient Egyptians.* London: Methuen.

6 Warlock, P. & Johnson, R. (1954): Western [*sic*] Papyrus . . . Manuscript of Mystery. *Magic Circular. 49,* 7–10.

7 Bailey, N. (1721): *An Universal Etymological English Dictionary.* London: E. Bell & Co.

8 Deacon, R. (1976): *Matthew Hopkins: Witch-Finder General.* London: Muller.

9 Strutt, J. (1841): *The Sports and Pastimes of the People of England,* Ch. 4. London: Tegg.

10 Chambers, E. K. (1903): *The Medieval Stage. 2,* 231. Oxford: Clarendon.

11 Farelli, V. (1948): A Chronological History of the Cups and Balls in *John Ramsay's Routine with Cups and Balls.* 10–36. London: Armstrong.

12 Clarke, S. W. (1924): *Magic Wand. 13,* 24.

13 Christopher, M. (1973): *The Illustrated History of Magic.* 9–11. New York: Crowell.

14 Warlock, P. (1976): Death of a Fallacy. *Magic Circular. 70,* 12–13.

15 Volkmann, K. (1956): *The Oldest Deception.* Minneapolis: Jones.

16 Cunnington, C. W., Cunnington, P. & Beard, C. (1960): *A Dictionary of English Costume.* 167, 171,
27. London: Black.

17 Cunnington, P. & Lucas, C. (1976): *Occupational Costume in England,* 289. London: Black.

18 Minguet e Yrol, Pablo. (1733): *Enganos a Ojos Vistas y Diversion de Trabajos Mundanos fundada en licitos Juegos de Manos.* Madrid.

19 Chaucer, G. (c.1381): *Canterbury Tales.* Prologue 357-8.

20 Chettle, H. (1592): *Kind-Hart's Dreame.* Reprinted 1923. Bodley Head Quartos, ed. by G. B. Harrison.

21 Spenser, E. (1591): *Prosopopoia, or Mother Hubberd's Tale.* 83-7. London: Ponsonbie.

22 Chaucer, G. (c.1381): *The Frankeleyne's Tale. ll.* 455 ff.; *The Hous of Fame, ll.* 186 ff.

23 Adams, W. H. D. (1865): *Dwellers on the Threshold or Magic and Magicians,* 208-13. London: Maxwell.

24 Godwin, W. (1834): *Lives of the Necromancers.* 260-63. London: Mason.

25 Thorndike, L. (1923): *A History of Magic and Experimental Science, 2,* 517-92. New York: Macmillan,

26 Wilkins, J. (1680): *Mathematical Magick,* 176. London: Gellibrand.

27 Robelly (1960): Albert Le Grand: *L'Escamoteur.* No 80, 1274-9.

28 Garreau, A. (1932): *Saint Albert le Grand.* Paris: Bruges.

29 Scheeben, H. C. (1931): *Albert der Grosse.* Leipzig.

30 I am indebted to Mr Alexander Adrion, noted German magician and historian of magic, and to the Historical Museum at Cologne, for the opportunity to examine this goblet.

31 Clarke, S. W. (1924): *Magic Wand. 13,* 38.

32 Wright, L. B. (1927): Juggling Tricks and Conjuring on the English Stage before 1642. *Modern Philology. 24,* 269–84. A valuable survey with many references to the original literature.

33 Hazlitt, W. C. (1874): *A Select Collection of Old English Plays originally published by Robert Dodsley in the year 1744.* London: Reeves & Turner.

34 Dr T. H. Hall advances the interesting thesis that Ady was a plagiarist, possibly appropriating a text by Arthur Wilson (1599–1652) to produce *A Candle in the Dark.* In *Old Conjuring Books* (1972), 133-46 London: Duckworth.

35 Butler, S. (1678): *Hudibras, The Third and Last Part.* Canto III, 235; (1970) Menston: Scolar Press.

36 Clarke, S. W. (1924): *Magic Wand. 13,* 88.

37 John Tillotson (1630–94), Archbishop of Canterbury: *Serm XXVI* (1742) 2, 237. 'In all probability those common juggling words *hocus pocus* are nothing else but a corruption of *hoc est corpus*, by way of ridiculous imitation of the priests of the Church of Rome in their trick of Transubstantiation.' Cited in *Oxford English Dictionary.* (1933) *5,* 320.

38 Harvey, P. (1967): *The Oxford Companion to English Literature.* 4th ed. 391.

39 Gee, J. (1624): *New Shreds of the Old Snare, containing the apparitions of two new female ghosts etc.* London.

40 Ferguson, J. (1959): *Bibliographical Notes on Histories of Inventions and Books of Secrets. 2,* 7th Suppl., 27–8. London: Holland.

2 *THE LEARNED ANIMALS* (pages 26-34)

1 *Dictionary of National Biography. 1,* 1045–6.

2 Halliwell-Phillips, J. (1879): *Memoranda on Love's Labour's Lost.* London: Adlard (Privately printed).

3 Chambers, E. K. (1923): *The Elizabethan Stage. 2,* 103. Oxford: Clarendon.

4 Toole Stott, R. (1958): *Circus and Allied Arts. A World Bibliography 1500–1957. 1,* 30–1. Derby: Harpur. A valuable listing of books relating to Marocco with interesting notes.

5 Greenwood, I. J. (1898): *The Circus. Its Origin and Growth Prior to 1835.* 10–11. New York: Dunlap Society.

6 Collier, J. P. (1842): Notes in *Fools and Jesters with a Reprint of Robert Armin's A Nest of Ninnies.* 63. London: Shakespeare Society.

7 Ralegh, Sir Walter (1621): *The History of the World. 1,* 178. London.

8 Johnson, S. (1810): *The Works of the English Poets.* Additional lives by Alexander Chalmers 6, 433–4.

9 Digby, Sir Kenelm (1644): *Two Treatises, in the one of which, the Nature of Bodies: in the other, the Nature of Mans Soule, is looked into; in way of Discovery of the Immortality of reasonable soules.* 466. Paris: G. Blaizot.

10 *Tarlton's Jests, and News Out of Purgatory.* Reprinted (1844) 23–4. London: Shakespeare Society.

11 Douce, F. (1807): *Illustrations of Shakespeare. 1,* 212–14. London: Longmans.

12 Chambers, R. (1864): *The Book of Days. 2,* 670–1. London: Chambers.

13 Caulfield, J. (1813): *Portraits, Memoirs and Charac-* ters of Remarkable Persons, from the Reign of Edward the Third to the Revolution. 2, 133–4. London: Kirby.

14 Altick, R. D. (1978): *The Shows of London.* 40. Cambridge, Mass.: Belknap.

15 Morton, Bishop Thomas (1609): *Direct Answer unto the Scandalous Exceptions of Theophilus Higgons.*

16 Quoted by Russell, C. (1904): *Notes and Queries.* 10th Series. *2,* 281–2.

17 Markham, G. (1607): *Cavelarice, or the English Horseman.* The eight Booke. 27–38. London: White.

18 Gardner, M. (1957): *Fads and Fallacies in the Name of Science.* 351–2. New York: Dover.

19 Rhine, J. B. & Rhine, L. E. (1929): *Journal of Abnormal and Social Psychology. 23,* 449–66; *24,* 287–92.

20 Christopher, M. (1971): *Seers, Psychics and ESP.* 40–6. London: Cassell.

21 Strutt, J. (1841): *The Sports and Pastimes of the People of England.* 245. London: Tegg.

22 Southey, R. (1951): *Letters from England.* ed. by J. Simmons. 340. London:

23 Frost, T. (1874): *The Old Showmen and the Old London Fairs.* 177–9. London: Tinsley.

24 Roose-Evans, J. (1977): *London Theatre from the Globe to the National.* 60. Oxford: Phaidon.

25 Hone, W. (1826): *The Every Day Book. 1,* 597.

26 Christopher, M. (1973): *The Illustrated History of Magic.* 57–9. New York: Crowell.

27 Ref. 23, 307.

28 Ref. 12, *1,* 293–5.

29 Ref. 23, 169.

30 Parke, W. T. (1830): *Musical Memoirs. 2,* 292–3 gives a good account but confuses Scalioni with Castelli. London: Colburn & Bentley.

31 Ref. 21, 255.

3 *BAGS, BUBBLES AND BOTTLES* (pages 35-51)

1 Hudson, D. (1945): *British Journalists and Newspapers.* London: Collins.

2 Houdini, H. (1908): *The Unmasking of Robert-Houdin.* New York: Publishers Printing Co.

3 *Weekly Journal, or Saturday's Post.* 9 March 1722/3.

4 *London Journal.* 19 October 1723.

5 *Daily Post.* 7 February 1724.

6 *Daily Post.* 11 January 1724.

7 Tennis courts were adapted for use as theatres from the middle of the seventeenth century.

8 Shenton, R. (1976): *Christopher Pinchbeck and His Family.* Ashford: Wright.

9 *Gentleman's Magazine. 1,* 79 (1731).

10 *Gentleman's Magazine. 1,* 120 (1731).

11 Caulfield, James (1819): *Portraits, Memoirs and Characters of Remarkable Persons, from the Revolution in 1688 to the End of the Reign of George II. 2,* 65–6. London: Young & Whiteley.

12 The relevant cutting, in the collection of the late James B. Findlay, was in storage and therefore not available for inspection at the time of preparing this book.

13 Speaight, G. (1955): *The History of the English Puppet Theatre*. 160. London: Harrap.

14 Paulson, R. (1971): *Hogarth, His Life, History, Art and Times*. *1*, 115. New Haven: Yale.

15 Paulson, R. (1965): *Hogarth's Graphic Works*. *1*, 102–3. New Haven: Yale.

16 Ref. 15, *1*, 154–8.

17 Chambers, R. (1864): *The Book of Days*. *2*, 264.

18 Morley, H. (1859): *Memoirs of Bartholomew Fair*. 392. London: Chapman & Hall.

19 Rosenfeld, S. (1960): *The Theatre of the London Fairs in the 18th Century*. 26. Cambridge University Press. Dr Rosenfeld quotes the opinions of Mr E. Croft-Murray and Mr James Laver on this matter.

20 *Harleian Manuscripts* 7190. I am indebted to Mr R. G. Bird, Borough Librarian of Tunbridge Wells, for drawing my attention to this and other sources concerning Loggon.

21 Barton, Margaret (1937): *Tunbridge Wells*. 269. London: Faber.

22 Richardson, S. (1804): *The Correspondence of Samuel Richardson*. Frontispiece to Vol. 3. London.

23 Wheatley, H. B. & Cunningham, P. (1891): *London Past and Present*. *1*, 111.

24 Gay, Mr (1727): *Fables*. London: Tonson & Watts.

25 Mackay, C. (1841): *Memoirs of Extraordinary Popular Delusions*. London: National Illustrated Library.

26 Hargrave, C. P. (1930): *A History of Playing Cards*. Republished by Dover (1966) 164–5.

27 Cole, A. H. (1949): *The Great Mirror of Folly. An Economic-Biographical Study*. Boston, Mass: Baker Library.

28 Swift, J., cited by S. W. Clarke (1924): *Magic Wand*. *13*, 197–8.

29 *Gentleman's Magazine*. *37*, 42 (1749).

30 *General Advertiser*. 18 January 1749, 1, col. 3.

31 Ref. 30, 2, col. 1.

32 *Catalogue of Prints and Drawings in the British Museum. Division I. Political and Personal Satires*. (1877) 3, Pt I, 737–43.

33 *London Magazine*. 35 (1749).

34 Williams, N. (1959): *Knaves and Fools*. 195–9. London: Barrie & Rockcliffe.

35 Sampson, H. (1875): *A History of Advertising*. 365–72. London: Chatto & Windus.

4 THE PHENOMENA (pages 52-60)

1 Caulfield, J. (1819): *Portraits, Memoirs and Characters of Remarkable Persons*. *2*, 22–5. London: Young & Whiteley.

2 *Gentleman's Magazine*. *61*, Plate 2, Fig. 5 (1791).

3 Wood, E. J. (1868): *Giants and Dwarfs*. 287–300. London: Bentley.

4 *Gentleman's Magazine*. *61*, 706 (1791).

5 Beckmann, J. (1797): *A History of Inventions*. *3*, 290–2. London: Bell.

6 Wilson, H. & Caulfield, J. (1869): *The Book of Wonderful Characters*. 30–1. London: Hotten. Records the activities of a number of fire-eaters,

stone-swallowers and water-spouters.

7 Clerk, T. (1810): *The Works of William Hogarth*. *2*, 69–71. London: Scholey.

8 Paulson, R. (1965): *Hogarth's Graphic Works*. 2 vols. New Haven: Yale.

9 Frost, T. (1874): *The Old Showmen and the Old London Fairs*. 235–6. London: Tinsley.

10 Clarke, S. W. (1925): *Magic Wand*. *14*, 138.

11 Houdini, H. (1920): *Miracle Mongers and their Methods*. 42. New York: Dutton. An historical survey of fire-, stone- and poison-eaters, sword-swallowers, water-spouters, etc., and their techniques.

12 Ref. 11, 55.

13 *The Times*. 27 February 1818.

14 *The Times*. 8 June 1826; see also W. Hone (1833): *The Every-Day Book and Table Book*. *2*, 771–5. London: Author.

15 Parke, W. T. (1830): *Musical Memoirs*. *2*, 290–2. London: Colburn & Bentley.

16 Altick, R. D. (1978): *The Shows of London*. 263–5. Cambridge, Mass: Belknap. References to various newspaper accounts are also given.

17 *Morning Chronicle*, quoted by W. Hone (1833) *Every-Day Book*. *2*, 775.

18 *New York Herald*. 1 September 1859.

19 *European Magazine*. March 1765. 194–5.

20 Ref. 6, 126–30, quotes full details from this pamphlet.

5 THE CONJURING QUACKS (pages 61-70)

1 Frost, T. (1876): *The Lives of the Conjurers*. 135–40. London: Tinsley.

2 *European Magazine* (1783). *3*, 406–9.

3 *Houdini on Magic* (1953) ed. by W. B. Gibson and M. N. Young. 57–66. New York: Dover.

4 *Dictionary of National Biography*. *8*, 323–6.

5 *Dictionary of National Biography*. *12*, 407–9.

6 Walpole, H. (1965): *Horace Walpole's Correspondence with the Countess of Upper Ossory 1778–1787*. 217. Vol *33* of the Yale Edition of *Horace Walpole's Correspondence* ed. by W. S. Lewis. London: Oxford University Press.

7 Sampson, H. (1875): *A History of Advertising*. 411–21. London: Chatto & Windus.

8 George, M. D. (1935): *Catalogue of Political and Personal Satires* (British Museum). *5*, 765–68.

9 *Gentleman's Magazine*. *69*, 1088 (1799).

10 William Alley, quoted by E. K. Chambers (1923): *The Elizabethan Stage*. *4*, 192. Oxford: Clarendon.

11 *Dictionary of National Biography*. *5*, 830–1.

12 *Gentleman's Magazine*. *59*, 756–8. (1789). C. H. Timperley's (1842) *Encyclopaedia of Literary & Typographical Anecdotes*, *2*, 764. London: Bohn, is based on this reference but makes two errors, giving Denton's first name as John and stating he was executed at Tyburn.

13 *European Magazine & London Review*. (1789) *16*, 86.

14 Clarke, S. W. (1924): *Magic Wand*. *13*, 209.

15 Hall, T. H. (1972): *Old Conjuring Books*. 157. London: Duckworth. Hall also discusses the error of

attribution of the English translation of Pinetti's *Physical Amusements* (1784) to Denton in Refs. 2, 3, 4 and 11.

16 Findlay, J. B. (1951): Thomas Denton. *Third Collectors Annual*. 20–4. Shanklin: Author.

6 LAUGHING GAS (pages 71-82)

1 Davy, H. (1799): *Nicholson's Journal*. *3*, 93.

2 Davy, H. (1800): *Researches, Chemical and Philosophical; chiefly concerning nitrous oxide, or dephlogisticated nitrous air, and its respiration*. London: J. Johnson.

3 Beddoes, T. (1799): *Notice of some observations made at the Medical Pneumatic Institution*. Bristol.

4 Robertson, J. M. (1897): *New Essays towards a Critical Method*. 131–90. London & New York: Lane.

5 Lowes, J. L. (1927): *The Road to Xanadu*. 377–88. Vintage Books: New York. (1959)

6 Horner, F. (1843): *Memoirs and Correspondence of Francis Horner*. Ed. L. Horner. *1*, 181ff. London: Murray.

7 Read, J. (1947): *Humour and Humanism in Chemistry*. 207. London: Bell.

8 George, M. D. (1947): *Catalogue of Political and Personal Satires*. (British Museum) *8*, 112–4.

9 Henry's Collection of Posters, Programmes etc. 1817–1829. British Museum Th. Cts. 364.

10 Schoenbein, C. F. (1842): *Mittheilungen aus dem reisetagebuche eines deutschen naturforschers*. Basel. See also Ref. 11.

11 Henry, Mr (*c.* 1826): *Conversazione: or Mirth and Marvels*. London: Duncombe.

12 Smith, W. D. A. (1965–7): A History of Nitrous Oxide Anaesthesia. *British Journal of Anaesthesia*. *37*, 790–8; 871–82; 958–66; *38*, 58–72; 143–56. These are the relevant articles from a much longer series. An excellent treatment of the subject on which I have drawn freely, and I am greatly indebted to Dr Smith for the mutual exchange of information on the use of nitrous oxide for entertainment purposes.

13 Honri, P. (1973): *Working the Halls*. 101–2. Farnborough: Saxon House.

14 Cary, L. (1961): *The Colt Gun Book*. Greenwich, N.Y.: Fawcett.

15 Robinson, V. (1946): *Victory over Pain*. 83–5. New York: Schuman.

16 Fulton, J. F. (1930): *Dictionary of American Biography*. *4*, 321–2. London: Oxford University Press.

17 Robert-Houdin, J. E. (1859): *Confidences d'un Prestidigitateur*. *2*. Paris: Libraire Nouvelle.

18 Webster, M. (1969): *The Same Only Different*. 78. London: Gollancz.

7 PHANTASMAGORIC PROFESSORS (pages 83-92)

1 Robertson, E. G. (1831/3): *Mémoires Récréatifs, Scientifiques et Anecdotiques*. 2 vols. Paris.

2 Poultier (1798): *L'Ami des Lois*. Du 8 germinal au VI. 28 Mars.

3 Oehler, A. (1811): *The Life, Adventures and Unparalleled Sufferings of Andrew Oehler*. Trenton, New Jersey: Fenton.

4 Brewster, D. (1832): *Letters on Natural Magic*. 80–82. London: Murray.

5 Hepworth, T. C. (1897–8): The Evolution of the Magic Lantern. *Chamber's Journal* 6th ser. *1*, 213–15.

6 See, for example, Olive Cook (1967): Victorian Magicians. *The Saturday Book*. *27*, 175–84. London: Hutchinson.

7 Hill, D. (1965): *Mr Gillray The Caricaturist*. 107. London: Phaidon.

8 *Dictionary of National Biography*. 22, 1131–2.

9 Layton, D. (1977): A Victorian Showman of Science. *New Scientist*. 1 Sept. 538–9.

10 *The Engineer*. 1 October 1858.

11 *Mechanics Magazine*. 7 October 1858.

12 Dircks, H. (1863): *The Ghost!* London: E.&F.N. Spon.

13 *Eastern Morning News*. 12 Jan. 1878.

14 Alma, W. (1975): *Magic Circle Mirror*. *5*, 123–4.

15 Fischer, O. (1935): *Magic Circular*. *29*, 107–9; 117–8; *Sphinx*. *36*, 143–5 (1937).

16 Armstrong, B. J. (*c.* 1963): *Armstrong's Norfolk Diary*. 103. London: Hodder & Stoughton.

8 THE JEWISH CONNEXION (pages 93-107)

1 Sachse, J. E. (1907): *American Jewish Historical Society Publications*. No 16, 73–83.

2 Saltarino, Signor (1910): *Das Artistentum und Seine Geschichte*. 127, 149. Leipzig: International-Artistischer Literatur.

3 Gibson, W. B. & Young, M. N. (1953): *Houdini on Magic*. 67–72. New York: Dover.

4 Ebstein, E. (1911): *Zeitschrift fur Bucherfreunde*. Neue Folge 3 (1), 22–8.

5 Geiger, L. (1907): *American Jewish Historical Society Publications*. No 16, 85–94.

6 Ersch & Gruber (1846): *Lexikon*.

7 Schubert, Chr. Fr. D. (ed.): *Deutsch Chronik*. No 81, 9 October 1775.

8 Boclo, L. (1815): *Fussreisen aus der Gegend von Cassel uber den Vogelsberg nach Heidelberg und Coblenz, von da zuruch uber einige Bader des Taunus*. Darmstadt, Seite 381f.

9 West (1833): *Dublin University Review*. *1*, 482, quoted by H. R. Evans (1928): *History of Conjuring and Magic*. Kenton.

10 Christopher, M. (1962): *Panorama of Magic*. 41–2. New York: Dover.

11 Lichtenberg, C. G. (1774): *Diary of a Tour of England, 1774*. Unpublished diary in the Archives of the University of Göttingen. I am indebted to Dr Haenel for access to this important document.

12 Rubens, A. (1975): Jews and the English Stage, 1667–1850. *Transactions of the Jewish Historical Society of England*. Vol. 24 and Miscellanies Part 9, 151–170. An excellent review with a section on conjurers.

13 Boase, F. (1965): *Modern English Biography*. 2, 44. London: Cass.

14 Frost, T. (1876): *The Lives of the Conjurers*. 215–20. London: Tinsley.

15 Clarke, S. W. (1926): The Annals of Conjuring. *Magic Wand*. *15*, 41–2.

16 *Hull Daily Advertiser*. 11 July 1845.

17 Alma, W. (1973): Australian Magic Review. *Abracadabra. 55*, 162–3; 229–30; 288–9; 350–1; 463–5. A valuable source of information concerning Jacobs' Australian tours with extensive quotations from contemporary newspapers.

18 *Jewish Record*. 31 October 1870.

19 *Jewish Record*. 28 October 1870.

20 I am greatly indebted to Mr Alfred Rubens for drawing my attention to these obituary and other notices (Ref. 21) traced for him by Mr C. R. Fincken of the Mocatta Library and recorded in his review (Ref. 12).

21 *Jewish Chronicle*. 11 March 1892.

22 *Melbourne Morning Herald*. 12 June 1855.

23 Stanyon, E. (1901): *Magic. 1*, 27.

24 Clarke, S. W (1928): *Magic Wand 17*, 38.

25 Ross, B. (1973): *Forward*. No 1, 10–11.

26 *Daily Telegraph*. 11 May 1911.

27 Christopher, M. (1973): *The Illustrated History of Magic*.

28 MacKie, A. (1971): *Scotland's Magazine*. May. 32–3.

29 MacGregor, A. A. (1945): *The Turbulent Years*. 209–16. London: Methuen.

30 Bentley, R. (1957): *Magic Circular. 51*, 167–71.

31 Bentley, R. (1957): *Magic Circular. 52*, 7–8.

32 *Magical World* (1913) New Series. No. 1, 4.

9   WIZARDS FROM THE NORTH
(pages 108–120)

1 *Biography of Professor Anderson: Sketches from his Note Book*. (c. 1865).

2 Houdini, H. (1908): *The Unmasking of Robert-Houdin*. 150. New York: Publishers Printing Co.

3 A Beckett, A. W. (1896): *Green-Room Recollections*. 159–60. Bristol: Arrowsmith.

4 *Hull Advertiser*. 24 July 1846.

5 *Eastern Counties Herald*. 30 July 1846.

6 Toole Stott, R. (1976): *A Bibliography of English Conjuring 1581–1876. 1*. Derby: Harpur.

7 Findlay, J. B. (1967): *Anderson and his Theatre*. Shanklin: Author.

8 Morley, H. (1891): *The Journal of a London Playgoer from 1851 to 1866*. 110. London: Routledge.

9 Wyndham, H. S. (1906): *The Annals of Covent Garden Theatre from 1732 to 1897*. *2*, 210–17. London: Chatto & Windus.

10 Christopher, M. (1973): *The Illustrated History of Magic*. 127. New York: Crowell.

11 *Eastern Morning News*. 10 July 1867.

12 *Eastern Morning News*. 27 July 1867.

13 Bridie, J. (1939): *One Way of Living*. 170–4. London: Constable.

14 *The College Courant* (1971) *23*, 35–7. Glasgow.

15 Bodie, W. (1905): *The Bodie Book*. London: Caxton.

16 Bodie, Dr W. (n.d.): *Strange Stories*. London: Simpkin, Marshall, Hamilton, Kent.

17 Bodie, W. (c. 1910): *Harley the Hypnotist*. London: Pearson.

18 *Magazine of Magic*. December 1916. *5* (1), 5.

10   SCIENCE ET LA PRESTIDIGITATION
(pages 121–130)

1 Robert-Houdin, J. E. (1878): *The Secrets of Conjuring and Magic*. Transl. and ed. by Professor Hoffmann. London: Routledge.

2 *Illustrated London News*. 23 December 1848. 397.

3 A reference to John Henry Anderson, the Wizard of the North (Chapter 9) and his imitators such as Barnardo Eagle, the Wizard of the South. It must have been galling for Anderson, who was appearing at the Strand Theatre at the time, to read in the same issue of *ILN*: 'For those who have not seen his great master, M. Robert-Houdin, his [i.e., Anderson's] exhibition is worthy of a visit.'

4 Sharpe, S. H.: *Salutations to Robert-Houdin*. This masterly survey of the life and work of Robert-Houdin appeared serially in the *Linking Ring* (monthly journal of the International Brotherhood of Magicians) from September 1967 to April 1974. A succinct article by the same author is 'Remarkable Robert-Houdin' in *Music Box. 8*, 341–7 (1978).

5 *Memoirs of Robert-Houdin. Ambassador, Author and Conjurer*, written by himself (1859). Transl. by L. Wraxall. A recent edition with a new introduction and notes by Milbourne Christopher was published by Dover (1964).

6 *Confidences d'un Prestidigitateur* (1858). Blois. For first English edition see Ref. 5.

7 *Les Tricheries des Grecs Dévoilées* (1861). Paris. First English translation *The Sharper Detected and Exposed* (1863). London: Chapman & Hall.

8 *Les Secrets de la Prestidigitation et de la Magie* (1868). Paris. For first English translation see Ref. 1.

9 *Magie et Physique Amusante*. Posthumously published in Paris (1877). English edition transl. and ed. by Professor Hoffmann, *The Secrets of Stage Conjuring* (1881). London: Routledge.

10 Seldow, M. (1971): *Vie et Secrets de Robert-Houdin*. Paris: Fayard. An excellent illustrated work.

11 Evans, H. R. (1909): *The Old and the New Magic*. 2nd ed. 162–6. Chicago: Open Court.

11   THEY ALSO CONJURED (131–140)

1 Grove, J. S. P. (1921): *The Dickensian. 17*, 211–14. The monograph by J. B. Findlay (1962) *Charles Dickens and his Magic*, Shanklin, is a useful treatment of the subject but exists only in a limited edition of 75 copies.

2 Dickens, C. (1854): *Household Words*. 11 November.

3 Dickens, Mamie (n.d. 1897): *My Father as I Recall Him*. 33–4. London: Roxburgh.

4 *The Letters of Charles Dickens* (1880). 2nd ed. *2*, 243–4. London: Chapman & Hall.

5 Colman, George, the younger (1830): *Random Records. 1*, 110–12. London: Colburn & Bentley.

6 Dark, S. & Grey, R. (1923): *W. S. Gilbert. His Life and Letters*. 212–13. London: Methuen.

7   Annemann, T. (1940): *The Jinx* No 102, 620.
    Theodore Annemann (1907–42), a well known
    American performer and editor of *The Jinx* (a
    magical periodical), did not cite a reference and I
    have been unable to locate the source of his infor-
    mation. Houdini first arrived in England in 1900
    when Gilbert was 64, at which age it is perhaps less
    likely that he would still be dexterous in rope
    manoeuvres and escapes.
8   Pearson, H. (1957): *Gilbert, His Life and Strife.* 97.
    London: Methuen.
9   Warton, C. (1931): Houdini saved the day for Sax
    Rohmer. *Sunday Herald.* Boston. 8 March.
10 Van Ash, C. & Rohmer, E. (1972): *Master of
    Villainy.* 134–7. London: Stacey.
11 Doyle, A. Conan (1930): *The Edge of the Unknown.*
    1–62. London: Murray.
12 Rohmer, S. (1939): *Salute to Bazarada and Other
    Stories.* London: Cassell. These stories first appeared
    in *Collier's Weekly* during 1937.
13 Collingwood, S. D. (1898): *The Life and Letters of
    Lewis Carroll.* London: Nelson.
14 Fisher, J. (1973): *The Magic of Lewis Carroll.*
    London: Nelson.
15 Green, R. L. (1953): *The Diaries of Lewis Carroll. 1,*
    195. London: Cassell.
16 Unpublished Lecture given at The Magic Circle by
    John Fisher on 15 May 1976. I am indebted to Mr
    Fisher for permission to quote from his talk.
17 Ref. 15, 2, 354.
18 Rolt, L. T. C. (1957): *Isambard Kingdom Brunel. A
    Biography.* 100–1. London: Longmans.
19 Donovan, T. B. (1951): Brunel and the Half-
    Sovereign. *Magic Circular. 45,* 89–90.

12 *EGYPT AND THE SPHINX* (pages 141–154)

1   Jenness, G. A. (1967): *Maskelyne and Cooke.
    Egyptian Hall, London* 1873–1904. Enfield: Author.
2   Shepherd, F. H. W (1960–): *Survey of London.*
    266–70. London: Athlone.
3   Hunt, Leigh (1861): *A Saunter through the West End.*
    43. London: Hurst & Blackett.
4   Jerdan, W. (1852–3): *The Autobiography of William
    Jerdan. 2,* 451. London: Hall.
5   Abrahams, A. (1906): *Antiquary. 42,* 61–4; 139–144;
    225–230.
6   ·Clair, C. (n.d. 1957): *Strong Man Egyptologist.*
    London: Oldbourne.
7   Disher, M. Willson (1957): *Pharoah's Fool.* London:
    Heinemann.
8   Mayes, S. (1959): *The Great Belzoni.* London:
    Putnam.
9   Smith, J. T. (1905): *A Book for a Rainy Day.* Ed.
    with introduction and notes by Wilfred Whitten.
    186–90. London: Methuen.
10 Chambers, R. (1864): *The Book of Days. 2,* 651–3.
    London & Edinburgh: Chambers.
11 I. W. (1864): *Notes and Queries.* 3rd Series, VI, 44.
12 Belzoni, G. (1820): *Narrative of the Operations and
    Recent Discoveries within the Temples, Tombs and
    Excavations, in Egypt and Nubia* etc. etc. London:
    Murray.
13 Bacon, G. (1902): *English Illustrated Magazine.
    28,* 298–308.
14 *Illustrated London News* (1846). 8 August. 96.
15 Barnum, P. T. (1927): *Struggles and Triumphs: or the
    Life of P. T. Barnum,* ed. by George S. Bryan. *1,*
    399–400. London: Knopf.
16 Fitzsimmons, R. (1969): *Barnum in London.* London:
    Bles.
17 *Punch.* (1844). 6, 157
18 Fitzsimmons, R. (1967): *The Baron of Piccadilly.*
    London: Bles.
19 Bellew, F. (n.d.): *The Art of Amusing.* 105–8.
    London: Chatto & Windus.
20 Ireland, J. (1791): *Hogarth Illustrated. 2,* 358.
    London: Boydell.
21 Frost, T. (1876): *The Lives of the Conjurers.* 320.
    London: Tinsley.

13 *MASKELYNE & COOKE—ROYAL ILLUSIONISTS* (pages 155–168)

1   Burlingame, H. J. (1897): *Herrmann the Magician.
    His Life; His Secrets.* Chicago: Laird & Lee.
2   Abrahams, A. (1906): *Antiquary. 42,* 229.
3   Jenness, G. A. (1967): *Maskelyne and Cooke.
    Egyptian Hall, London 1873–1904.* Enfield: Author.
    A splendid record of Maskelyne & Cooke's occupan-
    cy of the Egyptian Hall.
4   Maskelyne, J. N. (1910): 'My Reminiscences'. *Strand
    Magazine.* 39, 17–24.
5   Dawes, E. A. (1970): 'William Morton Remembers'.
    Magic Circular. 64, 116–26.
6   Morton, W. (1934): *I Remember.* Hull: Goddard,
    Walker & Brown.
7   *Maskelyne & Cooke. A Guide to their Original and
    Unique Entertainment of Modern Miracles* (c. 1877).
8   I am grateful to the late John Mulholland (1898–
    1970), Dean of American Magicians, for kind per-
    mission to reproduce this letter in his collection, now
    housed at The Players Club, New York.
9   Armstrong, B. J. (c. 1963): *Armstrong's Norfolk
    Diary.* 149. London: Hodder & Stoughton.
10 Carroll, C. M. (1975): *The Great Chess Automaton.*
    New York: Dover.
11 Maskelyne, J. (1936): *White Magic.* 62. London:
    Paul.
12 Burton, Jean (1948): *Heyday of a Wizard.* London:
    Harrap.
13 Hall, T. H. (1965): *New Light on Old Ghosts.* 86–119.
    London: Duckworth.
14 Maskelyne, J. (1949): *Magic—Top Secret.* London:
    Paul.
15 Hoffmann, Professor (pseud.); i.e., Angelo J.
    Lewis (1876): *Modern Magic.* London: Routledge.
    This classic text has gone through 17 editions. For a
    recent assessment of Hoffmann's important role in
    magic see J. B. Findlay & T. A. Sawyer (1977):
    Professor Hoffmann: A Study. Tustin, California.
16 Randall, H. (c. 1930): *Harry Randall Old Time
    Comedian.* 55–7. London: Sampson Low, Marston.

17 Devant, D. (1931): *My Magic Life*. London: Hutchinson.

18 Sharpe, S. H. (1978–9): Enchanted Hours with David Devant's Delightful Delusions. Serialized in *Linking Ring 58* (8) August 1978 *et seq*.

14 THE GREAT GUN TRICK (pages 169–183)

1 *Dictionary of National Biography. 1*, 679.

2 Hall, T. H. (1972): *Old Conjuring Books*. 157–8. London: Duckworth.

3 Clarke, S. W. (1925): The Annals of Conjuring. *Magic Wand. 14*, 41.

4 Odell, G. C. D. (1927): *Annals of the New York Stage. 1*, 262. New York: Columbia University Press.

5 Greenwood, I. J. (1898): *The Circus. Its Origin and Growth prior to 1835*. 65–6. New York: Dunlap Society.

6 Highfill, P. H. Jr, Burnim, K. A., & Langhans, E. A. (1973): *A Biographical Dictionary of Actors, Actresses, Musicians, Dancers, Managers and Other Stage Personnel in London, 1660–1800. 1*, 146–51. Carbondale and Edwardsville: Southern Illinois University Press.

7 Dexter, W. (1955): *The Riddle of Chung Ling Soo*. London: Arco. Republished by Supreme Magic Co, Bideford (1973).

8 Muir, P. (1954): *English Children's Books 1600–1900*. 131. London: Batsford.

9 Christopher, M. (1973): *The Illustrated History of Magic*. 193–5. New York: Crowell.

10 À Beckett, A. W. (1896): *Green-Room Recollections*. 161–3. Bristol: Arrowsmith.

11 Morley, H. (1891): *The Journal of a London Playgoer from 1851–1866*. 111–12. London: Routledge.

12 Frost, T. (1876): *The Lives of the Conjurers*. 257. London: Tinsley.

13 *Eastern Morning News*. Throughout the period 8–27 July 1867.

14 Hand, C. (1949): *I Was After Money*. 99–102. London: Partridge.

15 Hastings, M. (1963): *The Other Mr Churchill*. 71–5. London: Harrap.

15 SOUNDS, SHADOWS AND SHACKLES (pages 184–202)

1 Armstrong, B. J. (1963): *Armstrong's Norfolk Diary*. 48. London: Hodder & Stoughton. Armstrong consistently mis-spells Woodin as Wooding.

2 Duncan, B. (1963): *The St James's Theatre. Its Strange and Complete History 1835–1957*. 26–7. London: Barrie & Rockcliff.

3 *Hull Advertiser*. 27 June 1845.

4 *Illustrated London News*. 27 January 1855.

5 Brewster, D. (1832): *Letters on Natural Magic*. 174–5. London: Murray.

6 Hilliar, W. J. (1900): *Novel Hand Shadows. vi*. London: T. Nelson Downs Magical Co.

7 Gower, R. S. (1902): *Sir David Wilkie*. London: Bell.

8 *Punch* (1843). *5*, 230.

9 Bursill, H. (1859): *Hand Shadows to be Thrown upon the Wall*. London: Griffith & Farran. Reprinted by Dover (1967).

10 Bursill, H. (1860): *A Second Series of Hand Shadows to Throw upon the Wall*. London: Griffith & Farran. Reprinted by Dover (1971) as *More Hand Shadows*.

11 Miller, B. (1897): Hand Shadows. *Strand Magazine. 14*, 625–32 (December).

12 Devant, D. (1931): *My Magic Life*. 70–4. London: Heinemann.

13 *The Era*. 21 March 1896. 16.

14 Hammond, P. (1974): *Marvellous Méliès*. London: Gordon Fraser.

15 Barnes, J. (1976): *The Beginnings of the Cinema in England*. Newton Abbot: David & Charles.

16 Hertz, C. (1924): *A Modern Mystery Merchant*. 139–41. London: Hutchinson.

17 Stanyon, E. (1903): *Magic. 3*, 68.

18 *Parlour Magic* (1838). 25. London: Whitehead & Co.

19 The literature on Houdini is extensive, but an authoritative, scholarly and recommended text, based on material in his collection, is Milbourne Christopher's (1969) *Houdini the Untold Story*. London: Cassell.

20 Gibson, W. B. (1976): *The Original Houdini Scrapbook*. New York: Corwin Sterling Publishing Co. Principally an interesting pictorial record of original documents and photographs relating to Houdini. Other recent, well-illustrated treatments are Randi, J. & Sugar, B. R. (1976) *Houdini. His Life and Art*. New York: Grosset & Dunlap, and Henning, D. & Reynolds, C. (1977) *Houdini. His Legend and his Magic*. New York: Times Books.

21 Meyer, B. (1976): *Houdini. A Mind in Chains*. New York: Dutton.

22 *The Argus*. 19 March 1910. 18, col 8. I am indebted to Mr Will Alma, N. Caulfield, N.S.W. for drawing my attention to this report and the discordant dates. There is also 15 March given in the caption to a photograph reproduced in Gibson, Ref. 20.

23 *The Age*. 19 March 1910. 13, col. 2.

24 Ernst, B. M. & Carrington, H. (1933): *Houdini and Conan Doyle. The Story of a Strange Friendship*. London: Hutchinson.

25 Doyle, A. C. (1930): *The Edge of the Unknown*. 1–62. London: Murray.

26 Hall, T. H. (1978): *Sherlock Holmes and his Creator*. 91–143. London: Duckworth.

27 Lund, R. (1973): *The Budget*. March 76–7.

BIBLIOGRAPHIES

The literature of conjuring is extensive and the following bibliographic works are valuable sources of information.

Findlay, J. B. (1975): *Ninth Collectors Annual. A Catalogue of books on conjuring and the allied arts in the J. B. Findlay collection*. St Albans: D. W. Findlay.

Gill, R. (1976): *Magic as a Performing Art*. London & New York: Bowker.

Hall, T. H. (1957): *A Bibliography of Books on Conjuring in English from 1580 to 1850*. Lepton: Palmyra Press.

Hall, T. H. (1972): *Old Conjuring Books*. London: Duckworth.

Hall, T. H. & Muir P. H. (1976): *Some Printers and Publishers of Conjuring Books and Other Ephemera 1800–1850*. Leeds: Elmete Press.

Price, H. (1929): *Short-Title Catalogue of Works on Psychical Research, Spiritualism, Magic, Psychology, Legerdemain and Other Methods of Deception, Charlatanism, Witchcraft and Technical Works for the Scientific Investigation of Allied Abnormal Phenomena*. London: National Laboratory of Psychical Research.

Price, H. (1935): *Supplement to Short Title Catalogue*. London: University of London Council for Psychical Investigation.

Toole Stott, R. (1976, 1978): *A Bibliography of English Conjuring 1581–1876*. 2 vols. Derby: Harpur. This is the definitive work on English conjuring books.

Toole Stott, R. (1958–71): *Circus and Allied Arts: A World Bibliography*. 4 vols. Derby: Harpur.

GENERAL HISTORIES OF MAGIC

Christopher, M. (1973): *The Illustrated History of Magic*. New York: Crowell.

Christopher, M. (1962): *Panorama of Magic*. New York: Dover.

Clarke, S. W. (1924–8): The Annals of Conjuring. *Magic Wand*. 13–17. A scholarly, detailed history of magic. It is a great pity that this work has never been republished as a single volume other than in an extremely rare limited edition. *Note added in proof*. There are hopeful signs in the USA that this situation might soon be remedied.

Evans, H. R. (1909): *The Old and the New Magic*. 2nd ed. Chicago: Open Court.

Evans, H. R. (1928): *History of Conjuring and Magic*. Kenton, Ohio: International Brotherhood of Magicians.

Frost, T. (1876): *The Lives of the Conjurers*. London: Tinsley.

Houdini, H. (1908): *The Unmasking of Robert-Houdin*. New York: Publishers Printing Co. Reprinted 1978 by Magico Magazine, New York.

Lamb, G. (1976): *Victorian Magic*. London: Routledge & Kegan Paul.

Mulholland, J. (1936): *The Story of Magic*. New York: Loring & Mussey.

INDEX